COURAGE IN THE PEOPLE'S HOUSE

★ ★ ★ ★ ★ ★ ★ ★ ★

Nine Trailblazing Representatives
Who Shaped America

★ ★ ★ ★ ★ ★ ★ ★ ★

US Representative
JOE NEGUSE

SIMON & SCHUSTER

NEW YORK   LONDON   TORONTO   SYDNEY   NEW DELHI

*Dedicated to the two wonderful people whom I've been
blessed to share my life with—Andrea and Natalie*

With malice toward none; with charity for all; with firmness in the right, as God gives us to see the right, let us strive on to finish the work we are in; to bind up the nation's wounds; to care for him who shall have borne the battle, and for his widow, and his orphan—to do all which may achieve a just and lasting peace, among ourselves, and with all nations.

—ABRAHAM LINCOLN,
Sixteenth President of the United States (1861–1865),
Representative, House of Representatives (1847–1849)

Contents

Prologue   *1*

1   Joseph Rainey   15

2   Josiah Walls   41

3   William B. Wilson   63

4   Adolph Sabath   89

5   Oscar Stanton De Priest   113

6   Margaret Chase Smith   135

7   Henry B. Gonzalez   157

8   Shirley Chisholm   183

9   Barbara Jordan   205

Epilogue   *227*

Acknowledgments   *235*

Notes   *237*

Illustration Credits   *261*

Index   *263*

Courage in The People's House

Prologue

Awe overwhelmed us as my wife, Andrea, and I walked into the Library of Congress for the very first time on a cold evening in early November 2018. We had arrived in our nation's capital a mere few days after that year's general election, for what was billed as "New Member Orientation," a training session of sorts for newly elected members of Congress. Feeling far removed from our home in the suburbs of northern Colorado (with perhaps the only exception being the light snow that had apparently arrived with us in Washington, DC), we were scheduled that evening to join in a dinner with new and sitting members of the House of Representatives—my soon-to-be colleagues. As we walked through the ornate hallways of the historic library, two thirty-somethings from relatively modest means, we kept looking up at the cinematic grandeur of the place, and then, glancing back at each other with the same befuddled look. *What in the world are we doing here?* we thought, as we saw the many famous politicians all around the room, familiar from our television screen back in Colorado.

Neither of us had ever visited the Library of Congress before. And we were both transfixed with a fundamental sense of awe—not simply for the historic buildings, but for what they represented—the world's oldest and greatest constitutional republic. Not our nation's perfection, as I wouldn't have run if I didn't think it could be improved, but rather, the exceptional and unique idea of a republic that America's founders and framers had wisely created. As a son of African immigrants and a daughter of Mexican Americans, both firmly middle class with big dreams, we had somehow found our way here, to this extraordinary place, imbued with a real chance to do our part to try to make our country better.

And then, suddenly, we were face to face with one of our nation's heroes. Andrea and I recognized him immediately. It was John Lewis, the famous civil rights leader and representative from Georgia. Both of us had learned in high school about his bravery during the civil rights movement of the 1960s. And now, here he was, in the flesh—the man who inspired a generation with his fiery speech next to Dr. Martin Luther King Jr. on the Lincoln Memorial, and who had been beaten on the Edmund Pettus Bridge in Selma, Alabama, as he marched for justice, twenty years before either of us was even born.

He was a giant but small in stature, shorter than me. I was still wondering, nervously, how to make the right impression as I reached out to shake his hand—distracted by the thought that his hand was the same one that had once shaken Dr. King's—when he said, "Hello, young brother, how are you?"

I'm rarely at a loss for words, but I wasn't particularly articulate in my response. "I'm good, I'm good, Mr. Lewis," I said. "My name is Joe Neguse, and this is my wife, Andrea. I was just elected to Congress."

He recalled that I was the "young brother from Colorado" and congratulated me. I thanked him for everything he had done to make it possible for someone like me to even be able to raise my hand to run for office. I thanked him for all he had done for so many people. I thanked him for the opportunity to shake his hand. Andrea told me later that I was so nervous I even thanked him for a speech that evening he had yet to give! As the conversation came to a close, Mr. Lewis said, "Well, I appreciate that, young brother, but I appreciate you stepping up. We're proud of you, and I'm so glad the people of Colorado made that decision and made history."

As we parted, Andrea and I were moved beyond words.

We both were struck by his reminder of the barrier our state had broken in my election as Colorado's first Black member of Congress. But far more than that, we were deeply moved by the simple, yet profound experience of meeting one of America's most inspirational representatives, whose acts of courage had helped shape our country for the better.

I've long believed that America is the greatest democratic republic our world has ever known. For over two centuries, the United States has been a unique experiment in the ability of citizens to govern themselves through a constitutional structure, and to do so by a defining set of values, rather than an order imposed by a homogeneous ethnicity or creed—the values of freedom, liberty, equality, the rule of law, and more, enshrined in the Declaration of Independence, our Constitution, and the Bill of Rights. As the world's first and perhaps only truly multiracial republic, our country has been shaped over time by countless public servants—Republican and Democrat, liberal and conservative—who've worked to honor the meaning of those founding documents. And many of them served in the institution I would soon join: the US House of Representatives, or what some have colloquially referred to as the "People's House."

The historical record offers few answers as to why the House of Representatives has earned that moniker. Ostensibly, it refers to the simple fact that the House was originally the only part of our federal government elected directly by America's citizens. That is no longer the case, as members of the United States Senate are now also elected directly by the public, pursuant to the Seventeenth Amendment of the Constitution. Still, the House remains the only institution in which members must be elected by the American people when a vacancy arises (whereas senators may be, and often are, appointed). And there is little debate—among members of the House, at least—that the legislative chamber is the part of our federal government most closely connected to the "people," as amorphous a word as that may be.

The House has also attracted a far wider array of Americans than other governmental institutions, who, having earned the confidence of their fellow citizens, have made the journey to Washington, DC, to serve their constituency and their country. And with each of these history-making leaders whom Americans have sent to Congress—the first African Americans elected in the late nineteenth century; the first working-class White immigrants elected from crowded, polyglot cities soon thereafter; the first women elected to Congress in the twentieth century; and the late John Lewis himself—voters amended what it meant to be an American. They changed us all by making our country's promise truer and more open, and in that sense, helped shape our country, as every generation is called upon to do. This is an extraordinary legacy, and one about which most of us, myself included, know far too little.

This book seeks to change that.

In the pages that follow, we will explore acts of determination and political bravery by people many have never heard of—leaders who shaped our country as pioneers by opening the Congress to all Americans. For some of them, simply running for office required great courage. But the tales only begin with their elections. The greater lessons came after each was sworn in and began their service in the House, as they worked to represent their constituents, their districts, and their country.

My awe for the People's House has not faded since that night in November years ago when I first heard Mr. Lewis speak to the gathered freshman legislators. Perhaps that reverence is borne from the simple fact that I never intended to run for Congress and could never have imagined walking the halls of the Capitol.

When the opportunity to run first arose in the summer of 2017, I already had the best job I could imagine, leading my state's consumer protection agency as a member of the governor of Colorado's cabinet. Andrea and I had recently married, and we were thinking about starting a family. I had benefited from multiple opportunities to pursue my dreams, including practicing law and serving as an elected regent of the University of Colorado. All in all, it was clear to me that much about my life underlined the miracle of American opportunity and its amazing gift of freedoms to me and my family, which we could never take for granted.

My parents, Debesai and Azeib, put me here, in Colorado, with all these opportunities. They had left Eritrea, a small war-torn country in the Horn of Africa, separately as refugees, before they met in Bakersfield, California, and married. I was born four years after their arrival. To make their way in America, they worked many jobs—from fast-food restaurants to retail stores—and achieved success through sheer effort and hard work, my mother becoming a bank teller and my father earning his degree as an accountant. I was very young when we moved to the suburbs of Douglas County, Colorado, where my sister and I were lucky to grow up in a middle-class home and attend good public schools. I can still recall, vividly, traveling to Eritrea for the first time as a twelve-year-old, and the sense of profound shock I felt at how different our life had become in just one generation.

I knew I was incredibly lucky. And I felt a powerful responsibility not to waste the opportunity my parents and this country had given me. Although I never dreamed of serving in Congress, I always felt a need to be an active participant in our democracy, in part, because I knew so many others could not. In that sense, I felt it was up to me to make all their sacrifices worthwhile. Indeed, it's the same reason why I believe in America as strongly as I do. How could I not, after all my family and I had been given?

From the time Colorado entered the Union in 1876, until 2018, the state had never elected an African American to the US House of Representatives. And yet, when I decided to run for Congress, breaking that barrier was not top of mind. Protecting our environment, expanding access to public education, reducing gun violence, and a steadfast belief in our ability to build a more hopeful future—those were the issues, among others, that animated my desire to serve, and they ultimately became the core of my first congressional campaign.

Still, on occasion, after a long evening of phone banking or knocking on voter doors during our primary campaign, I'd indulge, if only for a moment, the thought that maybe—just maybe—we might make state history. Months later, having won a heated primary campaign and earned the Democratic nomination, that same thought waned for a time as Andrea and I welcomed the birth of our daughter, Natalie. Enthralled and fully engaged with the new light of both of our lives, there were days I would genuinely forget that we were still campaigning. Life was moving very fast.

Although many assumed we would win, I didn't want to take victory in the general election for granted, so we didn't slow the pace. Meanwhile, a looming awareness began to take hold—that, besides the wonderful and total life change of becoming a father, I might also be going to Washington and uprooting a life that had been lived almost entirely close to home, in the suburbs of Colorado. Besides worrying about those rapidly approaching changes, however, I also began thinking seriously about what role I might play were I lucky enough to be elected. Of one thing I was sure: at a time when so much of our politics had become consumed by division and fear, I'd endeavor to focus on the hope I knew firsthand that our country promised.

That inspiration crystalized in another moment near the end of the campaign, in late October 2018. During the closing weeks of the campaign, I had the opportunity to tour Children's Hospital Colorado in Aurora. While on the tour, we were shown a school room for seriously ill children who were patients at the hospital. As we walked through the room, our tour guide showed us a wall where students had posted inspirational quotes from various famous people.

On that wall, I saw the sentence "Fear is contagious, but so is hope."

I had never heard that phrase before. The statement had no attribution, and I didn't know who had put it on that board. But I was deeply struck by it. And I held tight to that idea through the rest of the campaign. In my victory speech a few weeks later in November, I said, "There was a whole lot to be fearful of yesterday, and the day before that, and the day before that, and the last two years, but tonight, because each and every one of you is standing up and reclaiming our democracy, the hope for tomorrow has never been brighter."

That was my frame of mind when we arrived in Washington just a few days later, amid this whirlwind of change in our lives, and met John Lewis for the first time. It was then that I really took in the historic sweep of what service in the People's House truly means. Shaking his hand was one part of that dawning awareness, the sense of being in the presence of living history. Another part was the realization of the historically large and exceptionally talented class of representatives I would have the privilege of entering Congress with. They were proof of the hope infused in our country's premise and the truth that a thriving republic, inclusive of all its citizens, is not a dream but instead a reality bequeathed to us by those brave members of Congress who came before.

I began thinking seriously about who those people had been.

Since our nation's founding, more than twelve thousand Americans have been elected to Congress. On the Congressional Historian's website, I found a page detailing many of these Americans—some famous, a few infamous—and others, completely unknown today. As I scoured the webpages, my astonishing realization was that I knew very little about most of them. Dipping into the biographies on the congressional website, I learned about former slaves who were elected to Congress after the Civil War and fought valiantly for civil rights. I learned about an immigrant from Scotland who labored by hand as a young boy in the coal mines of Pennsylvania and then led the fight nationally for the rights of miners and working Americans. And I learned about the first woman elected to Congress from Maine, who courageously confronted Senator Joe McCarthy's tactics in the 1950s.

None of their names was familiar to me.

The seed of an idea for this book was born. I was determined to learn more about how this institution came to be, who made it what it had become, and to spread that knowledge widely. Most of all, I wanted to show the remarkable acts of courage of these legislators—representatives of all races, genders, religions, and political affiliations—who, *as Americans*, loved their country and were prepared to give up their honors and power, if necessary, to cast votes of conscience for the greater good. And I promised myself that, if given the opportunity to perhaps one day write a book and share a story, I would share theirs.

One reason their stories are less well known is, in my view, the institutional preference among many historians for other parts of our federal government: the presidency, the Senate, the Supreme Court—indeed, it seems, everything *but* the House of Representatives. And yet, the People's House is truly an institution like no other.

The Senate is certainly the more famous legislative chamber, long described as the greatest deliberative body on Earth, with one hundred individually powerful members whose six-year terms were meant to provide the "select and stable member of the government" as described by Founding Father James Madison in *The Federalist Papers*, some of the most important essays ever written in American history. The House, on the other hand, has 435 individual members who, per *Federalist* No. 52, "have an immediate dependence on, and an intimate sympathy with, the people," secured through far more frequent elections—every two years—than any other part of our government.

In turn, the House looks much more like the country: younger, more diverse, and with a greater variety of occupations. Indeed, as Madison presciently noted more than two hundred years ago, "the door of this part of the federal government is open to merit of every description, whether native or adoptive, whether young or old, and without regard to poverty or wealth, or to any particular profession or religious faith." In many respects, the People's House fulfills the founders' intent as the most democratic part of our federal government. And true to form, over the decades this system has worked to open up access to more of our citizens.

However, despite that fact and the House's close proximity to the American people, presidents still receive the bulk of attention from many historians and most Americans. So do the many colorful senators from years past and their famous debates. But the most fundamentally American stories emerge from the House, where ordinary people have mustered the courage and skill to do extraordinary things.

Put simply, members of the House must earn their places in history. And the individuals profiled in the pages that follow have done precisely that.

It bears noting that some of the most profoundly important laws in our country's history started in the House, including legislation to protect the fundamental rights of every American, often starting their path when a member dropped a bill in the "hopper"—a tradition that still exists today and is open to any Member, simply by walking onto the House floor and inserting legislative papers. Madison—one of America's most important and pivotal founders—served four terms in the House before he became president and introduced the Constitution's Bill of Rights as legislation on the House floor in 1789. One of our nation's greatest leaders, Abraham Lincoln, served a term in the House before he became president, during the years when the body convulsed with controversy over issues leading up to the Civil War. During that same era, John Quincy Adams served as a congressman for nine terms—having already served as president—and fought to defeat a gag rule that prevented debate on the House floor over abolishing slavery (a rule he objected to as unconstitutional). While the Civil War still raged, the Thirteenth Amendment began its path to inclusion in the Constitution, forever ending slavery, as a bill introduced in the House. A century later, the Civil Rights Act of 1964 began there, too. With each law, and with each election, ordinary Americans who came to Congress helped shape our republic, extending its protection and promise to more Americans, as they fulfilled the meaning of the words of our founding documents.

A stranger to the Capitol before that winter night in November 2018, I have become a constant inhabitant these past few years. As I walk the bustling halls after a meeting or finish taking constituents on a quiet, late-evening tour of the building, I remind myself that all of us who have the honor of being there are in the presence of all those who went before, whose deeds remain so profound and present because they have not ended, as Americans continue the fight to advance and protect our country. Our inspiration comes from those unsung representatives whose words and work brought us there, so we can add to their work, and together make the more perfect union that we dream of without expectation of perfection, but always moving closer to it.

My own faith in our democratic experiment goes back, in part, to a book I picked up as a teenager in high school in the suburbs of Colorado. I can't exactly recall where I first got my paperback version of John F. Kennedy's *Profiles in Courage* or precisely why it fell into my hands. But I can still bring to mind the feelings of excitement, fascination, and purpose that the book engendered as I flipped its pages and learned for the first time about the political life of the Congress, captivated by the elevated prose through which Kennedy told of a series of unique acts of political courage by each of eight senators throughout American history. The impact was indelible, and the inspiration enduring.

My original interest had been in President Kennedy himself. As a student, I read with great interest the commencement address he delivered at American University in June 1963, five months before his assassination. The address, commonly known as the "Peace Speech," still represents to me one of the best expressions of a more hopeful political philosophy—one undergirded by our common sense of humanity. Coming after the Cuban missile crisis, when President Kennedy faced down the Soviet Union in a test of nuclear brinkmanship, he called on Americans to recognize the humanity of our adversaries and described a lasting, pragmatic peace that could be based on rules, institutions, and mutual respect. "For, in the final analysis," President Kennedy reminds us, "our most basic common link is that we all inhabit the same planet. We all breathe the same air. We all cherish our children's future. And we are all mortal."

It was because of that speech that I had found President Kennedy, and perhaps, in turn, found *Profiles in Courage.* And I found his stories about other senators I had never heard of—and the portrayal of their sacrifices and acts of daring to do what they believed was right—absolutely riveting. One reason for the book's enduring popularity is its retelling of an aspect of politics many never consider, one of true service, in which individuals reached positions of power and prestige but chose to go against their own political interests, and often the desires of their constituents, in the service of conscience. The setting struck me powerfully, as I could see in my imagination the great debates and decisions of state playing out on the floor of the Senate, with the course of history determined by an individual's battle with their own sense of right and wrong.

The stories Kennedy recounted in *Profiles* continue to echo throughout our country's history in interesting ways. As a House impeachment manager in February 2021, I studied extensively the impeachment trial of President Andrew Johnson more than one hundred fifty years earlier, in 1868. He avoided removal from office by only one vote, a vote unexpectedly cast by an obscure senator from Kansas, Edmund G. Ross, who had been Johnson's ardent critic. Kennedy profiled Ross, approvingly quoting a historian who called his vote "the most heroic act in American history." While some have a different view, as President Kennedy noted in *Profiles*, the book's subject was courage, not justification of the decisions made by the politicians about whom he wrote, and part of its strength comes from his choice of surprising characters with unique perspectives.

This book humbly attempts to do something similar.

The goal is simple: to tell a story about America though the nine profiles that follow of House of Representatives members of all political stripes who showed great courage—not only in the determination to overcome the odds and break barriers just to serve in Congress, but in the risks they took, as they faced off against powerful interests and sometimes their own allies, and what they sought to accomplish as the fruits of those labors. After all, moral courage in dedication to what one believes is right and best for our country is often a prerequisite to real leadership and the opportunity to improve the lives of our fellow citizens. These leaders had those qualities. And while none of them was perfect, their service made a difference.

So we begin with courage, and with the important premise that the story of political courage in Congress includes all Americans. These members' impact reaches beyond the issues of their day and includes the whole meaning and sweep of our democracy, as they redefined who it includes and how we can manifest a government of, by, and for the people. These profiles tell that story even as the story of our nation continues to unfold, and as we decide our part in it daily. My hope is that long after I've left office, someone may read about these nine public servants, many of whom history has made little note, and be, at least in part, as inspired as I was when I read President Kennedy's book, many decades after his death—and that perhaps they could come to see themselves as someone who could also step forward with the hope of someday contributing to their country.

That hope, or goal as it were, is not an inconsequential one. Our democracy has rarely been at greater risk or in more desperate need for people of good faith to step forward and help save it. And yet we have diminished the stature of government so substantially in the minds of our citizenry that one would be hard-pressed to find many who believe that serving in public office is an honorable profession, much less a forum in which to demonstrate courage and improve our union.

We diminish this birthright at our own peril.

Centuries ago, one of America's greatest presidents, our nation's first, George Washington, wisely noted that "[a] primary object should be the education of our youth in the science of government," for in a republic like ours, "what species of knowledge can be equally important? And what duty more pressing than communicating it to those who are to be the future guardians of the liberties of the country?" He was certainly right. We know that across the arc of human civilization, whenever a republic has failed, that loss was usually precipitated to some extent by a loss of commitment to being a citizen in every sense of the word, which requires being an active participant, not a passive subject. As we drive down our knowledge of—and esteem for—our institutions and lose our respect for them—as we have done—we open the door for those who disdain the rule of law and constitutional norms that enable our system to function. Cynicism is easy, loss of respect can feel justified in the bitterness of the present, and disconnection from each other as fellow citizens—*fellow Americans*—happens all by itself. Meanwhile, the opposite—rebuilding the connective tissues that make us one nation—can appear impossible.

It is not.

We can refresh those muscles by recalling some of our best examples, ordinary people who served and did extraordinary things. They stepped forward for election to Congress, some of them at great personal peril, and when they left office, they didn't become wealthy. To the contrary, some were impoverished and died with little, banished to the appendices of history, rarely to be read about or heard of again. Their stories inspire the unavoidable implication that we are responsible to sustain the precious republic they lent to our generation, for our temporary use, and to protect it from cynicism and demagoguery so that we can lend it onward to the next generation.

Without a doubt, Congress itself deserves some of the blame for losing the public's respect. As a deliberative body, it is broken. Gone are the dramatic speeches and fiery debates that played out the nation's great controversies—powerful speeches over the Thirteenth Amendment, the annexation of Texas, or World War I. In fact, today, many speeches on the House floor are made to an empty chamber for the benefit, it seems, of only the C-SPAN cameras.

During my first term, I was thrilled to address a full body, as I was called upon to speak for five minutes on a "motion to recommit" during debate on an immigration bill, a rare motion that generally requires all members to be present. During my speech, I offered the following:

> " 'It is bold men and women, yearning for freedom and opportunity, who leave their homelands and come to a new country to start their lives over. They believe in the American Dream. And over and over, they make it come true for themselves, for their children, and for others. They give more than they receive. They labor and succeed. And often they are entrepreneurs. But their greatest contribution is more than economic, because they understand in a special way how glorious it is to be an American.' That quote, those are not my words, [Mr. Speaker]. Those are the words of President Ronald Reagan. They were delivered by President Ronald Reagan in 1980, the same year that my parents came to the United States."

As I orated about my own family's immigration experience, amid cheers of encouragement from some colleagues and loud jeers from others, I felt all the energy of real legislative debate. But I was, unfortunately, one of the last to do so. The next year, in the following Congress, the motion to recommit was eliminated from the House rules, as the majority believed it had been abused by the minority.

Now, those infrequent in-person debates rarely happen at all.

In committee proceedings, I have seen but a few votes ever change—on either side of the aisle—because of a point raised by the member of the other party. Quite simply, the Congress has changed dramatically since the early days of our republic. And while this book profiles nine members who overcame far greater barriers to serve than these, I sometimes wonder if they would have bothered to make those sacrifices to be a part of the Congress as it operates today.

Such speculation ends, however, when I consider the work of the giants from the modern history of the Congress who have had such a profound influence on me, including representative John Lewis, who awed me into silence with a single handshake and gave me the gift of his mentorship before he passed away, particularly during the challenging days of the presidential impeachment of 2019. That story is perhaps as good a place as any to end this prologue, as it connects to both the first and last profiles in this book and to the reason I was inspired to write in the first place.

The responsibilities came swiftly when I was sworn into office on January 3, 2019, and joined the House Judiciary Committee, one of the oldest committees of the Congress. I had chosen the committee because of its primary jurisdiction over immigration, an area of interest to me as a son of immigrants, and gun violence prevention, an issue that had driven me since my days in high school, when the terrible massacre at the neighboring Columbine High School had deeply shaken our community and our state. As fate would have it, the Judiciary Committee is also responsible under House rules and centuries of precedent for initiating, when necessary, articles of impeachment. And that put us squarely in the middle of both presidential impeachments that would ensue over the following two years.

During the 2021 impeachment trial, I studied closely the trial of Secretary of War William W. Belknap, who was impeached in 1876. And it was during that research that I learned of Representative Joseph Rainey, one of the first and most remarkable African Americans to ever serve in Congress, from 1870 to 1879.

Quite fittingly, Rainey is the first member profiled in this book.

The late Representative Barbara Jordan of Texas is the subject of this book's last chapter. In 1974, during impeachment proceedings against President Richard Nixon, Jordan sat, like me, as a freshman on the Judiciary Committee. When I arrived on the committee nearly half a century later, I was deeply influenced by her words, especially her extraordinary, televised speech on the Constitution and the Congress's responsibility, which has come to be known as one of the finest speeches in congressional history. As my colleagues and I worked on the impeachment proceedings, Jordan's speech was rightfully referenced as a North Star, for guidance on how to explain such constitutionally weighty subjects to the American people. I was grateful for the wisdom her remarks imparted to me and my colleagues during such a tumultuous time for our country, which I hoped would soon pass.

As we now know, that was not the case. Less than a year after President Donald J. Trump's first Senate impeachment trial, following the attack on our nation's capital on January 6, 2021, he was impeached a second time, in the final weeks of his presidency. A second impeachment trial soon followed, and I was selected by the Speaker of the House to be a House manager, prosecuting the trial before the Senate. Again, I dipped into the speeches and decisions of the past for guidance on how to best carry out that heavy responsibility. It had been years since I had read *Profiles in Courage*. But it was then, reviewing the 1868 trial of President Johnson, and the vote of Senator Ross, that I began rereading the weathered paperback copy I had kept from my time in high school. I then began to think seriously about how a book elevating the best of those who served in the People's House—people like Rainey and Jordan—could begin to heal some of the lost faith that has damaged our democracy today.

I firmly believe that their stories can still inspire us, as we reach back into history and find courage in people who are mostly forgotten, and as we seek courage today, in the struggle to safeguard our republic and preserve freedom and liberty for all Americans.

Their stories can speak for themselves.

1

Joseph Rainey

★ ★ ★ ★ ★ ★ ★ ★ ★

I view it in the light of the Constitution—in the light of the amendments that have been made to that Constitution; I view it in the light of humanity; I view it in the light of the progress and civilization which are now rapidly marching over this country.

—JOSEPH RAINEY

On the morning of April 27, 1874, members of the US House of Representatives gathered—solemn, chastened, and dressed in black—for a special floor session. They had assembled with a single purpose: to mark the death of a senator whose soaring oratory had, in the view of many, carried the moral argument behind the nation's deadliest war and had helped bring freedom for four million enslaved Americans.

Senator Charles Sumner of Massachusetts, dead at sixty-three, had never given up fighting for equality for African Americans. He had worked for years after the Civil War to pass legislation barring racial discrimination, but ultimately, was thwarted by his foes and even his own allies, some of whom viewed him as sanctimonious and had wearied of his implacable righteousness. At one point, Sumner's opponents went to the length of assembling in the Senate chambers in the dead of night to defeat his bill while he was sleeping. And for a time, they succeeded. Sumner's inability to secure his civil rights bill's passage haunted him until his dying days. On his deathbed, he told the vice president of the United States, Henry Wilson, "If my works were completed and my civil rights bill passed, no visitor could enter that door that would be more welcome than death."

Now, on this day of remembrance, Sumner's absence appeared to close an era. His passing inspired a series of laudatory eulogies, including from those who, during his life, had bridled at his stubborn ethics and haughty manner, and from some who had even opposed his life's work. One representative's speech, however, stood out from the others, and for more reasons than one. As the middle-aged and well-dressed congressman rose on the House floor to deliver his remarks, it was clear—to members and onlookers alike—that his grief and anguish were profound.

The congressman began his speech by fondly recalling his personal and warm friendship with Sumner. And then, he reminded the House of Sumner's unfinished legacy. For on that spring day, he planned to offer more than a eulogy. He intended to continue picking up the mantle, invested with the Civil War's 720,000 lost lives, to pass the Civil Rights Act. He and Sumner had previously advocated, as a legislative strategy and to attempt to secure its passage, the linkage of the civil rights legislation to a grant of amnesty for former Confederates. Their approach had not been without criticism. But the humble and intensely driven Congressman would soldier on, committed to doing everything in his power to ensure a true democracy of equals.

The man was Joseph Rainey, a former slave from South Carolina, who became the first Black congressman ever elected in American history.

As Rainey began his speech, he recounted meeting in Sumner's apartment—they had lived near each other in Washington, DC—where Rainey, a self-educated former barber who was born into slavery, enjoyed Sumner's evident respect, and soaked in the wisdom of his famous intellect. "His friendship, when formed, was sincere and advantageous," Rainey solemnly told his colleagues that day. "I can never forget so long as I have the faculty of recollection the warm and friendly grasp he gave my hand soon after I was admitted a member of this House. On my first visit to the Senate, he said: 'I welcome you to this chamber. Come over frequently; you have rights here as well as others.'"

Those gathered in the House—like countless others across the country—were well aware that Sumner's advocacy had nearly cost him his life. After one of his speeches in 1856, inveighing against the immorality of slavery, an enraged representative from South Carolina, Preston Brooks, walked onto the floor of the Senate and beat him bloody and unconscious with a cane. Sumner barely recovered from his injuries and was unable to return fully to service in the Senate for four long years. In his eulogy, Rainey described Brooks's attack as the first blows of the Civil War, an assault on "God's chosen advocate for freedom." Many African Americans, Rainey included, had considered Sumner to be *their* senator. And like a Christian martyr, Rainey said, Sumner had accepted blows for them:

> "The unexpressed sympathy that was felt for him among the slaves of the South, when they heard of this unwarranted attack, was only known to those whose situations at the time made them confidants. Their prayers and secret importunities were ever uttered in the interest of him who was their constant friend and untiring advocate and defender before the high court of the nation. Mr. Speaker, it is said that 'the blood of martyrs is the seed of the church.' With equal truthfulness and force, I think it may be said that the blood of Charles Sumner, spilled upon the floor of the Senate because he dared to oppose the slave power of the South to interpose in the path of its progress, was the seed that produced general emancipation; the result of which is too well known to need comment. It spoke silently, but effectively, of the cruelty and iniquities of that abominable institution."

Those listening to the eulogy in the House chambers were surely moved by Rainey's powerful and vivid oratorical analogies. But as Rainey brought his speech home, he shelved the soaring rhetoric. For it was now time to address the crux of the matter—civil rights, the unfinished business that lay before the House, that Rainey himself would see through to its end. He demanded the House recall Sumner's last words, "Do not let the Civil Rights bill fail," repeating them twice and gently shaming his colleagues by noting, "This sentence, we trust, will prove more potent and availing in securing equality before the law for all men than any of his former efforts." The passage of the bill would be Sumner's best memorial, Rainey suggested, uniting all the struggles of his service.

> "How remarkable the connecting incidents of his history! This is particularly apparent when we recall the fact that he began

as an advocate of human rights, continued through an eventful career the same, and closing his last hours on earth, facing the judgment-seat of the very God, he looked back for a moment and repeated these words, which will be ever memorable, *'Do not let the Civil-Rights bill fail!'* "

Rainey, a junior member of the House, assumed this responsibility for Sumner's quest, which had eluded the senator with his twenty-three years of tenure. He was not the only African American in the House, but his three years of seniority were already greater than any other in the Congress. Rainey had entered the House first, by a matter of months, when he won a special election to fill a vacancy in 1870, a mere five years after the end of the Civil War. His claims on history's attention are many. He would become the first African American to preside in the Speaker's chair and earned the respect of many colleagues for his remarkable oratory skills and integrity. Nonetheless, Rainey also endured repeated acts of disrespect and humiliation against him on the floor of the House and in his daily life. The historical record reveals he more than held his own in debate, meeting insults with thrilling comebacks and exposing the hypocrisy of many of his House colleagues. And he did so despite constant threats of violence to his own safety and that of his family—which, for a time, forced him to move his wife and children from South Carolina to Connecticut.

During Reconstruction, which lasted approximately eleven years after the Civil War, federal troops protected African Americans in the South and their ability to vote and hold office, while, under section 3 of the Fourteenth Amendment to the Constitution, those who had held government offices and rebelled against the Union were barred from any role in the government or military unless they applied to the Congress for restoration of their full political rights (which could be granted only by an amnesty vote of two thirds in each body). Rainey and his African American colleagues in the House would often point out that some of the former rebels who desired to return to political power were still fighting against Reconstruction, including through the Ku Klux Klan and other violent organizations, assassinating hundreds of Black and White Republican leaders, and intimidating voters. Indeed, it still "wasn't safe to fly the Stars and Stripes in Georgia," said Jefferson Long, one of the six African American Congressmen at the time.

Rainey, however, supported full rights for former Confederates—so long as that restoration of political rights came linked with full civil rights for African Americans. He had adopted this linkage from the beginning of his political career, in the immediate wake of the war, long before he entered Congress, and before he had ever met Sumner. And despite the hardship and hazards Rainey and his constituents faced, and the implacable opposition of his foes, he would never waver in his commitment to that view. Later, some other leaders would also adopt the idea, and it finally became a centerpiece of the five-year fight for Sumner's Civil Rights Act.

Rainey had been a small child and was still owned as a slave when Sumner began his career as an abolitionist. Rainey was born in 1832, in Georgetown, South Carolina, a coastal town of rice plantations. His father, Edward Rainey, a barber, saved money while still in slavery to buy his own freedom and that of his wife, Grace, and their children, including Joseph. The family then moved to Charleston, where Edward began accumulating wealth as a barber at an exclusive hotel. At the time, South Carolina maintained brutal laws of control to keep the system of slavery in place, including forbidding education of Black children, whether slave or free. Joseph Rainey did learn his father's trade, however, and he too did well as a barber.

Rainey later traveled to Philadelphia, where he met his wife, Susan, and then successfully evaded punishment for making that trip to a free state, which was illegal for African Americans, regardless of their status. When the Civil War broke out, he was forced to dig trenches for the Confederate army back in Charleston. He also worked on a ship running through the Union Navy's blockade of the South, and likely gained the ability, through that experience, to escape with Susan to free, British-ruled Bermuda. It was a safe place to settle for the duration of the war, and the island's economy was booming, with smugglers attempting to run supplies to the South. Warehouses were full, and as many as a dozen ships anchored in the bustling port of St. George, their sailors crowding the streets. Joseph's barber shop and Susan's dressmaking shop were busy, bringing them both financial success and status in the community. When an epidemic hit St. George, the Raineys moved to Hamilton, Bermuda. As usual, Joseph kept busy. He operated a barber shop in a hotel, and the historical record indicates he joined an African American fraternal organization there as well, Alexandrina Lodge No. 1026, adding his name to a resolution the organization passed expressing mourning for the assassination of President Lincoln.

In the autumn of 1866, with the war over and conditions improving at home, the Raineys returned to South Carolina. An advertisement they bought in a Bermuda newspaper thanked their patrons for their success, and the street where Rainey's shop had stood was named Barber's Alley. A resident would later recall, "He was invariably courteous to everyone, a good listener, hard worker, and possessed a strength of character."

When Rainey returned to South Carolina after the war, his relative wealth and education made him a valuable asset in a political setting where members of a newly freed Black majority in his state desired skilled leadership to help achieve progress. So-called Black Codes, enacted by many southern legislatures soon after the war, sought to force former slaves back to work on plantations, restricting African Americans in South Carolina, for example, to employment as servants and field hands and allowing them no political rights. Rainey participated in a statewide Colored People's Convention to protest these laws, and the Union military commander of the area, General Daniel Sickles, listened to their call, nullifying the codes.

As South Carolina politics opened to African Americans, Rainey served in a variety of offices on his three-year path to the Congress. In 1867, he became a county chairman for the Republican Party, and the next year, a delegate to the state constitutional convention. He served as an agent for the state land commission and brigadier general in the state militia, and then, in 1869, performed as census taker in Georgetown. Finally, in 1870, he won election to the State Senate, where he was appointed chair of the Finance Committee.

Rainey's work on the new state constitution during these early years of his political career presaged the philosophy he would later advocate for in Congress, which was eventually adopted by Sumner and other allies. For African Americans, the state constitution would secure political rights, while building literacy and the social capital to govern by instituting compulsory public education for all. But Rainey also advocated for reconciliation as a long-term path for African Americans to preserve their new rights in the South. Although the new constitution denied the vote to former rebels until they received amnesty from Congress, he proposed a resolution asking Congress to restore the political rights of all South Carolinians. He had already begun linking civil rights to amnesty.

Remarkably, Rainey took that position under the threat of real violence happening in his state, including arson, beatings, and lynching. Attacks against Black politicians and voters, and Reconstruction Republicans more generally, were common, as a strategy to recover power and roll back the changes brought by the South's loss in the Civil War. One particular South Carolina militia even wore gray military uniforms, much like the Confederate Army's. A legislative committee found that four Black politicians had been assassinated over two months in just one Congressional district, after which the committee itself was then threatened.

A leader of Rainey's prominence was particularly at risk.

In the face of all that danger, Rainey refused to back down. In fact, he did just the opposite. He decided to run for Congress. In the ninety-four years since the Declaration of Independence was signed, no African American had ever been elected.

Many expected him to fail. Rainey intended to prove them wrong.

In the fall of 1870, he stepped forward to run in a special election. His predecessor, Benjamin Whittemore, a Republican from Massachusetts who had come to South Carolina as a chaplain in the Union Army, had been censured by Congress for selling appointments to the US Naval Academy and resigned from office. After Rainey's success in state politics, he was a natural candidate for the Republican nomination to replace Whittemore, representing a district that spanned the northeast corner of the state. After a short, spirited campaign, in October and November of 1870, he won two elections, both by wide margins, first to fill out the brief remainder of Whittemore's term and then to serve the next full term. He had become the first African American to serve, to be joined shortly after by five others chosen around the same time in elections across the South.

When he arrived in Congress, newspapers reported on his unprecedented presence on the floor of the House, and noted Rainey's courtesy, eloquence, and well-dressed style. A reporter for the *Cleve-land Daily Plain Dealer* described the scene in December 1870, as Rainey was sworn in: "Taking a position in front of the Speaker, he put his heels together like a soldier, and raised his hand to take the oath, which was administered by the Speaker, Blaine, in his usual manner, while the whole House looked on in amazement." The reporter noted that Rainey "[b]owed courteously to the Speaker, and punctuated the oath with an inclination of the head as every sentence was pronounced."

Within a few months, Rainey would be plunged into the fights in Congress over both amnesty and legislation to calm the violence that was making political participation for African Americans so deadly. In the House of Representatives, numerous amnesty bills came through as each former rebel was voted on by name in the Congress. Rainey called, in exchange, for approval, passage, and enforcement of the Ku Klux Klan Act, which was intended to protect voters in the South and prosecute their attackers.

One of Rainey's African American colleagues from South Carolina, the fiery Robert Elliott, initially disagreed, as did some others who had been oppressed in the antebellum South. On March 14, 1871, Elliott responded to an ally in his own party who sought to approve amnesty and remove the political disabilities of southerners, explaining:

> "Sir, I say that this removal would be injurious, not only to the loyal men of the South, but to the Government itself. To relieve those men of their disabilities at this time would be regarded by the loyal men of the South as evidence of the weakness of this great Government and of an intention on the part of this Congress to foster the men who today are outraging the good and loyal people of the South. It would be further taken as evidence of the fact that this Congress desires to hand over the loyal men of the South to the tender mercies of the rebels who today are murdering and scourging the loyal men of the southern States."

While the amnesty question continued as a perennial issue before the Congress, Rainey advocated powerfully for the Ku Klux Klan Act, which would empower prosecutions by equipping the federal government with its own criminal justice system, a decisive shift and centralization of power from the states, which had largely controlled criminal law. Critics loudly charged that the act would be unconstitutional. A heated debate ensued. Rainey jumped into that debate with full force, despite having served in the House for less than five months. He rose near the start of the evening session on April 1, 1871, just after 7:00 p.m., in the flickering gas light of the House chamber.

It was his first major speech to Congress. And he was ready.

Beginning with a mournful tone, he recalled the death and terror facing his constituents, saying, "Mr. Speaker, in approaching the subject now under consideration, I do so with a deep sense of its magnitude and importance, and in full recognition of the fact that a remedy is needed to meet the evil now existing in most of the southern states, but especially in the one which I have the honor to represent in part, the state of South Carolina. The enormity of the crimes constantly perpetrated there finds no parallel in the history of this Republic in her very darkest days." He cited slavery as the cause, and the work of the Civil War as unfinished. "Even now, sir, after the triumph achieved at such a cost, we can yet see the traces of the disastrous strife and the remains of disease in the body politic of the South."

Rainey's prescription for that disease called for, first of all, a restoration of law and order. In responding to the bill's opponents, he said their arguments, with narrow interpretations of the Constitution, should not stand in the way of assuring that basic necessity.

> "For my part, I am not prepared, Mr. Speaker, to argue this question from a constitutional standpoint alone. I take the ground that, in my opinion, lies far above the interpretation put upon the provisions of the Constitution. I stand upon the broad plane of right; I look to the urgent, the importunate demands of the present emergency; and while I am far from advocating any step not in harmony with that sacred law of our land, while I would not violate the lightest word of that chart which has so well guided us in the past, yet I desire that so broad and liberal a construction be placed upon its provisions as will insure protection to the humblest citizen, without regard to rank, creed or color. Tell

me nothing of a constitution which fails to shelter beneath its rightful power the people of a country!"

As he finished his oration in defense of the bill, Rainey reminded his colleagues that he and the five other African American representatives serving in the House were personally at risk. And yet, his chief desire was peace—for his constituents, his state, and his country.

"I can say for my people that we ardently desire peace for ourselves and for the whole nation," Rainey declared. He made clear, in no uncertain terms, "Come what will, we are fully determined to stand by the Republican party and the Government. As to our fate, 'we are not wood, we are not stone,' but men, with feelings and sensibilities like other men whose skin is of a lighter hue." And he reminded his colleagues that "When myself and colleagues shall leave these Halls and turn our footsteps toward our southern homes, we know not but that the assassin may await our coming, as marked for his vengeance. Should this befall, we would bid Congress and our country to remember that 'twas 'bloody treason flourished over us'" (a quote from Shakespeare's *Julius Caesar*, as Mark Antony condemns Caesar's murder).

It was a matter of life and death for Rainey. However, "Be it as it may," Rainey explained, "we have resolved to be loyal and firm, and if we perish, we perish!" As his colleagues awaited his final words, Rainey closed his remarks humbly, stating simply, "I earnestly hope the bill will pass."

Rainey's earnestness, among others, clearly won the day. The bill ultimately passed. And the administration of President Ulysses Grant successfully prosecuted enough Klan leaders, especially in South Carolina, to tamp down the violence, at least temporarily. But the work remained unfinished.

Senator Sumner had introduced his Civil Rights bill in 1870, around the time that Rainey joined the House, and it was still pending. Sumner had always argued for both racial equality and abolition of slavery, and he regarded the bill as the final piece of his crusade that began before the Civil War and would conclude, he hoped, with Reconstruction. Rainey also recognized the bill as the best way to cement in law the status as citizens that Black Americans had won in the war but that remained precarious and incomplete during Reconstruction. The bill would outlaw discrimination in jury service; on trains; and in hotels, restaurants, bars, and other public accommodations, including churches. It also mandated the desegregation of schools.

Opposition to the bill came from multiple sides. For many Democrats, including former Confederates now largely restored to full political rights and their allies, the bill threatened a full racial equality that they opposed and had fought against, even in the face of the three constitutional amendments intended to bring it about. Some predicted apocalyptic consequences, as when a Kentucky representative said passage of the bill might cause a race war, threatening, "When that occurs, the Black race will be exterminated in this country." And for some Republicans who had supported Reconstruction and the constitutional amendments, the bill created a political hazard, as they feared it would drive away the support of less affluent voters, particularly in mountain areas where slavery had not been prevalent. The bill languished for two years in the Senate Judiciary Committee, where two key Republican Senators, although former abolitionists from the North, pronounced it too extreme and too much of an intrusion into the private conduct of Americans.

But in 1872, Sumner found a way to bring his bill back to life.

By that year, Congress had granted amnesty to most former Confederates, but the topic remained an important symbolic issue and key to the year's presidential politics. The Republican Party had recently split, with Liberal Republicans meeting in Cincinnati, Ohio, in early May to nominate Horace Greeley to run against President Grant, adopting a platform of amnesty and reconciliation with the South. Months later, the Democrats would nominate Greeley, too. Republicans on President Grant's side sought to undercut Greeley by removing the issue of amnesty from the political lexicon. In short, they advanced legislation to end the debate once and for all by granting amnesty to nearly everyone eligible. But, as that amnesty bill moved forward in the Senate, Sumner, who supported Greeley, took the opportunity to revive his Civil Rights bill. On May 9, 1872, he made a motion on the Senate floor to bypass the Judiciary Committee's blockade entirely by adding the text of his bill as an amendment to the pending amnesty bill.

And in a surprising vote, he won.

Sumner's allies had supported him sincerely. But some senators voted for his amendment hoping to kill both bills, without appearing to do so: the amnesty bill could only pass with a two-thirds majority in both houses, which it was less likely to receive when paired with civil rights. By the same token, the civil rights measure would now need two-thirds support to pass instead of a simple majority.

Whatever the hidden strategies, however, Sumner's move showed he had adopted the pairing that Rainey had first begun pursuing years before, at the South Carolina constitutional convention. Sumner now made the explicit appeal. Many of Rainey's colleagues had also come to accept the logic of pairing amnesty and civil rights, recognizing a republic couldn't function permanently with many citizens excluded from holding office. At the time, others also asserted that moves for reconciliation could calm the insurgency gripping the South, which they believed drew power, at least in part, from resentment against the Reconstruction amnesty rules themselves. Instead of suppressing political participation, their philosophy demanded that Black voters should be protected at the same time former rebels were reincorporated into the democratic system.

Among the most powerful statements for the bill, Rainey and his colleagues could testify to their own experience of discrimination even as members of Congress. During one notable speech, Rainey asked the House:

"Why is it that the colored members of Congress cannot enjoy the same immunities that are accorded to white members? Why cannot we stop at hotels here without meeting objection? Why cannot we go into restaurants without being insulted? We are here enacting laws for the country and casting votes upon important questions; we have been sent here by the suffrages of the people, and why cannot we enjoy the same benefits that are accorded to our white colleagues on this floor? . . . I say to you, gentlemen, that you are making a mistake. Public opinion is aroused on this question. I tell you that the negro will never rest until he gets his rights. We ask them because we know it is proper, not because we want to deprive any other class of the rights and immunities they enjoy, but because they are granted to us by the law of the land. Why this discrimination against us when we enter public conveyances or places of amusement? Why is a discrimination made against us in the churches; and why in the cemeteries when we go to pay that last debt of nature that brings us all upon a level? Gentlemen, I say to you this discrimination must cease."

As politicians, the Black Congressmen of the era never gained the status of insiders. Some of their own party leaders discriminated against them, assigning them to lesser committees and giving them rank on those committees lower than their seniority would have dictated. Nor was Sumner himself an insider in 1872, despite his fame and soaring oratory. His unyielding moral stands and unwillingness to compromise had alienated his colleagues, many of whom regarded him as self-righteous. He had also quarreled with President Grant in opposing Grant's plan to annex the Dominican Republic, and was expelled from his own party caucus, reducing his status to that of a freshman senator, and, observers said, precipitating a decline as well in his health.

On May 13, four days after Sumner's amendment combining the Senate's amnesty and civil rights bills (which had not yet passed), Rainey and his African American colleague from South Carolina, Robert Elliott, attempted to link the two issues in the House as well. A House version of the amnesty bill was approaching final passage when Rainey sought to speak.

The House was noisy, members walking and talking among themselves, sharing lists of names of individuals from across the South for inclusion in the bill for restoration of the rebels' full political rights. In hopes of ending the amnesty debate and remove it as an issue from presidential politics, the Republican leadership had thrown open the amnesty bill for any member of Congress to add whomever he wished to its list of approved individuals. An initial list of sixteen thousand names had grown by dozens of pages, with blanket language that covered almost anyone. Members walked to the desk at the front of the chamber to turn in their own lists of names, each of which the House added by unanimous consent without having them read.

Amid the hubbub, the Speaker twice declared he had lost control of the House and pleaded for order amid laughter and jokes by members. All but about one hundred fifty former rebels would now receive full amnesty—some had even been given amnesty twice. Benjamin Butler of Massachusetts, chairman of the Judiciary Committee, tried to speak over the noise, pushing through the confusion for a rapid vote.

At that moment, Rainey rose and sought to speak. Members shouted out objections, calling for the House to hurry onward. But Rainey persisted.

Finally, the Speaker granted him the floor.

Rainey spoke now with a serious voice and purpose, emphasizing the weighty decision the House would soon make. Slowly, the members returned to order and paid attention. But he and Elliott would face a major obstacle. The process of parliamentary procedure would not easily allow them to link civil rights to the amnesty bill. Democrats had filibustered and used various procedural delays against the Civil Rights bill, which remained in the House Judiciary Committee. Rules adopted by their own party leaders barred amendment of the amnesty bill to add the text of the Civil Rights bill, as Sumner had done in the Senate. As explained by Chairman Butler, adding the Civil Rights bill to the amnesty bill could kill it, since amnesty would need a two-thirds vote. Rainey and Elliott's best hope was to pass a motion suspending the rules and to bring the Civil Rights bill to the floor immediately after the amnesty vote, sending both bills to the Senate simultaneously as separate pieces of legislation, where Sumner's paired bill was waiting. But the motion to suspend the rules would require a two-thirds vote.

While both parties waited for the vote that would finally end the amnesty issue, Rainey told the House that he and his constituents agreed with them. He wanted to give the former rebels their full rights—in fact, he had been advocating to do so in state and national politics for four years. Ignoring the insults and threats he had suffered as a member of Congress, he said:

"We are desirous, sir, of being magnanimous; it may be that we are so to a fault; nevertheless, we have open and frank hearts toward those who were our former oppressors and taskmasters. We foster no enmity now, and we desire to foster none for their acts in the past to us, nor to the Government we love so well. But while we are willing to accord them their enfranchisement, and here today give our votes that they may be amnestied; while we declare our hearts open and free from any vindictive feelings toward them, we would say to those gentlemen on the other side, and also to those on this side who are representing more directly the sentiment and wishes of our disenfranchised fellow citizens, that there is another class of citizens in this country who have certain dear rights and immunities which they would like you, sirs, to remember and respect. . . . We now invoke you, gentlemen, to show the same magnanimity and kindly feeling toward us—a race long oppressed; and in demonstration of this humane and just feeling give, I implore you, give support to the civil rights bill, which we have been asking at your hands, lo! these many days."

He added that he and Elliott, and their Republican colleagues, had not filibustered the amnesty bill, as the Democrats had done to their Civil Rights measure. "It is because we are disposed to facilitate and assist the furtherance of those measures we believe equitable and just to our fellow man, thus doing unto others as we would they should do unto us," Rainey said. "I hope you will assist us in securing our civil rights. I need not say to you that we fought for the maintenance of this Government while those who are about to be amnestied fought to destroy it."

Rainey had certainly met the moment. But even after he concluded his powerful remarks, opponents attempted to block Elliott from making his motion. When Elliott finally got the floor, he declared he now would vote for amnesty—although he had opposed it before—but asked in return for support of an immediate vote afterward on civil rights. And as soon as the amnesty bill passed, he made his motion to suspend the rules and bring up the Civil Rights bill.

The vote was called immediately thereafter. And when it was all said and done, the motion received a majority, but not the necessary two-thirds support.

It had failed.

Some hope remained, however, because Sumner's bill remained a part of the amnesty bill still under consideration in the Senate. Democrats mounted a filibuster, holding the floor and talking day and night. The issue dragged on. President Grant's supporters wanted the amnesty bill enacted and listened to some southern Republicans' warnings that the Civil Rights bill would hurt him in that fall's election. But it would not be easy to bypass Sumner in the Senate, potentially disrespecting his legacy of abolitionism, notwithstanding his diminished status as an exile from the Republican caucus.

Finally, on May 22, 1872, as the filibuster dragged on and on through the night, Senator Matthew Carpenter, a Wisconsin Republican and Grant stalwart—and Sumner's bitter enemy—devised a clever strategy to outmaneuver him. Carpenter made a deal with the Democrats to drop their filibuster as soon as Sumner was out of the room; in exchange, Republicans would bring up an immediate vote on the House amnesty bill and, shortly after, a version of the Civil Rights bill that Carpenter had drafted, which left out the most important provisions. As the session wore on, overnight, Sumner left the floor of the Senate to get some sleep, whereupon Carpenter activated his plan. With a bare quorum present, the filibuster ended at 5:45 a.m. The Senate passed the House's amnesty bill and then passed Carpenter's emasculated Civil Rights bill, sending it over to the House.

Sumner rushed to the floor just as the plan reached consummation and cried out, "Let it go forth that the sacrifice has been perpetrated. Amnesty has been adopted, but where are the equal rights of the colored race?"

Carpenter's version of the Civil Rights bill would not win support from true advocates of civil rights in the House. But the stronger version of the bill remained in committee. A week later, the House took a test vote, and the strong Civil Rights bill failed to gain enough support to go forward. The issued died for that year. And in the fall, President Grant won the election over Greeley by a landslide.

In 1873, Sumner tried again, dropping church desegregation from the Civil Rights bill—a provision some contended would run afoul of the First Amendment's guarantee of freedom of religion—but his ill health kept him from advocating strongly for the legislation. Meanwhile, time was clearly running out for Rainey's vision to establish a basis for southerners of all races to coexist in a democratic system through equal rights. In April 1873, the Supreme Court had handed down the *Slaughterhouse* decision, hollowing out the applicability of the Fourteenth Amendment's promise of equal protection, making it, as a dissenting justice wrote, of little meaning, a "vain and idle enactment," and stripping the federal government of power to enforce its protections.

All the while, newspapers alleged the failure and incompetency of southern Reconstruction governments, even in northern publications that had supported equal rights, with exaggerations and distortions that painted Black leaders as corrupt and incapable of holding office. The falsehoods proved so durable that they would live on into the middle of the twentieth century, with some historians still contending that the era's elevation of such leaders was a tragic mistake. For practical politicians such as Rainey, the changing mood meant that troops and federal prosecutors could not be expected to stay in the South forever to guarantee political rights. Rainey knew that the need to codify civil right protections was urgent.

Sumner's death came in the spring of 1874. Rainey gave his moving eulogy. Tributes came from many others, as well, as the nation grappled with the passing of Sumner's generation of abolitionists, whose principled crusade had helped end slavery during the most tumultuous time in America's history. Rainey's speech, however, proved especially powerful and prescient when he twice intoned Sumner's last words: "Do not let the Civil Rights bill fail." Those words, repeated by Rainey, would seemingly prove more effective than all of Sumner's many erudite floor speeches for the bill. Moved by respect for Sumner's legacy, the Senate rapidly passed the bill in the wake of his death, without amendments.

Now the fight moved to the House, where it would play out over the next year.

Rainey continued to make the case linking civil rights to amnesty as a moral argument, even though the two could no longer be connected in legislation now that the amnesty bill was law. The year before, in March 1873, Rainey excoriated a colleague for complaining about being prevented from putting forward yet another amnesty bill for "a few men who had raised their traitorous hands against this Government," and stating "if there are any people in this country who have a right to find fault, it is the class to which I belong, because that gentleman and his political friends would not allow the civil rights bill to be acted upon. . . . I say we should be generous to all, not simply to a few."

In one particular exchange in 1874, Rainey sat in the House chamber as he listened to a long speech delivered by Representative Robert

Vance of North Carolina, a former slave owner and brigadier general in the Confederate Army who opposed the Civil Rights bill. As Vance concluded his remarks, he stated his firm belief that "we have really extended to the colored man everything that I think he ought to ask at our hands," and further, that "[i]f [he] belonged to the colored race," he would "not stand here and ask the passage of a law to force me into what are termed my civil rights." Vance declared to the members listening on the House Floor that, "[i]f I belonged to the colored race I would come up by my own merit . . . and I would not ask any help from Congress. I would not stand here as a beggar asking for these social rights."

Rainey, an eloquent debater, stood upright. "Before the gentleman sits down, I would like to ask him a question," Rainey calmly stated. "Certainly," Vance replied. Well, Rainey explained, "this gentleman has just said that if he was a colored man, he would not ask Congress to pass the civil rights bill, which has for its object the removal of disabilities imposed upon us by prejudice." Then, Rainey cleverly proceeded to pose Vance a simple question: "I ask him what he thinks of those Southerners who ask Congress to remove from them *their* political disabilities on account of their action toward this Government?" Vance's eventual attempt at an answer—that the southern rebellion was, "under the circumstances," right in his view—only lent further credence to the urgent necessity for the Civil Rights bill.

Exposing the opposition's true colors, however, would not solve the legislative gridlock, as violence resurged in the former Confederacy, and as some in the Republican Party, which had used its majority power to send troops, lost their resolve. As the 1874 midterm elections approached, the economic depression and corruption scandals in the Grant administration hurt the party's chances. Republican leaders in the House continued to bottle up the Civil Rights bill, fearing it would hurt them at the polls. Only after the Democrats won a devastating victory that fall, taking control of the House, did some Republicans, including Judiciary Committee Chairman Butler, push for a package of bills to protect the party's Black southern members, including Sumner's Civil Rights bill, while their party still held the majority during the lame duck session.

Butler led that fight, which extended into early 1875, even after he had lost his own reelection bid in 1874. Before the Civil War, he had been a self-proclaimed "state's-rights" Democrat, but his experience as a Union general had apparently changed him. Desperately needing reinforcements, he had raised regiments of Black soldiers, at first feeling doubtful whether the former slaves could fight, but soon thereafter, inspired by their courage.

In support of the Civil Rights bill, Butler delivered a spellbinding oration that brought repeated and long cheering and applause—until the Speaker threatened to clear the gallery—as he told of sending a column of three thousand Black soldiers against a strong fortification atop a steep hill on Virginia's James River, without permitting them to fire their guns. Under a hell of cannon and rifle fire from behind the Confederates' wall, the soldiers hacked at the defenses with axes, picking up the tools and the flag from men who fell, until they broke through and the position was taken, leaving 542 of them dead in the narrow space where they attacked the wall, and where Butler picked his way among their bodies on his horse. "I looked on their bronzed faces upturned in the shining sun to heaven as if in mute appeal against the wrongs of the country for which they had given their lives," Butler said, "feeling I had wronged them in the past and believing what was the future of my country to them—among my dead comrades there I swore to myself a solemn oath, 'May my right hand forget its cunning and my tongue cleave to the roof of my mouth if I ever fail to defend the rights of these men who have given their blood for me and my country this day and for their race forever' and, God helping me, I will keep that oath."

But Butler and Rainey, and their Republican colleagues, faced a daunting political environment. The opposition could point to the *Slaughterhouse* decision, quoting the Supreme Court's majority opinion to insist the Civil Rights bill was unconstitutional. And with those arguments and extensive procedural delays, Democrats endeavored to prevent passage of the Reconstruction bills until they could take over with their new majority.

It was during this final effort to enact civil rights legislation that Rainey delivered perhaps his greatest speech. It came in response to a lengthy legal criticism of the Sumner bill by Representative James Burnie Beck, of Kentucky, who concluded his remarks with the Democrats' argument that the legislation would interfere with Americans' lives by attempting to create social equality. Rainey quickly rose to his feet and requested the floor.

"Mr. Speaker," Rainey sternly began, "I did not expect to participate in this debate at this early period." He pointed out that in the presidential election, when they had called for reconciliation, the Greeley campaign—representing both the Democrats and Liberal Republicans—had said they would advocate for the friendship and rights of "the race to which I belong," as well as amnesty for southerners. Now, however, they were opposing the part of that equation that would give African Americans equal rights. Directly addressing Beck's remarks, Rainey stated:

> "The gentleman from Kentucky [Mr. BECK] has taken a legal view of this question, and he is undoubtedly capable of taking that view. I am not a lawyer, and consequently I cannot take a legal view of this matter, or perhaps I cannot view it through the same optics that he does. *I view it in the light of the Constitution—in the light of the amendments that have been made to that Constitution; I view it in the light of humanity; I view it in the light of the progress and civilization which are now rapidly marching over this country* [emphasis added]. We, sirs, would not ask of this Congress as a people that they should legislate for us specifically as a class if we could only have those rights which this bill is designed to give us accorded us without this enactment."

As Rainey had attested, unlike many of his colleagues, he was not an attorney, nor had he received any legal training. And yet, his words were arguably more compelling than those of the most accomplished lawyer. This self-made man, who through sheer determination had broken countless barriers and landed in the People's House, invoked during the debate the two most powerful tools available to him, and to all Americans, of every race and creed: the Constitution and their common humanity. And having supported reconciliation, he eloquently implored his colleagues to, finally, honor their end of the bargain.

The Congress eventually heard his call. And the Civil Rights Act of 1875 passed in the final hours of the 43rd Congress. The rest of Butler's package of legislation, however, had been stripped, and the education clause eliminated from the bill. The compromise left only equality in jury service, transportation, and public accommodations—and with no enforcement mechanism to bring an end to discrimination in places such as restaurants and railroads, except by lawsuits brought in federal court by those who had been victims of discrimination (an impossibility at that time for most African American citizens). Then, in 1883, the Supreme Court overthrew that part of the law, as well, leaving only the section on juries intact. The long fight had brought little real change for those denied equality, and would not until, in another century, another cast of characters carried on the cause.

Reconstruction ended in 1876 with the contested presidential election between Republican Rutherford B. Hayes and Democrat Samuel Tilden. With widespread violence and intimidation of Republican voters across the South, the election resulted in a near-tie, with contested results from southern states tipping the balance either way in the Electoral College. As the dispute built for months, fears of another Civil War became real, and Congress sought a path to compromise by creating a commission to decide the contested results. Rainey voted against the commission, perhaps foreseeing the final compromise that ultimately emerged—in exchange for allowing Hayes to take the presidency, the Republicans agreed to remove troops from the South, essentially ending Reconstruction.

For Rainey personally, and his history-making colleagues, the end of Reconstruction meant the end of their political careers. After being easily reelected the first time, in 1872—his stance of reconciliation attracting voters of both races—Rainey's election wins were legally contested in both 1874 and 1876. With Democrats in the South emboldened by their strengthening position, violence increased across the region even before the electoral compromise of 1876. On July 4 of that centennial year, a dispute arose in Hamburg, South Carolina, when Black militiamen celebrating Independence Day at first refused an order by two White men to move out of the way of their carriage. The dispute escalated, and the area's leading Democratic politician, a former general, gathered a large group of men with heavy firepower—including a cannon—that attacked the militia, killing one member and capturing twenty-five, five of whom were murdered in cold blood during the night. The general was not punished—he was elected to the US Senate. Two weeks after the Hamburg Massacre, Rainey condemned the murders on the floor of the House. Ordinarily a mild-mannered and respectful debater, he finally lost his temper when a New York Democrat blamed the Reconstruction South Carolina government for the deaths.

In 1878, when Rainey ran again, his South Carolina colleague, Robert Smalls, was attacked while campaigning by eight hundred mounted and armed men—led by the state's leading Democrats—who cornered him with forty supporters in a store and threatened to burn them out; Smalls survived only because an even larger body of his supporters descended on the scene.

Rainey lost his seat in that election. He was not alone. African American leaders lost their positions across the South with the end of Reconstruction, and with it, the removal of federal troops and federal oversight of elections. The voting and civil rights that had been achieved in the post–Civil War amendments and laws were soon rolled back.

Rainey tried to return to politics in various roles. He served in a position with the Treasury Department. Later, he ran an unsuccessful business in Washington. But he eventually returned to South Carolina. And it was there, back in Georgetown, the city of his birth, that Rainey died of heart failure in 1887. He was fifty-five years old.

For nearly a century, Rainey's accomplishments received little attention. Many historians repeated the fiction that Reconstruction-era leaders were incompetent and corrupt. But perspectives eventually changed, and the heroism of these leaders was rediscovered. Rainey's reputation, in particular, rose, as historians noted his symbolic status as the first and longest- serving of the Reconstruction Congressmen. The House of Representatives commissioned his portrait in 2005 and in 2022 accorded him the rare honor of naming a room in the Capitol for him.

Of course, Rainey is to be remembered for far more than his symbolism. He, more than many, perceived a need for reconciliation as the foundation for sustainable equal rights, no matter the difficulties. His decision to link political amnesty and civil rights as a legislative strategy, calling on the Constitution's power both to protect the individual rights of all Americans and to create equal opportunity for all, may not have been popular. Nor did he and those who shared his views have the power to bring about that future in their lifetimes. But he, undoubtedly, used the moment given him by history to the best of his ability. Though he had great reason to harbor animosity toward his adversaries, he showed remarkable courage in reaching out to them instead, while at the same time vigorously demanding his rightful place—as an *equal* citizen, under the law.

2

Josiah Walls

★ ★ ★ ★ ★ ★ ★ ★ ★

[W]hen from every corner of this broad land . . . millions of the free citizens of a free government shall . . . exchange with each other the mutual grasps and the meaningful glances of a common citizenship, there will be aroused in the bosoms of all a higher and purer sense of the honest and sincere attachment cherished by all in common for those free institutions whose origin and beneficent sway they are now to celebrate.

—JOSIAH WALLS

As representatives slowly shuffled across the House floor, meandering through the aisles to their seats, the atmosphere was tense. The mood in the House chamber was, for some members, as bitter as the icily cold weather outside. The date was February 4, 1875. Members had gathered in the historic chamber, during the waning days of the 43rd session of Congress, in the wake of a political typhoon. Democrats would soon be taking the reins of the House for the first time in a generation, having won a resounding victory at the polls a few months earlier. Republican representatives grumbled as they made their way on and off the House floor. The winds had shifted. Many political careers would be ending unceremoniously in a matter of weeks—prematurely, in the view of those politicians who had lost. But the business of the House, and the country, would go on. And the business at hand this morning was a weighty matter indeed: the House's final consideration of the Civil Rights Act of 1875.

The path to this final vote on the fateful bill had been an arduous one. Members of Congress had labored for many years to pass the legislation. Among such members was a young, impassioned representative from the South. The lush wetlands and immense hardwood trees near his home in the backwoods of Alachua County, Florida, must have felt a world away from the marble walls and carved furnishings in the nation's seat of government where he now served.

His name was Josiah T. Walls, a man born a slave who, through sheer determination and grit, became Florida's first Black congressman. His eyes surely conveyed a heaviness beyond his years. He had toiled, long and hard, for years with his colleagues to push civil rights legislation forward, believing such laws would crown the struggle of the Civil War and Reconstruction by guaranteeing true equality for all Americans, particularly in public education. Now, after years of struggle and grid-lock, endless parliamentary maneuvers, and heated legislative debates, the bill had finally come up for final passage.

The congressional session began that day without fanfare, just a few minutes after noon. The chaplain offered a solemn prayer. The journal from the day before was perfunctorily read. And then, the rhetorical battle commenced.

It was a rancorous debate, to be sure. The congressional record makes clear that the Speaker was compelled to bang his gavel multiple times. Passions were high. But finally, after hours of fiery pronounce-ments, indignant rebuttals, and the like, the yeas and nays were ordered.

It was time to vote.

As the clerk called the roll, Republican members, one by one, bel-lowed their support of the measure. Among them were the Black rep-resentatives whose elections had made American history just a few years earlier. Joseph Rainey, the first African American ever elected, voted aye. His fellow South Carolinian Richard Cain voted aye, too. Mississippian John Lynch, a former slave, joined them. Alabaman James Rapier did the same. As the final count was tabulated, it was clear that not only had the bill earned the votes of the vast majority of Republicans, but it had, finally, passed the House. The legislation—the late Senator Charles Sumner's dying wish—would finally become law. And the members who had worked so hard to achieve that dream were undoubtedly pleased as they heard the clerk announce the bill's passage.

But it is doubtful that Josiah Walls celebrated with them. For, unlike so many of his colleagues, Walls did not vote for the bill.

He abstained.

Walls's compatriots must have wondered what rationale he could possibly muster for doing so. And how could he ever defend his decision not to support the civil rights legislation?

History does not indicate whether Walls offered such an explanation on that day, and if so, to whom. But he had his reasons. Of that, one can be certain.

What Walls surely knew in his heart was that the central core of the famed measure had been given up to what some deemed an unacceptable compromise. In their final days controlling the body, his party's Republican leaders had stripped a provision federally funding public schools and prohibiting racial segregation in them in order to gain the bill's passage. Walls, as much as anyone, knew that education could open the passageway for four million former slaves to escape poverty and take their place in society and civic life. He had made that journey himself—escaping slavery, learning to read, and becoming a miliary leader, a teacher, a successful farmer and businessman, and a congressman—all during just ten short years. His belief in the universality and promises of public education was bone deep.

As a member of Congress, Walls envisioned a new South, industrialized and welcoming to immigrants, that could sustain prosperity and equality for everyone, Black and White. And throughout his political career and private life, he placed building blocks toward that future, with educational improvements in his state of Florida as the cornerstone. His own extraordinary achievements were recognized in his time, so much so that he even gained respect from his adversaries. However, he also knew the status of African Americans in the South remained precariously fragile—as did his own service in the House— and largely depended on the continued resolve of Republican leaders in Washington to station troops to protect his constituents' rights. Many hundreds of his supporters were being terrorized and killed by the Ku Klux Klan, and he survived an assassination attempt while campaigning. Reconstruction presented an opportunity for something more lasting. In his own vision of reconciliation and economic development, Walls sought a firmer basis of equality through one of life's most indestructible and profound gifts: education.

When the Civil Rights Act passed the House on that February day in 1875 without the education provision, Reconstruction was already ebbing away, eroding Walls's dream of a new South. His resolute anger is recorded by history. The day after President Grant signed the bill, Walls waited restlessly in his seat in the House, holding a lengthy speech in his hand. He had carefully prepared a scathing and thorough indictment of the forces that sought to reverse the results of the Civil War through violence and intimidation. Walls's speech reviewed the history of Reconstruction, beginning with the days just after the war had ended. He quoted extensively from Democratic southern newspapers that vowed to use any means necessary—including violence—to overthrow Reconstruction governments and exclude African Americans from political power. The words jumped off the page.

"I reluctantly confess, after so many long years of concessions," Walls dejectedly noted, that those who lost the Civil War were now attempting to win what they had "lost by the bayonet" and would bring "a complete reign of terror and anarchy." He returned to the call for federal funding of public schools for citizens of all races, and asked, in desperation, for protection of African Americans in the South to continue.

"Sir, when I say that we cherish no animosity toward those who were once our masters, I speak for all the colored people of this broad land," Walls continued. "Yet we demand that our lives, our liberties, and our property shall be protected by the strong arm of the Government, that gives us the same citizenship that it gives to those who it seems would, if it were possible, sink our every hope for peace, prosperity, and happiness into the great sea of oblivion."

He was never allowed to rise to his feet to give his speech, as the congressman speaking for the other side refused to yield to Walls the time that party leaders had planned to give him. A mere year later, he would be expelled from the House after a partisan investigation of claims of election irregularities lodged by his opponent, a former Confederate general. The Democrats refused to allow any of his congressional colleagues to speak on his behalf. And it would take well over one hundred years—until 1993—for another African American to be elected to Congress from Florida.

Walls had been forced to spend much of his six years in the House battling attempts to push him out of office, prompting some historians to question how much he accomplished. But after he left office, he again won election to the Florida State Senate, continuing his lifelong advocacy for compulsory public education. Later, he returned to teaching, as director of the agricultural college that would eventually become Florida A&M University. Florida public schools grew rapidly during Reconstruction and survived, to a diminished degree, even after Reconstruction ended. Indeed, by 1890, half of Black Floridians were literate—up from almost none after the Civil War—the highest level of Black literacy in any former Confederate state.

Walls had made a difference.

He rose from slavery to wealth, power, and respect and then fell to obscurity. Walls left no record of his life beyond what historians can find in official documents, newspapers, and the written memories of others. One must piece together his story largely without knowing how he felt or what he expressed in his personal letters or diaries, because all that is lost.

Virtually nothing is known about Walls's mother or the rest of the family into which he was born, except the man who was likely his father, and who was believed to have owned his mother as a slave and Josiah himself from the moment of his birth on December 30, 1842. Dr. John Walls practiced medicine in Winchester, Virginia; Josiah lived there in his boyhood and later in another Virginia town. How did Josiah Walls become an educated man, able to lead political conventions, craft legislation, and deliver complex, powerful arguments on the floor of the House? In the world of his youth, educating a person in slavery was a crime, and there is no evidence he received any schooling before he was eighteen. At that age, he was swept up by the Civil War, when the Confederate Army forced him to serve as a slave and servant for an artillery detail. In May 1862, Walls was captured at the Battle of Yorktown, in Virginia, and Union troops gave him his freedom. He eventually made it to Harrisburg, Pennsylvania, where he attended a year of school before joining the Union Army himself. Perhaps he received more schooling as a soldier, as many Black soldiers did, or, given his remarkable abilities, may have been able to parlay his single year of formal education into the impressive skills he later developed. In either event, the difficulties he faced clearly gave him a powerful appreciation for the value of education that he retained for the rest of his life.

African American units fighting for the North earned admiration for their courage, but they also faced discrimination, with lower pay, worse clothing and equipment than their fellow servicemembers, and difficult assignments. Walls's unit at first received scant training and was assigned to dig sod and perform other manual labor. But Walls ultimately saw combat and rose in the ranks to become a first sergeant and artillery instructor. His regiment was sent to Florida, and among their assignments, Walls's patrols found and freed slaves to bring them to the Union side. On one raid in St. Augustine, a patrol of twenty-five soldiers freed seventy slaves.

When the war ended, Walls possessed a special status among his peers in Florida. Unlike many freedmen, he could read and write, and moreover, had some financial resources, having left the army with a little over $100 in compensation. He had married his wife Helen, known as Ella, while still in uniform and went to work briefly at a sawmill before becoming a schoolteacher in Gainesville. At the time, many freed slaves were eager for education and flooded new schools funded by private benefactors in the North, often in buildings the students built themselves out of logs and whatever material they had at hand. Or they studied outdoors, alongside children on the ground and graying elders on benches, all gathered around a fire with slates and books in hand. Teachers were scarce, and Walls was more qualified than many who had the job. Among Black Floridians, very few had the literacy to teach, and White teachers, who demonstrated courage to come from outside the state, were often physically threatened.

Before the Civil War, education in Florida was paid for privately, thereby leaving people of all races who lacked financial means locked out of the system. Walls himself touched on this policy in 1872, in one of his first speeches in the House, stating that to educate a slave "was to set him free, and . . . to deprive him of all the advantages necessary to enable him to acquire an education was to perpetuate enslavement." He explained further that, in his view, states like Florida had declined to offer public education to citizens who did not have financial means because slaves "more directly associated with" such individuals, rather than "with that class who controlled the destinies of slavery." Thus, "[s]o fearful were they that the Negro would become educated . . . they enacted laws prohibiting him from being educated even by his own master . . . and if by chance [he] did learn to read, and it was found out, he was whipped every time he was caught with a book, and as many times between as his master pleased." Walls implored his colleagues to "remember that this state of affairs existed only about six years ago."

In the aftermath of the Civil War, former slaves overwhelmed new schools with their eagerness to learn. In fact, citizens of different races sometimes came, as the freedmen's schools provided an opportunity to become literate for those who could not afford to enroll in a private school. Observers reported that the freedmen regarded reading as something almost sacred: an ability that could make their freedom real and could open a world of meaning that had been always denied to them. With their students' intense interest, classes with qualified instructors advanced extraordinarily rapidly. To Walls and others, the evidence was clear that education promised to remake the social, economic, and political order. Indeed, within five years, almost 16 percent of Black Floridians over the age of ten had gained literacy.

But moving faster would require more schools. It would require more teachers and an adequate, stable source of funding. And, perhaps above all else, it would require a leader to champion it all.

It is against that backdrop that Walls's political career began in 1867, shortly after Congress put the United States Army in charge of Reconstruction, with laws requiring former Confederate states to adopt new constitutions, ratify the Fourteenth Amendment, and allow African Americans to vote in order to end military rule and gain readmission to the Union. His status as a veteran and a teacher surely helped as well. Newspapers attested to his courtesy and remarkable intelligence, but also said his lack of education remained noticeable. As the constitutional convention approached, Walls began attending political meetings, and he won a seat as a delegate from his county at the convention, which convened in January of 1868. After the new government was formed, he also won election as a state assemblyman and the following year became a state senator.

Politics were volatile and dangerous in Florida then. Some Democrats resisted Reconstruction with violence—from 1868 to 1871, political murders claimed nineteen people in Walls's Alachua County alone. In Jackson County, near Tallahassee, 153 people were killed. Elections were chaotic affairs, with voters often in danger and needing protection to cast their ballots. At first, many Democrats either boycotted elections or were disqualified from voting by the Fourteenth Amendment due to their status as former rebels, giving Republicans a powerful majority. The Republican coalition included Black freedmen, White Republicans originally from Florida (pejoratively called "scalawags" in the jargon of the day), and those Republicans who had newly arrived in the state (known as "carpetbaggers"). But the Florida Republican Party was divided bitterly among various factions, weakening attempts at reform. The more conservative group of Republicans sought the backing of African American voters to boost their party's electoral chances, but without making the changes the freedmen insisted upon for equality and advancement. At the 1868 constitutional convention, that faction kept control, and the results disappointed many Black leaders. The first legislative session under the new constitution also produced little progress. Walls was shunted to an unimportant committee, with the demeaning task of procuring new inkwells and paperweights for the legislators' desks. That legislature also defeated legislation to create a system of public schools in Florida; the bill would have prohibited schools from integrating children of all races, and the African American chair of the education committee would not advance it with that provision.

Walls was a fast learner, however, and when he returned to the legislature the next year, as a state senator, he was ready. This time, he won a place on the education committee. That committee turned out a new bill creating a system of public schools, along with the establishment of a state university. And an agreement was reached on the issue of segregation. The bill would not mandate it, but rather, would allow local school boards to choose whether their schools would be segregated or integrated. The bill passed and was signed into law in January 1869, marking the founding of Florida's existing public school system today.

Walls also prospered personally during those years. In 1868, he bought a sixty-acre farm, presumably using the money he had saved from his work as a teacher, and developed a reputation as a highly successful farmer, soon adding more acreage to his holdings. Even later, after he was elected to Congress, he would work side-by-side with the hired hands in his fields.

In August 1870, Republicans from across Florida gathered in Gainesville to nominate a candidate for the state's sole at-large seat in the House of Representatives. In Walls's day, Florida was sparsely settled, with a population smaller even than that of tiny Rhode Island. Gainesville had been incorporated as a city only the year before the convention. The dusty town looked like a scattered collection of houses and didn't even have a hall appropriate for the gathering. For Walls, however, the area was fertile ground for both his farming ventures and his burgeoning political career. Land was cheap and easy to buy, and the fluid political situation meant anything could happen.

The Democrats' strategy to win the 1870 elections in Florida brought a campaign of violence to deter voters from going to the polls. That, in turn, put pressure on Republicans to unify their factions and nominate a Black candidate who would draw freedmen to the polls. Various names were put forward, and the convention, amidst the sweltering heat, nearly collapsed in chaos and rioting through a series of ten ballots. Attendees cast ballot after ballot.

Finally, on the eleventh ballot, a candidate won the nomination for election to Congress. It was Josiah Walls, only twenty-seven years old.

Walls became a compromise candidate because he had not aligned closely with any faction and had qualities that appealed to all sides. Some in the party favored his advocacy for economic development—canals, railroads, and port projects—while many others supported him as a strong advocate for equality and education. But winning the general election would prove a larger challenge. The statewide respect Walls had earned in the legislature would not be enough. His opponent from the Conservative Party (as the Democrats in Florida briefly called themselves at the time) was a Confederate veteran, Silas Niblack, who charged that a former slave would be too ignorant to serve in Congress. In response, Walls challenged Niblack to debate, so he could defend his intelligence. When Niblack refused, Walls, speaking at a rally in Gainesville, with members of both parties present, suggested Niblack was a coward, afraid to face him on the stage. Unrest erupted in the crowd. Enraged Democrats attacked an African American handing out Republican leaflets, and gunfire broke out.

A bullet missed Walls by inches.

The violence continued on Election Day, as Niblack's allies set out to keep Walls's supporters away from the polls. Men armed with guns blocked roads miles from the towns where African Americans could cast their ballots. And in at least two cases, when groups of voters gathered together for safety in numbers to defeat the blockades, the men trying to stop them fired on them. In Marianna, Klan leaders attacked voters outside the polling place and as many as two hundred fled the area.

The polls closed during the fighting and also closed early for the day, at 4:00 p.m. And when the statewide count was completed, and after the canvass board had thrown out results from various areas where problems had occurred, Walls was declared the winner by 627 votes. He would soon make the long journey from Florida to Washington, DC, to take his seat and begin serving in the People's House.

The race, however, was apparently far from over.

Niblack contested the election. At the time, a congressional committee heard contests, taking evidence like a court of law. During Reconstruction, however, the committee was constantly busy, as elections routinely blew up in charges of violence and fraud; in fact, in Walls's district alone, five of the next six elections would be overturned, usually on partisan lines. In this instance, Niblack raised technical issues with some of Walls's ballots, pointing to a polling place that closed an hour late and other precincts where election officers had failed to put proper signatures on returns. Walls, for his part, raised the issue of voter intimidation and violence, which he said had reduced his count by many hundreds of votes, robbing him of an even larger victory. After two years, when Walls's term was almost over, the committee ruled in favor of Niblack, accepting his arguments about flawed paperwork, but giving Walls credit for only twenty-nine votes from Black voters who had been deterred from the polls—those who testified or presented sworn statements, rather than the hundreds of others who had been chased away.

For Walls, these challenges would dominate his service. He was reelected by a large margin in 1872, after federal troops and law enforcement quieted the violence and due to the popularity he had gained from his work in Congress. But the Niblack case was still pending in committee when he won that election. For that reason, Walls experienced the rare—and strange—situation of being removed from office on

January 29, 1873, only to be sworn in again as a member of Congress on March 4 of that same year thanks to his reelection victory. Soon enough, he would be fighting against another election contest. But, in the meantime, he became a major national leader for the policy issue that would define his service: universal education.

In October of 1871, the nation's top Black leaders, including abolitionist Frederick Douglass, met in Columbia, South Carolina, to chart a course for advancing their rights and expressing their views to the public—a constant problem for leaders who faced implacably negative newspaper coverage in the South. Walls served as the organizing chairman of the Southern States Convention of Colored Men, and later managed issues on the floor using the legislative skills accumulated in the Florida legislature. He also made the convention's biggest waves politically when, during a heated debate over whether to endorse President Grant's reelection, he made a motion to nominate Black abolitionist John Mercer Langston for vice president—an idea so radical, even to his contemporaries, that the body quickly set it aside and adopted the Grant endorsement with little additional discussion.

As a member of the committee to draft the convention's statement to the public, arguably the most important task of the body, Walls helped guide the group toward a strong stand for national support of education, his life's passion, and work. Fittingly, parts of that same statement would appear five years later in his final speech to Congress, when he reviewed the history of Reconstruction. In the convention's statement in 1871, one sees the start of a recurring theme in Walls's work: that the nation should assure public education for *all* citizens, Black and White. The statement to the nation said:

"While we have, as a body, contributed our labor in the past to enhance the wealth and promote the welfare of the community, we have, as a class, been deprived of one of the chief benefits to be derived from industry, namely: the acquisition of education and experience, the return that civilization makes for the labor of the individual. . . . We ask that your Representatives in Congress may be instructed to afford such aid in extending education to the uneducated classes in the States we represent as may be consistent with the financial interests of the nation. *Although we*

urge our unrequited labors in the past as the ground of this appeal,
yet we do not seek these benefits for ourselves alone, but for the
whole portion of the laboring class in our States, whose need is as
great as ours."

Put another way, education—for all—was the key, as Walls made clear.
And he would be relentless in his pursuit to secure it.

In his first term in Congress, Walls pushed hard for education and
the economic development of his state. He was a prolific legislator, introducing more than fifty bills as a member of Congress, many of them
for improvements in Florida, and won a number of victories. He proposed new mail routes that sped postal service, new customs houses,
navigational improvements, life-saving stations, telegraph lines, and a
rail link to a port that would aid transportation to Cuba. And he received widespread praise in Florida's newspapers for his efforts, leading
to his lopsided reelection victory in 1872, despite the ongoing challenge
to his election of 1870. But through it all, the pursuit of accessible education was clearly dearest to Walls. His bill to grant a million acres of
land to endow the state's agricultural college was cut to 90,000 acres,
but still, it passed. He also attempted to endow a theological institute
and to donate unused federal buildings in Florida as schools. And in
his first and most important major speech to the Congress, he chose
education as his topic—more specifically, his advocacy for a national
education fund, in a bill that had come to the floor in February 1872.
The bill would dedicate money from public lands to be distributed to
the states solely for education, under the eye of a national superintendent. Every child between six and sixteen—irrespective of race—would
be guaranteed a public education.

During debate on the bill, Walls rose to speak in response to Archibald MacIntyre, a Georgia Democrat and former Confederate colo-
nel, who had argued that, while he supported education, the bill would
violate states' rights because the Constitution did not explicitly provide
the federal government authority over education and, moreover, states
in his view could be counted on to educate children on their own. Walls
began his remarks by detailing the history of denial of education, not
only to African Americans, but to citizens of all races who lacked financial means. When MacIntyre interrupted to defend himself, Walls

responded firmly, but courteously, explaining that "[t]he gentleman will be answered in the course of my remarks. I must ask him not to interrupt me now, as I did not interrupt him when he addressed the House." MacIntyre did not interrupt again.

Southern states had received grants for education, but several failed to use those resources to teach children, Walls reminded his colleagues. He further pointed out that education would strengthen democracy, make citizens more productive, and give them the power to overcome oppression and injustice. And to the specious argument that African Americans were incapable of learning, he gave examples of scholars and leaders and, coming near the end of his own striking oration, presumably the example of himself. "Notwithstanding all the laws enacted prohibiting the Negro from being educated, in spite of the degradation of over two hundred and forty-seven years of the most inhuman and barbarous slavery ever recorded in the history of any people, and coupled with five years, subjugation to the reign of terror from the Ku Klux Klan, the dastardly horrors of which those only know who have been victims, and those who commit the deeds. Notwithstanding all these obstacles and oppositions, we find in nearly every town and village, where the whipping-posts and auction blocks were once visible, schoolhouses and freedmen's savings banks erected in their stead, which are the growth of only five years, and which stand today as living refutations to the foul, malignant, unjust, and untrue arguments used against the Negro."

One can imagine the profound conviction in Walls's voice when he spoke those stirring words as a man recently freed from slavery himself. At the heart of his argument, however, was his central thesis that simply funding public education, the purpose of the bill under consideration, would not be enough, because some states could not be trusted to carry out the intent of the law.

"I am in favor, Mr. Speaker, of not only this bill, but of a national system of education, because I believe that the national Government is the guardian of the liberties of all its subjects. And having within a few days incorporated into the body politic a class of uneducated people, the majority of whom, I am sorry to say, are colored, the question for solution and the problems to be solved, then, are: can these people protect their liberties without education; and can they be educated under the present condition of the society in [those] States. . . ."

He answered his own question in the negative—stating plainly that education for former slaves would require federal intervention—and explaining the connection between slavery and knowledge:

"Education constitutes the apprenticeship of those who are afterward to take a place in the order of our civilized and progressive nation. Education tends to increase the dignity and self-respect of a people, tends to increase their fitness for society and important stations of trust, tends to elevate, and consequently carries with it a great moral responsibility. This is why the Democratic party in the South so bitterly oppose the education of all classes. They know that no educated people can be enslaved. They know that no educated people can be robbed of their labor. They well know that no educated people can be kept in a helpless and degraded condition, but will arise with a united voice and assert their manhood."

After Walls's impassioned speech, the bill creating the national education fund faced a series of amendments and a final vote. Most of these amendments were compromises necessary to secure the bill's passage, with which Walls concurred. He voted to allow states more discretion in how to use the money. And he voted to allocate funding among the states based on the level of illiteracy in each. Indeed, Walls voted for each of the compromises that would help the bill pass—all except one. He opposed, on principle, the one amendment that assured the bill's approval, which dictated that education money could never be withheld from a state because it segregated its schools by race. That amendment passed, without Walls's vote, and then the bill passed on its final vote. After passage, the legislation was never funded. And it was clear where Walls would draw the line.

Walls's profound and unyielding views on the vital necessity of education were unusual among his colleagues. Having once been denied education, and having won his learning through war and personal struggle, he saw and keenly appreciated its benefits as he became a federal lawmaker and a success in farming and business. One can also deduce, however, based on his other speeches and how he lived his life, that education was only part of his vision for equality and economic freedom in the South. He was sincere in his work to improve the economy through federal projects, and in his call for immigrants and African Americans from elsewhere in the country to migrate to Florida and develop its abundant productive land. And he also fought by the side of his congressional Republican colleagues for the passage of Senator Sumner's Civil Rights bill.

In 1871, during his first term, Walls anticipated the strategy Sumner would adopt the next year, to pair civil rights with amnesty. To that end, Walls himself introduced a bill to grant amnesty to all former rebels in Florida, and then sought to attach his bill as a rider to Sumner's, explicitly linking rights for former Confederates with rights for former slaves. The Washington *New National* praised Walls for "this happy suggestion," stating, "He deserves the thanks and support not only of his colored constituents in Florida, but of every colored man of the nation; nor does it stop here; he deserves consideration at the hands of every lover of justice." Of course, not everyone felt the same way. Walls was harshly criticized for what some saw as doing favors for former Confederates and Democrats who nonetheless opposed the equality he strove for. He defended himself in a published letter to his Alachua County constituents, arguing that, in his view, freedmen had nothing to gain from antagonism or conflict with others, but instead could advance more by enlisting them to their cause. "Let us all labor for the financial advancement of our State, and to secure equal civil and political rights to all," he firmly declared.

After returning from his first term in Congress in 1873—and after being both removed from the body *and* reelected to it—he used the money he had earned from his salary to buy a large antebellum cotton plantation and a newspaper. The newspaper, where he installed a fellow veteran as editor, would help advance his political point of view. The plantation would become his base for the agricultural business he developed over the next decade. Walls gained admiration as one of Florida's most successful farmers—so much so that journalists visited to report on his operations. The plantation had already been known as among the best in the state, with excellent land and nearby access to shipping by water and rail. Walls employed roughly seventy-five farmhands and another twenty-five workers at his sawmill. He grew tomatoes and other vegetables, shipping them as far away as New York for large profits, and planted an orange orchard, even eventually building a rail spur to the property to carry the produce. At his peak, he was a rich man, worth an estimated $60,000—a multimillionaire by today's standards. And yet, even though he lived in one of the finest houses in the county, he still worked much of the time in the fields, "[t]aking the lead among his employees," as one reporter attested.

Walls also used his experience in Congress to begin practicing law, forming a law firm with several partners. In rural areas of the South, a lawyer did not require formal legal training; the skills were in too short supply, especially for African Americans who required legal assistance. Walls had presumably gained enough knowledge of law from his work in public office and political and business dealings to be of significant aid to his clients. (Several years earlier, Walls had addressed the shortage of Black lawyers as a state legislator, as well, by passing a bill to allow county clerks—many of whom were Black—to become lawyers without passing the bar.)

In his second term in Congress, Walls advanced a resolution to recognize Cuban rebels as belligerents against Spain. He posed his position in moral terms, seeking to extend freedom from the recently freed to those still held as slaves by the Spanish, and compared the rebels to the American revolutionaries of 1776. "Pride in the perpetuation of African slavery in the western world is a continued menace to our institutions," Walls orated. "The existence of the so-called republic of Spain, professing to be inspired by the Magna Carta of American liberty, which pronounced 'all men are created equal,' is a travesty upon humanity and a libel upon civilization while it extends the protection of Spanish government to the most pronounced slave oligarchy that has ever existed among men."

Party leaders did not allow Walls time on the floor to make that speech—it was read into the record—as the few lone Black congressmen continued to struggle for respect, even from their own party, and as Reconstruction lost momentum due to the combined headwinds of the economic downturn of 1873 and the rising violence in the South. Walls nonetheless continued to work with his colleagues for the Civil Rights bill, with its promise of funding and desegregation for southern schools, even as party leaders were backing away from the legislation.

In this difficult political setting, Walls delivered perhaps the broadest statement of his philosophy of reconciliation, in a speech supporting a $3 million appropriation for the upcoming centennial celebration, a huge exposition to be mounted in Philadelphia in 1876. Again, he was not given time to deliver his speech on the floor. But the clarity and strength of his words rang out, nonetheless. Opponents had attacked the celebration as an overgrown Fourth of July celebration, and the appropriation as excessive and even unconstitutional. Walls disagreed. He met each of their arguments, one by one, but the heart of his speech described his dream for the future of the country. In short, he contended that by developing its resources, increasing industry, modernizing production, and training workers, the South, which had been plunged into poverty, could rise in prosperity for everyone and leave its past behind. And the exposition, he explained, would demonstrate these benefits to the world, encouraging capital investment and attracting immigration from overseas, which he saw as key to the rising industrial might of the US.

The most powerful part of the speech—and most poignant, considering the reversals leaders like Walls would soon face—came when he extolled America as an example of freedom for the world, speaking with the deep patriotism of one who knew what freedom meant. Walls imagined the centennial as an opportunity for Americans of all races to come together under the banner of national pride and, again, in the words of the Declaration of Independence, "that all men are created equal." In introducing that concept, he acknowledged the vicious struggle of politics he was forced to deal with, saying, "Long ago, patriotism was said by an eminent English novelist to be 'The love of office,' and politics 'The art of getting it'; and I am not ignorant of the common supposition that, in southern politics particularly, the actual truth of old Fielding's allegation is being continually illustrated; but coming from the South, as I do, I desire to say that the patriotic tendency of the centennial is not the least attractive or least important feature of it in the estimation of southern men, 'without respect to previous condition' [a phrase Walls borrowed from the Fifteenth Amendment to refer to former slaves]."

He compared the American Revolution and the Civil War to great fights for freedom in the past, calling on patriotic feelings to rejoin the American nation in unity. "I believe that when from every corner of this broad land, from every State and Territory, thousands and millions of the free citizens of a free government shall assemble in the very cradle and place of the birth of all that politically they hold dear, and exchange with each other the mutual grasps and the meaningful glances of a common citizenship, there will be aroused in the bosoms of all a higher and purer sense of the honest and sincere attachment cherished by all in common for those free institutions whose origin and beneficent sway they are now to celebrate than they have ever before been permitted to feel, and which will strengthen all the bonds which can unite freemen to their native land, and kindle a blaze of patriotic feeling in whose dazzling light all questions of minor differences and all hurtful recollections of past disagreements will be blotted out."

Later that year, Walls won reelection to a third term, but this time by a small margin. His opponent was former Confederate General J. J. Finley. As before, his opponent charged irregularities, mainly technical—the most important being the failure of election officials in one of Walls's stronger areas to accurately administer an oath to voters—but the political situation was stacked against him, making the case difficult or impossible for him to win. The fight also consumed most of his effort, making him less active as a member of Congress. Among his difficulties, his key witness was mysteriously murdered, and the county clerk's office containing the evidence burned. But most important, Democrats had captured a majority in the House. *They*, not he nor his party, would make the decision about who had won the seat, based on a majority vote.

And so, facing the likelihood he would be removed, Walls joined his African American colleagues in strong support for the Civil Rights bill during the lame duck session in 1875, before the swearing in of the new Democratic majority. This would be the Republicans' last chance to outlaw segregation in public accommodations and in public schools. When the bill came up for final approval, however, party leaders had removed the education provision to assure its passage. Walls refused to cast his vote in favor of an act that was nonetheless considered the final achievement of Reconstruction. He abstained, and in so doing, took the opposite view of the vast majority of his own party colleagues. The day after President Grant signed the bill, he delivered his stinging rebuke in a speech on the political violence in the South and the dying of freedmen's hopes for Reconstruction, as they lost the possibility of desegregated schools, and more, universal schooling, both of which Walls had worked long and hard to achieve.

Some historians believe Walls was right, describing the hollowed-out Civil Rights Act of 1875 as Reconstruction's "dead letter" which failed to make a significant difference in advancing equal rights. But irrespective of the historical verdict, it is clear that Walls believed Reconstruction and the advancement of freed slaves depended on more than laws passed in Washington. The school system he had supported in Florida did rapidly increase literacy in his state. And although the Democrats removed him from Congress in 1876 on a party-line vote, as expected, he continued for another twenty years to build his successful farming business and maintain his career in politics. He lost renomination to Congress from the fractured and chaotic Republican Party, but his county elected him that fall to the State Senate.

Walls's return to the state capitol in Tallahassee was marked by his advancement of the only resolutions of the 1877 session that would benefit Black residents. And unsurprisingly, both resolutions were squarely focused on the same topic: public education. The first was an investigation of the public schools, which passed, and the second, a bill that would make schooling mandatory for all children ages six to fifteen, which did not. The latter received only one other vote besides his own. Later, when Democrats took full control of Florida government, they would dismantle some of Walls's education work—including drastically reducing funding for schools, rendering some unable to operate. Nevertheless, the system remained better than it had been when Walls helped start it. That much was clear.

In February 1884, Walls again helped lead a convention, this time the State Conference of the Colored Men of Florida, held at Gainesville. And again, education became the key plank of the group's platform. At the convention, many Black leaders decided to leave the state's Republican Party, and Walls ran for Congress as an independent. After a disastrous campaign, he was soundly defeated in the election.

This time, he left politics for good. Months later, his wife Ella died, leaving him on New Year's Day, 1885, with his six-year-old daughter, Nettie. Walls's health declined, and a freeze in 1895 destroyed his crops and ruined him financially. He moved to Tallahassee and became director of the Florida Normal College, now Florida A&M University, where he brought his successful farming techniques to students learning in the college's fields, often wearing suits befitting his former career rather than farming clothes. He was living there when another terrible tragedy struck: his beloved Nettie reportedly experienced a mental health crisis and became reclusive, and then killed a child. She was committed to a mental institution immediately thereafter, where she died within a year. Walls never recovered from his shock and grief. He lived only a few years more.

On the day Josiah Walls died, May 15, 1905, it had been forty years since the Civil War ended, and nearly thirty years since he had walked the halls of the Congress. The last African American to serve had left the House at the turn of the century, in 1900, and it would be almost thirty years until another was elected. The rollback of Reconstruction was complete, as Jim Crow laws negated the Fourteenth and Fifteenth Amendments to the Constitution by undermining the right to vote and equal protection under the law.

Walls's death would go unnoted in the media of his day. Official records would denote no will or even a death certificate.

He disappeared.

He was buried in an African American cemetery in Tallahassee. To this day, no one knows exactly where, as many such cemeteries were later destroyed.

His legacy remains, however, in his enduring words and the educational advances he championed that would one day lead to generations using their knowledge to fight for freedom. And those heirs of the educational advances Josiah Walls helped plant would eventually reassert the demands for equality that he had fought for.

3

William B. Wilson

★ ★ ★ ★ ★ ★ ★ ★ ★

I am a poor man, and I shall die a poor man. I have had a
very hard life, and I am suffering today from the fatigue of it.
I care not for riches, or power, or credit. But I do want people
to say, when they meet about my bier, that I have always kept
my word and that I have tried to be fair.

—WILLIAM B. WILSON

The eldest surviving child in his family, the six-year-old boy armed himself with a sharp knife as he stood in the snow with his mother, Helen, at the door of their small, two-room brick cottage, guarding against eviction by the coal mining company that owned the house. The boy's father, Adam Wilson, had joined a strike that February 1868. And although he had the money for rent, the company expelled all striking workers from their homes, which were stacked in a row in a tiny village ten miles from the streets of Glasgow, Scotland. The local bailiff's men emptied the home, strewing their belongings in the snow. Left with no other options, the family moved into an abandoned stable.

The strike ended a few weeks later, with the workers eventually relenting and returning to work. But not Adam. He would not return to the mine under the conditions he had opposed. Nor would he work in any other mine in Scotland, as mine owners all over the country had blacklisted him for striking.

Things were bleak. Adam Wilson couldn't find a job anywhere to support his wife and four children. So, he did what countless others did and would continue to do in the decades to come.

He struck out for America.

And as he embarked on the long journey across the Atlantic Ocean, Adam Wilson could never have imagined that his son—the young, stoic boy who had stood guard outside their home—would one day rise to the highest levels of government.

Looking back fifty years later, William B. Wilson, who would follow in his father's footsteps as both a miner and labor leader, laughed heartily at the memory of his six-year-old self, grabbing the biggest kitchen knife that he could find to hold off the bailiff. The incident, to be sure, had helped inspire his drive to seek justice for workers. But, perhaps more remarkable than that, Wilson felt no animosity toward the mine owners who had thrown out his family, telling others that they had been within their rights.

Wilson would endure many trials and tribulations throughout his life. But anger and resentment were emotions he would rarely countenance. A life of hardship, poverty, and struggle had not left him embittered, but rather, equipped him with an inviolable commitment to fairness and justice for working people, and an enduring faith in the American political system to bring about that change. His calm demeanor and rational approach to the political and labor battles he would wage earned him many admirers—and, harsh critics, too. But, in the final analysis, his effort to protect the rights of workers would make a real difference.

"One of my earliest recollections was that of being turned out of our home, evicted in midwinter, and finding shelter in the stables of the tollhouse nearby," Wilson would later recall. "I am glad that my days have been laid at a period and in a country where there is opportunity for exercising vigor and intelligence in moving toward higher planes with more splendid ideals."

After their arrival in America, his family settled in Pennsylvania. And it was there that Wilson went deep down into the dark and cavernous coal mines of the Keystone State to earn money for his family.

He was nine years old.

Wilson never supported himself other than by hard, physical labor until, at the age of forty-four, he was elected to Congress. And he never forgot where he came from, leveraging his considerable political skills to pass landmark legislation protecting miners, and working for years in the House to successfully establish—for the first time in our country's history—a Department of Labor as a cabinet-level agency. In a final twist of fate, when faced with the decision of whom to appoint to lead the new department as the nation's very first secretary of labor, the choice for President Woodrow Wilson (no relation) was an obvious one.

He chose William B. Wilson.

As secretary, Wilson created and built the agency from the ground up. Later, he managed industrial policy during the depths of World War I. And in the process, he became the president's trusted confidant—indeed, President Wilson twice halted campaigns seeking to draft Secretary Wilson to run for governor of Pennsylvania, saying that he needed him more in his cabinet.

William Wilson was a big, muscular man with rough hands from a lifetime of labor, known for his balanced temperament and an even-handed approach to his adversaries. President Wilson, famous in some quarters for being unwilling to take advice, nonetheless listened to Secretary Wilson and strongly defended him from attacks by his critics. During the brutal Colorado coal strike of 1913–14, in which more than fifty people tragically died, the president responded directly to those who claimed Secretary Wilson was biased against mine owners. "Allow me to protest with great earnestness against the implications of your letter," the president wrote back to one critic. "I have never known a more careful and judicial mind than that of Secretary Wilson."

The wonder of William Wilson's story comes not from his political courage *per se*—although that, too, was legendary—but from the quality of his character and his dedication to fairness, despite the cruel inequities he endured in his life. He nearly died in a mine accident. He was blacklisted by employers and forced to migrate across the country to find work to support his family. He would be arrested on false charges and literally kidnapped by company bosses. And later, when he couldn't make his living at his occupation because of his union leadership, he taught himself to farm on a poor, rocky patch of land.

Yet, despite all he endured, Wilson never resented his opponents. He worked to gain their praise, because he saw conciliation and dialogue as the keys to progress and believed that production and prosperity for workers and companies alike would lift all boats. In 1919, toward the end of his time in the president's cabinet, Wilson's friend and biographer, Roger Babson, asked him why he had bent over backward to work with "anti-union" employers and protect the freedom of workers to have open shops, in which those who declined to join unions still enjoyed the fruits of labor negotiations. Wilson replied, "Mr. Babson, my great ambition is to have people say of me these two things: first, that I have kept my word, and second, that I have been fair."

As a child in Pennsylvania, William grew up in a company-owned mining town populated largely by immigrants from the British Isles. Arnot had been named for—and was largely owned by—a distant financier who also owned the coal mine. The residents of the unpainted, plank-walled shacks lived on the company's land, shopped at its store, and worked underground digging its coal by hand, with picks and shovels. Their pay, based on the tons of coal they dug each day, left them in deep poverty, subsisting from backyard vegetable gardens that were green oases on muddy streets with few trees or landscaping. William's first impression of America was of ripe red tomatoes, which he had never seen before—he took a big bite of one and spat it out, thinking it was poison.

William's parents intended their son to be educated, and as a young child, he burned through readers faster than they could afford to buy the next one. His mother Helen helped teach him, and he briefly attended public school in Arnot. He also worked hard to earn money as a boy, carrying loads and doing other odd jobs for neighbors, and accumulated two dollars, which he used to buy a secondhand encyclopedia, *Chambers's Information for the People*. He read the book aloud to his father, who had received no education at all and was nearly illiterate. They discussed what they learned together from that book and others, including Adam Smith's *Wealth of Nations*. Adam Wilson used this knowledge to hold his own in the daily debates at Hugh Kerwin's local cobbler shop, where miners gathered in a backroom to discuss the issues of the day with each other and with Kerwin, who owned the town's largest library and subscribed to various periodicals, including the *Congressional Record*. William, bright-eyed and eager, sat daily in the shop, soaking in the older men's debates and discussions like a sponge, until one day the cobbler noticed and began encouraging the young boy, lending him books and discussing ideas.

He soon showed himself a prodigy. Adam would call on him during the discussions with other men to recite the facts and statistics they had read, bolstering his arguments and showing off his clever son. There, in the backroom of Kerwin's simple shop, William learned to marshal and retain facts to support arguments in a logical way—first as his father's helper and then in his own right. And he would continue studying on his own his whole life, especially pursuing a love of poetry (his favorite was Robert Burns) and writing his own poems, which he later gathered into a book.

William's formal schooling, however, would last less than a year.

His father's years of hard labor had taken their toll. And eventually it became clear that the back injuries Adam had sustained working in the mines meant that he could no longer manage the job underground. If he remained sitting, he could still chip out the coal, but he couldn't bend over to pick it up. The only solution for the family's survival would be for his nine-year-old son to go down into the mine with him every day to pick up the coal and put it into the carts that carried it to the surface.

And so William did what was expected of him. He joined many other boys his age at work, ending their education to begin toil that would last a lifetime, or until their bodies and health gave out, riding down each early morning into the mine and remaining there in the black dust and foul-smelling darkness until night.

"For quite a while, I did the loading, my father and I working side by side," Wilson told a reporter, many years later. "I worked in the mines until I grew to be a man. But before I was ten years old, I met with an accident. . . . The rock where we were working was unsound— loose, as a miner would call it. My father had detected this fact by a peculiar ring of his pick when he struck it. This is one of the familiar dangers incidental to coal mining, and resort was had to the obvious precaution of putting in an extra prop. It then seemed to be reasonably safe. I was engaged in chipping coal from a big fragment of fallen rock when the material overhead gave way. The extra prop was thrown out of plumb, and great masses of rock came down upon me like an avalanche. I was knocked down and buried beneath the debris [several tons of rock]. But, by lucky chance, it so happened that I fell in such a way as to lie prostrate between the fragment of rock I had been chipping and the prop, which had assumed a horizontal position on the ground. The prop and the rock fragment together upheld the mass, so that when I was dug out it was found that practically the only injury I had suffered was cut on the back of my head."

Wilson became a "half member" of the local miners' union at age eleven. Barely a teenager, he was elected secretary of the union just a few years later, at age fourteen, despite not even being old enough to be a full member (the age requirement was sixteen). It was clear the young man was destined to lead others.

At twenty-one, he married his wife Agnes, and they eventually had eleven children, nine of whom survived. But by the time he was married, Wilson had already been fired from the coal mine because of his union work. Coal company blacklists—and his reputation as a union leader—spread far beyond Arnot, blocking him from work in mines and for many other large employers as well.

Like father, like son.

And so, for the duration of his twenties, William was forced to travel to find work. Tramping back and forth across the country, from New York to Ohio, Indiana to Illinois, and as far west as the farmlands of Iowa, he sought to escape his name as a union man. He dug ditches and quarried stone. He sawed lumber and he cut down trees. He prospected for coal, peeled bark used in leather tanning, and shoveled coal on a freight locomotive. He did it all.

All the while he kept at his unpaid union work, leading strikes and settling disputes by putting committees of workers across the bargaining table from employers. At that stage of the labor movement, many employers denied that workers had a right to organize and refused to recognize unions or engage in collective bargaining. Among his contributions as a leader, Wilson explained the basis in fairness for both sides to negotiate by recognizing the rights of each.

At one particular mine, where Wilson had established a system of collective bargaining, a new owner arrived and refused to recognize the union. The company's stockholders owned the mine, the owner explained, and in his view, they had the right to decide how work would be done there. The response formulated with Wilson's leadership was, in a word, surprising.

The union told the mine owner that he was right.

"We recognize that the mines are the property of the stockholders and as such the stockholders are free to do with these mines as they see fit so long as they do not interfere with the natural rights of others," Wilson's committee wrote to the mine owner. But, by the same token, the message went on to assert, "We, however, have also concluded that our bodies belong to us wage earners and that we are likewise free to use these bodies as we would, provided we do not interfere with the just rights of others. The stockholders have decided that they will operate the mines only under certain conditions. We have decided that we will operate our bodies only under certain conditions."

At the time, local governments in towns controlled by mining companies often took their side in labor disputes, with some agencies and courts acting, in effect, as agents for the mines and large companies. Wilson was repeatedly arrested on spurious charges. On one occasion, agents for a company tricked him into boarding a train and whisked him away incommunicado to be arrested in another city where his supporters could not find him. Courts frequently issued injunctions against strikers, ordering them back to work or barring the provision of food and financial support to families of striking workers. After receiving one of those injunctions, Wilson declared, "An injunction that restrains me from furnishing food to hungry men, women, and children, when I have in my possession the means to aid them, will be violated by me until the necessity for providing food has been removed or the corporeal power of the court overwhelms me. I will treat it as I would an order of the court to stop breathing."

Years later, when he was serving in Washington, his refusal to obey that injunction would be used by Wilson's critics as an example of his lawlessness.

In the 1890s, to build a base of financial stability for his family, Wilson took up farming, first leasing and then buying a 100-acre tract in Blossburg, Pennsylvania, less than ten miles from Arnot. He knew nothing about farming, and the land he bought was steep, rocky, and unproductive. But he eventually scratched out a living. A team of oxen bought to pull his plow had been trained for logging, not farming, and they walked too fast for him to keep up. When he first started working with the animals, they paid no attention to his orders. "Although I 'hawed' and 'gee'd' to the best of my ability, the furrow was a zigzag," he recalled years later. "Finally, I said to the oxen, 'Go as you please! It's all got to be plowed, so take it any way you like.'" As difficult as farming proved, however, it provided Wilson with a safe place for his family to live, where they could not be evicted by a company owner and which supplied food and a little money should he be unable to work because of his union activities. But he had to pay a $1,500 mortgage, a huge sum for a man who had never earned more than $80 a month, and usually half as much.

During a large strike Wilson led at the turn of the century, in 1899 and 1900, mine owners came to the farm to meet him secretly. They offered to pay off the mortgage if Wilson would simply board a train and leave the area, giving word that he had been called away unexpectedly. Without his leadership, they assumed the strike would collapse. And they were confident they could purchase Wilson's assent.

They were wrong.

In the depths of the lengthy and controversial strike, Wilson was broke. A less principled man may have taken the offer. But not Wilson. As the labor leader Mother Jones later recounted, he rose to his feet, trembling with rage, and threw the owners out of his house for suggesting he break faith with the miners.

When the story got out, the residents of Arnot declared a holiday in honor of Wilson. His reputation for refusing the bribe helped spread his name. And when the strike settled, with partial success, Wilson was elected international secretary-treasurer of the United Mine Workers of America (UMW), with responsibility for one of the nation's key industries and a budget of millions of dollars.

In that position, Wilson helped lead the anthracite coal strike of 1902, once called the "most important single incident in the labor movement" by no less an authority than the legendary president of the American Federation of Labor (AFL), Samuel Gompers, who explained, "From then on, the miners became not merely human machines to produce coal but men and citizens." Hard anthracite coal, produced for the most part only in a few counties in Pennsylvania, heated the cities of the northeast and powered much of the nation's industry. A few companies and railroads controlled the supply, and they refused to recognize or bargain with the UMW. When the union struck, demanding a living wage, honest measurement of the coal that workers dug, and an eight-hour workday, the owners took a hard line, refusing any dealings with the union, which they considered illegitimate.

The mine operators had reason for confidence. In past national strikes, a series of presidents had put the federal government on the side of business, using troops to force workers to capitulate. A representative of the operators declared the union unnecessary, writing that the "rights and interests of the laboring man will be protected and cared for—not by the labor agitators, but by the Christian men to whom God in His infinite wisdom has given the control of the property interests of the country."

Such statements helped the union in the all-important fight for public opinion, which its leaders recognized as a critical tool for success. They offered firm but conciliatory statements that contrasted with the high-handed intransigence of the owners. With Wilson at his side, John Mitchell, who had become the union's president in 1898, at the age of twenty-eight, convinced miners of bituminous coal, who had a contract with owners, not to mount a sympathetic strike that would alienate the public. That decision proved so popular it brought a flood of contributions to support the strikers. For arguably the first time in a national strike, the union was winning public sympathy rather than blame for the hardships caused by the work stoppage. And the hardship was great, as the strike continued for more than five months. Fuel shortages and rising prices began to paralyze the cities.

In the fall, with winter approaching, President Teddy Roosevelt intervened, warning that cold weather could bring famine, death by exposure, and rioting in cities lacking fuel for heat.

He called both sides together at the White House on October 3, 1902.

As the meeting began, President Roosevelt delivered his opening remarks. And then, the coal industry's representatives spoke. They raged over the strike, exaggerated their accusations of union violence, insulted the union leader to his face, and even disrespected the president. Mitchell remained calm and offered to enter mediation or arbitration led by the president. The owners refused.

Roosevelt was angry. And he did little to hide it.

As he left the meeting, his frustration with the owners was readily apparent. "There was but one gentleman present, and I was not that man," he said following the meeting, issuing a standing invitation to Mitchell to visit the White House. More important, he ultimately pushed the owners to accept arbitration with the union. The strike ultimately settled with a deal that split the difference. A precedent was established for the federal government to act as a neutral party to settle labor disputes. Mitchell's and Wilson's public standing rose dramatically, as did that of other moderate labor leaders, with a new acceptance of the rights of workers to organize and bargain as equals with their employers.

Union officials remained frustrated, however, that basic legislation for worker safety and recognition of unions could not pass the Congress. Corporations had largely kept the law on their side, with court injunctions and even the military, on occasion, helping them break strikes. In fifty years, more than one hundred bills to create a cabinet-level department of labor had been introduced in Congress. None had passed. In 1903, Congress had established a Department of Commerce and Labor, but its purpose focused on encouraging business, with workers an afterthought and programs in that arena confined mostly to compiling statistics. Anti-union organizations maintained a powerful political and lobbying arm in Washington and had allies in the chairmen of the House and Senate labor committees. One such association's spokesman boasted to members that they need not worry about any pro-labor legislation passing, "[w]ith you gentlemen intelligently and forcefully backing up [certain] Congressmen." The situation prompted Gompers and his AFL to change course, abandoning a policy of avoiding direct involvement in elections, and instead searching far and wide to recruit their own members to run for office.

In Pennsylvania, they wouldn't need to look very far.

In 1906, William B. Wilson, an immigrant who had never been elected to any public office, local or otherwise, announced his run for Congress. He would humbly seek to represent not only the citizens of his community in Blossburg, but also the working people of the country he had served his entire career.

And, surprisingly to many, he won.

His victory was remarkable. No Democrat had been elected to the northern Pennsylvania seat in more than thirty years, and Wilson's opponent, an incumbent running for a fourth term, was a Civil War veteran and the wealthy owner of a lumber company with an established political organization in each county of the district. Wilson, on the other hand, had run without financial backing or any organization to speak of. Traveling from town to town to speak to groups in Grange halls, churches, and public parks, he spoke plainly as he called for change. And rather than trying to excite his audiences with political rhetoric, he spoke calmly and earnestly of fairness, conciliation, and hard work.

At the county courthouse in Wellsboro, with its rough stone walls and tall windows, a crowd filled the seats and spilled into the aisles to hear Wilson carefully list the plans he would pursue in Congress. He concluded by saying, "I will stand for those things which I believe will be beneficial not only to the people of this district, but to the great mass of the people of the whole country. And I promise you that if I am elected, I will return here two years hence and render to you an account of my stewardship."

Perhaps the very lack of fire Wilson brought to his campaign helped elect him. As a leader in some of the most violent and divisive conflicts of his times, he had gained a reputation for defusing confrontation and appealing to rationality and compromise. Even some pro-business Republicans endorsed him when he ran. At a meeting during the 1906 campaign, William Nearing, the superintendent of a mine near Blossburg, declared, "Wilson is a constructive man, a friend of capital as well as of labor, and one whom no just man need fear." The next speaker responded, "I will go one better than Nearing by voting for Wilson, although I am a Republican. For when all is said and done, Wilson had done more to keep conditions peaceful in these counties than any other man in the district. It is impossible to estimate the millions of dollars in time and property which he has saved by his conciliatory methods."

Wilson's conciliatory approach worked, and he won his election. Now it was time for the next part of his journey—a journey that began on the shores of Scotland and had taken him from the coal mines of north-central Pennsylvania to the marble hallways of the Capitol of the United States.

But his first few months of service would not be as eventful as he had hoped.

When Wilson first entered the House, his party was in the minority, evidenced by the poor committee assignments that he received. Nonetheless, Wilson remembered why he was there. And so, as a legislator, he worked actively, even against long odds, speaking out when he could address issues affecting the rights of workers or when he could apply his vast knowledge of mining and other practical topics from industry and labor relations. He advocated for workers in Puerto Rico and on the Panama Canal, opposed a law undermining rights of munitions workers, and fought consolidation of coal claims in Alaska that could favor monopolists. He also favored improved safety rules on railroads and in the manufacturing of matches, and introduced one of the first old-age pension bills in Congress, thirty years before the Social Security Act passed. He wasn't the wittiest speaker or skilled at turning a phrase.

A strong, ruddy, slow-moving man, he was at his best when bringing his knowledge to bear, using the skill he had learned as a boy in the cobbler shop in Arnot decades before to organize the facts in support of his arguments. As if recognizing that debt, he even hired the son of the cobbler, Hugh Kerwin, who had died years earlier, to be his office secretary and aide.

His most ambitious effort in those early days in Washington was his attempt to establish a bureau of mines and mining. Over the prior seventeen years, mine accidents had killed more than twenty-two thousand people, with greater numbers dying all the time—twenty a day, on average, when he entered the House. Wilson knew the heavy toll they exacted on workers and families across the country. And he was determined to create an agency that could investigate these accidents and, he hoped, prevent them.

Near the start of the day on a Wednesday in April 1908, Wilson slowly rose from the House floor, armed with tables listing death statistics from countries in Europe and from US states. The numbers painted a grim picture. Taken together, they showed that American mining was far deadlier, with a gruesome death toll far higher than those of other countries.

Papers in hand, Wilson began his speech by praising American miners, applauding their productivity and skill, but then quickly turned to the sobering numbers, demonstrating that countries with deeper and more inherently dangerous mines had far fewer deaths per capita. The reason, he suggested, was that in those countries, a national authority studied mine disasters and made rules to prevent their recurrence. His argument was straightforward and logical. But he had spoken for only a few minutes before members began to rise from their seats and pointedly ask him to yield for questions. Of course, some were less honest questions than implicit—or explicit—criticisms of his argument.

Other members might decline to yield their limited speaking time on the House Floor for such theatrics, preferring to deliver their speeches in full.

Wilson, however, would yield to them all.

Didn't the states have investigative agencies already? Weren't the supervisors of mines already qualified and licensed? Wouldn't a federal agency duplicate state efforts and waste money?

In each case, Wilson responded calmly and candidly. Confident in his own position, he readily acknowledged the part of his colleagues' statements that were true. Members listened intently as Wilson then brought his own deeper knowledge and well-considered case to bear. He fielded so many hostile questions that his time expired before he had given half of his speech. But the enormity of the problem and the sincerity of his plea began to win the sympathy of the House.

Once his time ran out, leaders from *both sides* volunteered to give him more. Loud applause from their colleagues echoed through the House.

Republican Martin Madden—a Chicago representative and the president of the nation's largest limestone quarrying company—came at Wilson sharply with a series of rapid-fire questions, like a prosecutor conducting a cross-examination. Each probing question pierced the stuffy air of the chamber. Wilson waited patiently. And then, he parried the rhetorical blows the only way he knew how—with disarming candor. He admitted, honestly, that each state's mine inspectors were qualified. They did normally investigate accidents, Wilson conceded, and when they found deficiencies, they typically identified improvements.

Madden was incredulous.

"Have they the right to order changes made?" he demanded.

"Yes, within certain limits," Wilson again acknowledged.

It appeared to some that Madden had won the day. But they would soon conclude otherwise.

As Wilson took the floor back, he proceeded to deploy an encyclopedic knowledge on mining disasters that only he—a man who had, as a child, mined with his own hands in the deep coal mines of his state—would possess.

"Now, Mr. Chairman," Wilson began simply, "the great difficulty is that even those learned in mining and understanding the whole business, understanding the limitations of resources at their disposal, are not in a position to determine what are the causes of these explosions in many instances." Then, he painstakingly reviewed a series of recent disasters by name, in each of various states, many of which had the state agencies Madden had extolled, along with the granular facts of the unexplained accidents that had killed groups of men. It was an intellectual *tour de force* that most were simply not expecting from the humble and understated Wilson.

"There has been a difference of opinion as to whether or not dust will ignite without a mixture of gas in it," he explained. Likewise, "[t]here has been doubt as to whether the sprinkling of dry mines, required by some of our laws, increases or reduces the danger of explosion. There are differences of opinion as to whether a silent electric current on a wire introduced into a mine, that does not come into contact with anything that will create a spark, will ignite the gas in a mine." And then came his core argument—that "there are other things at the present time in doubt, and under this bill proposed here, if it is enacted into law, a bureau is established furnishing the necessary equipment to make an investigation, and then these things can be determined through tests and experiments, and information furnished to the various state governments so that they may construct their laws accordingly."

The House burst with applause. And the questioners henceforth remained silent as members carefully listened to the rest of what Wilson had to say. He had won the respect of his colleagues, not with a soaring, emotional appeal, but by patiently listening to their objections and then responding with substantive information that reflected a total command of the facts, as well as a well-constructed piece of legislation that would actually save lives.

But Wilson could orate, too.

As he finished his speech—the House now listening attentively, without interruption—he called his colleagues' attention to the humanity and courage of the men underground. "The miners of our country are an intelligent and courageous class of men," he declared. "They are engaged in production of material that is the basis of our modern industrial and commercial activities. They are daily taking great risks in the hard and hazardous occupation which they follow. When accident has befallen any of their number, when the caving in of the roof, the flooding of the mine, or an explosion of coal dust or fire damp has cut off all means of escape, the innate courage of the miner asserts itself, and he will yield to no hardship, however great, nor shrink from any danger, however perilous, in his efforts to relieve his fellow men."

Left unsaid, Wilson could have been speaking of his very own father, who had once gone down into the mine back in Pennsylvania to find men after an explosion. Wilson was among the family and friends who waited on the surface as his father's crew went in for the search, and then saw a second blast belch forth, with a roar and a pillar of smoke, from the mouth of the mine. Were the rescuers now dead, too? Only after a long, agonizing wait would they learn that Adam Wilson and the others had been miraculously spared from the second explosion by good luck—they had been checking a side tunnel when the blast ripped past them in the main shaft.

Indeed, as William Wilson spoke of brave rescuers on the House floor over forty years later, he could have been speaking of himself as well. For he too had once gone into a collapsing mine to look for a co-worker, while the rock above cracked with a sound like gunshots and the stone ceiling visibly sagged. As Wilson later recalled privately, they had kept looking for the missing man until they found him, buried and dead under a pile of shale.

Wilson could have told any one of those compelling personal stories in his speech on the House floor that day.

He shared none of them.

True to form, he didn't want to draw any attention to himself.

Instead, he kept the focus on the brave miners laboring across the country. "Those sturdy sons of toil," he concluded, "deliberately enter the dark and dangerous caverns of the mines to carry relief to their suffering fellow men or perish in the attempt. It is for the benefit of men of this character that I appeal to you to establish and equip a bureau of mines and mining."

Again, the House erupted into sustained applause.

Notwithstanding the cheers, Wilson and his allies would have to wait until more like-minded members had won seats in the House to make much progress on labor bills. Unions were only beginning to build and flex political muscle. In 1908, the AFL asked both major political parties to add its pro-union legislation to their platforms. The Republican Party took the opposite action, adopting a plank supporting the use of injunctions against strikes, while the national Democratic Party made an alliance with organized labor, adopting planks against injunctions and in favor of creating a separate department of labor whose secretary would serve as a member of the president's cabinet.

A Republican, William Howard Taft, won the presidency that year. Republicans held their strong majorities in the House and the Senate, too. And yet, despite the strong political headwinds, Wilson, carrying the Democratic banner, easily won reelection. In the next Congress, he redoubled his efforts to create the bureau of mines, imploring his colleagues to support his legislation.

And this time, it passed.

Then, in 1910, the Democrats won control of the House. And the former miner and labor leader—who had fought his entire life for better labor conditions—became chair of the House Labor Committee.

Wilson, gavel in hand, assumed the chairmanship with three other union men joining his committee as members—a hatter from New York, a coal miner from Maryland, and an iron worker from Illinois. He made use of his new power—and new allies—to push through bills that changed working conditions for millions of Americans. The new Children's Bureau would battle against child labor and investigate other threats to the well-being of children. Wilson's Seaman's bill would address the safety of sailors and shipping, especially the manning of lifeboats—coming in the months after the infamous sinking of the *Titanic* in 1912—and outlaw criminal penalties for seamen who quit their jobs in American ports and American seamen who did so in foreign ports. (Under the law at the time, ship owners could have crew members criminally imprisoned for "jumping ship.") Gompers presented other ideas to Wilson, too, and testified to his committee, telling his AFL membership, "With a true and tried unionist, William B. Wilson . . . as chairman of the House Committee on Labor, that committee has ceased to be a mere graveyard of labor measures and has become a potent power responsive to social and economic conditions and requirements."

The most important bill, however, to come from Wilson's committee, would create the Department of Labor.

The department, as conceived by Wilson and his colleagues, would combine existing labor-related divisions from other agencies, including immigration and naturalization, and elevate its head, the secretary of labor, to be a member of the president's cabinet. In addition, Wilson planned for a new agency within the department, which was his top priority: a conciliation service to mediate labor disputes, preventing strikes or ending them before they could become bitter and intractable. The service, run by the secretary, would enter into mediation only with the agreement of both parties to a dispute, and it would not make public recommendations. Further, its advice would be nonbinding—it would simply be a peacemaker. The concept, in many respects, reflected the core of Wilson's governing philosophy. For even after the many abuses he had endured, he assumed basic good intent from all whom he interacted with. As he later told his biographer, Roger Babson, "So long as there is understanding, there is peace. But when understanding is lacking, then the germs of trouble take root and grow."

As the Labor Committee chairman, Wilson rose on the House floor to manage the debate when the bill came up for final consideration shortly after noon on July 10, 1912. He had achieved a unanimous bipartisan recommendation for approval from his committee, but the debate with the full House would not be easy. The sticky heat in the chamber that day far exceeded normal, even for a hot, humid Washington summer. Men on the floor, sweating in stiff shirts, vests, and wilting suit coats, repeatedly allowed their tempers to flare. Opponents of the bill veered the discussion to unrelated topics to make political points and burn up time. Partisans of each side accused the other of hypocrisy and playing to the gallery. In the midafternoon, as the debate wore on hour after hour, two members from Connecticut clashed in personal accusations of corruption and dishonesty, boiling over with bitterness until William Sulzer of New York, an ally of Wilson, who officially had the floor at the time, broke the spell, saying, "This is a hot day. Let us keep cool." As laughter rolled through the body, he added that the matter between the two members "will no doubt be thoroughly discussed on the stump in the cooler days of the autumn."

As if to demonstrate his dedication to conciliation and reason, Wilson refused to engage with the discussion when it turned rancorous and irrelevant, repeatedly bringing the House back to the issue at hand. His Republican opponents brought up amendments to the bill on the floor. Wilson listened to their ideas, and in several cases accepted them, allowing the Republican minority to make significant changes to the shape of the new department, including with an amendment defining its purpose, and another eliminating several assistant secretaries presiding over divisions for various industries, which instead left the department's organization flexible with just one assistant secretary. Surely surprising some of his more partisan colleagues, Wilson admitted the amendments were improvements, or at least, reasonable changes he didn't feel he had to block.

His approach was certainly a novel one.

But Wilson knew when to stand his ground as well. When a Republican member offered a "poison-pill" amendment that could have sunk the bill, Wilson blocked it with a point of order. And when it came to his prized program for mediating labor disputes, he didn't give an inch.

Oddly enough, the mediation provision of the bill received the Republicans' most aggressive attack, betraying their suspicion that the new agency would put the government on the side of unions against employers. Wilson argued the point at length, responding to one challenger after another.

J. Hampton Moore, a Philadelphia Republican, questioned whether Wilson thought employees were more important than employers. He responded, "I think that a lifetime of work in the line of endeavoring to bring employer and employee together for the purpose of making wage contracts satisfactory to both parties, without resorting to the strike—a lifetime of work along that line is a sufficient answer to the gentleman's question." The minority leader, James R. Mann of Illinois, then joined the fray, challenging Wilson's concept of voluntary mediation and charging that the mediators would inevitably grow in power to become coercive after the bill passed. "I do not know what they will do," Mann complained. "If they have not any authority to take evidence, swear witnesses, and take testimony, what else can they do?"

Wilson responded plainly. "There is an immense field for them to work in," he replied. "That is the field of getting the two parties to a dispute together before they have reached that point where they are at each other's throat; before they have reached the point . . . where the employer looks upon the employee as an anarchist and lawbreaker, and the employee looks upon the employer as a bloodthirsty tyrant and oppressor of labor. If you can get them together before they reach that point, then you can accomplish some good."

Mann dropped his questioning. And the debate continued for hours more.

Later in the day, Madden, the Chicago quarry owner, brought up the same concerns, questioning if the new secretary of labor would be able to impose his decisions in a dispute, with binding arbitration. Wilson had already explained that he opposed binding arbitration. But Madden would not relent.

"There is not anything, then, the gentleman from Pennsylvania thinks, that would lead to any compulsory settlement of any labor dispute?" Madden asked.

"Nothing whatsoever," Wilson assured him. "I may say to the gentleman . . . that if it gave any power of compulsory arbitration I would be opposed to the bill."

Madden and the other opponents seemed satisfied. And as the day wore on, Wilson tried to bring the bill to a vote. Finally, after the sergeant at arms was dispatched to enforce a quorum, and after six and a half hours of uninterrupted debate, he won the day.

The bill passed the House.

And that November, a Democrat, Woodrow Wilson, won the White House, boosted to victory with labor support and with promises to fulfill. Unions now had their best access to political power yet. But that political power, it seemed, would no longer include William Wilson.

He had lost his reelection bid to Congress.

A socialist candidate had challenged Wilson from the left and siphoned off enough votes to allow his Republican opponent to win. It had been a difficult race. He would remain in Congress for only a few more months, through inauguration day on March 4. His short political career appeared fated for an unceremonious end.

But Wilson would not wallow in defeat. It simply wasn't in his nature.

Instead, he would use his remaining time in the House to continue pushing through his labor agenda, while hoping the bill creating the Department of Labor would pass the Senate and be signed by the outgoing chief executive, President Taft. Gompers and the AFL used their newfound political clout to urge it forward, and the Senate finally approved the bill in February 1913. After many decades, it seemed as though the legislation would finally become law. But yet another obstacle remained.

As the final days of the administration sped by, it became clear that the legislation was languishing on the president's desk.

Something was wrong.

President Taft didn't want to sign the bill. He believed the cabinet was large enough, with nine members. And he preferred for the government to be reorganized before creating any more departments. At the same time, he also realized that, with Democrats taking over the White

House and controlling Congress, any veto he issued would not stop the bill from becoming law in the next Congress. And as he contemplated whether or not to sign the historic legislation, there was one more factor to consider.

The defeated, three-term congressman from Pennsylvania. William B. Wilson.

Taft believed that if he signed the bill, Wilson would most likely be the new secretary of labor. Indeed, Wilson's friends had begun lobbying for his appointment after his reelection defeat, including John Mitchell, of the UMW, who told Wilson in early November of a major push to get him the job—to which Wilson replied that he would not ask for a job "of such great dignity." Gompers and the AFL also lobbied the president-elect for Wilson's appointment, as did the railroad unions and other pro-labor congressmen, including Sulzer, who had been elected governor of New York. And the historical record reveals that, unbeknownst to William, Woodrow Wilson had in fact made his decision well before knowing if the new job would actually come into existence.

Wilson's probable selection for the job appeared to be an open secret in Washington. He would be an appealing choice to be the new secretary, with respect from both parties. Still, there were no guarantees. And on March 3—literally, the day before Woodrow Wilson would take the oath of office—Taft's decision remained unknown.

For his part, William Wilson's mind was elsewhere. In the final hours of the 62nd session of Congress, he was focused on the continuing fight for his Seaman's bill, to make ships safer and give seamen the freedom other citizens had to quit their jobs—changes he expected to help build a professional merchant marine in the United States. On the last full day of the Congress, the bill had finally come back over from the Senate, where it had picked up new amendments at the request of the shipping industry. The bill had gathered bipartisan support. Even the Republican minority leader, James Robert Mann of Illinois, praised it, saying, "There can be no question but that this bill marks a forward step in the progress of humanity and in attaining the object of man, and I hope the Senate amendment will be agreed to."

And then, Mann surprised everyone.

"Mr. Speaker," the minority leader began, "one gentleman who has been most prominent in connection with this bill, both in the committee and on the floor, is a member of this House, who has been also prominent in other labor legislation that has been enacted by Congress for years, and I hope that we are saluting the next Secretary of Labor."

The House exploded in applause.

Democrat Joshua Alexander of Ohio, the committee chair leading the debate, joined in, declaring, "I yield five minutes to the next Secretary of Labor."

After more applause and laughter, the Speaker of the House said, "The Secretary of Labor is recognized for five minutes."

True to his modest and calm, deliberative style, Wilson took no notice of the jokes, or the honor they entailed. The hour was already well past midnight, and the Congress was trying to complete work on many bills before it ran out of time—it would stay in session until 4:20 a.m. on the morning of March 4, Inauguration Day.

The Department of Labor bill still sat unsigned on Taft's desk. And the fate of the department, and perhaps Wilson's own political career, remained in doubt.

Wilson put that out of his mind and steeled himself to the task at hand. With only a few hours left in the congressional session, he had a job to do. The complex piece of legislation that he had crafted and labored to enact was before the House for a final time. Making matters more difficult, the exceedingly late hour meant there was no time left to address the changes made by the Senate.

Members would have to vote it up or down.

Wilson addressed the moment with his trademark clarity and sound logic. As dawn broke across the nation's capital, he lucidly explained the Seaman's bill and the Senate changes, the impact on safety and technical aspects of the handling of ships. And when his five minutes were up, Alexander allotted five more minutes to complete the explanation. It would be Wilson's last speech in the House.

Again, he offered no bombast or lofty rhetoric. Just a technical and intellectually honest explanation of the bill before them. And his humble belief that, all things considered, the bill should be approved.

The members, grumbling and tired as they voted in the wee hours of the night, concurred.

And the bill was passed.

It was one of Wilson's finest moments. The passage of his Seamen's

legislation was among Wilson's most significant legislative accomplishments. But the euphoria was short-lived. For President Taft would leave
the legislation unsigned in the final hours of his presidency. The bill
would one day become the law of the land, but only after William Wilson had left the Congress.

It was a stinging defeat. And yet, all was not lost. For in the concluding hours of his presidency, there was, ironically, another piece of
legislation that President Taft *had* decided to sign. Seated at his desk in
the White House, a mere few hours before the new president would
take his oath of office, Taft finally took out his pen and signed the Department of Labor bill.

It was now law.

And Wilson — the Scottish immigrant who had toiled on behalf of
workers since he was a boy — would ascend to become a member of the
presidential cabinet soon thereafter, when President Woodrow Wilson
appointed him the nation's first secretary of labor.

The department he headed at first lacked offices, furniture, or a
budget. Putting it together would be a struggle. Congress was often
uncooperative, and the conciliation agency took time to gain willing
clients for its mediation services. But over the eight years of Wilson's
leadership, the department became an important positive force in the
lives of working people. Wilson created a worker safety agency, a
worker health agency, and an agency to help workers find jobs around
the country where they were needed. He influenced the president, who
relied on him heavily, to sign a bill stopping the use of injunctions to
break strikes. And when the government made its first big investment in
public housing, the president assigned Wilson to oversee the funds and
decide where to build. At Ellis Island in New York, the immigration
station Wilson now oversaw as a cabinet member, he ordered improved
facilities and safety measures for immigrants and staff.

During World War I, Wilson stepped up to an even more important
role, as mobilization and the need for weapons manufacturing strained
the labor force and created new conflicts between employers and workers. He recruited women into the workforce and set up a new agency to
manage the immense challenges of wartime production. After the war,
massive strikes, race riots, and anarchist bombings swept the country,
and Wilson's work for conciliation and labor peace became even more

crucial. At one point, Attorney General A. Mitchell Palmer ordered more than three thousand immigrants arrested and deported for their political views. Wilson and his agency, citing their fidelity to the rule of law, refused to carry out mass deportations without proof of lawbreaking, and released all but a few hundred of those Palmer had rounded up.

After ending his service in Washington in 1921, Wilson moved back to his farm near Blossburg. He remained involved in politics and mediated labor disputes.

He lived a full life.

In 1934, at the age of seventy-two, Wilson passed away, leaving behind an impact on the country much larger than his limited fame would suggest. Still, he seemed to have been satisfied with his accomplishments for their own sake, regardless of his lack of personal profit. Babson, his biographer, recalled a meeting in Wilson's office at the Labor Department, one winter day toward the end of his service in the cabinet, with five chiefs of the department's agencies gathered for an organizational meeting. The secretary became philosophic about his life.

"My many years' experience in Washington has convinced me that the only men who secure and permanently retain the love of their countrymen are those who put service before everything else," he told them. "The men who seek money are always doomed sooner or later; the men who seek power or fame are continually taking chances and running risks of disaster; but those who are actuated by a simple desire to serve are the ones who ultimately win. The paths of such men may be long and tedious. It may be necessary for them to go through sloughs of despond and to climb treacherous heights; but by keeping the one star in mind they ultimately win, and become an honor to their families, to their communities, and to their nation."

4

Adolph Sabath

★ ★ ★ ★ ★ ★ ★ ★ ★

*Let us ... show them that our country ever extends the warm
hand of sympathy and fellowship to the oppressed people of
the earth.*

—ADOLPH SABATH

The two men met alone in a lush garden pavilion near the New Jersey shore on an unusually pleasant afternoon in late July 1912. They could hardly have been more different. Adolph Sabath, a relatively new member of Congress from Chicago, was short and stocky, with a round face and a bushy dark mustache. He spoke with a thick Czech accent that attested to his arrival in America, nearly penniless, thirty-one years before. He radiated kindness and good cheer and was known, even among his most ardent adversaries, as a warm and considerate man. Woodrow Wilson, the governor of New Jersey and the Democratic nominee for president, was tall and slender, with a narrow face that often wore a pinched expression. Ten years Sabath's senior, Wilson was a patrician intellectual and academic, the renowned former president of Princeton University, known by many for inflexibility, coldness, and a willingness to discard old friendships over matters of principle.

By the measures of the day, most people would have considered Wilson the superior of the two politicians. He had come from a privileged social class, possessed fame as a thinker and leader, and beheld the nation's most powerful office, his life's dream, beckoning for his grasp in the general election, just a few months away. But on this warm day near the shores of Sea Girt, New Jersey, it was Wilson who was the supplicant, not Sabath.

For the nominee had seriously alienated a voting bloc he desperately needed. And the congressman's endorsement would be critical to getting those voters back.

Wilson and Sabath both knew it. Indeed, they both understood well the stakes. But Sabath was clear-eyed about his plans. He had come to the expansive Governor's Summer Cottage with the specific intent of denying Wilson the support he so desperately needed.

Sabath had refused an earlier invitation. And Wilson had plenty of reason to doubt that Sabath would change his mind and back his candidacy. His own campaign team had maneuvered to deny Sabath political power he had earned, robbing him of his delegation in the just-concluded Democratic National Convention of 1912 in Baltimore, Maryland. Wilson had advocated for temperance and was suspected of supporting prohibition of alcohol, which Sabath and many of his constituents strongly opposed. And, most vexingly, Wilson had grievously insulted Sabath's national heritage with writings that also suggested he would restrict legal immigration from the European region Sabath had come from, keeping apart families—like Sabath's own—whose members had been divided between the US and the old country. As a result, Sabath went to the meeting, as he later recalled, "[s]ore, piqued, dissatisfied, and disgruntled." He agreed to attend only at the pleading and behest of party leaders, and in the company of most of the Democratic caucus of the House, one hundred sixteen members in all, including the Speaker of the House himself, who was Sabath's friend and had been narrowly defeated for the presidential nomination by Wilson, under questionable circumstances.

While large groups of members of Congress from across the country congregated and waited on the broad, green lawn and wide, shaded porch, Wilson spoke intently with Sabath as the two men huddled in the garden for nearly an hour. The historical record indicates that, as they exchanged views, Wilson sipped an alcoholic beverage to prove he wasn't a prohibitionist.

Wilson's efforts notwithstanding, the ultimate outcome of the meeting appeared to be more a credit to Sabath's openness than to Wilson's persuasiveness. Fortunately for both men and their mutual political efforts, Sabath demonstrated on that day an extraordinary level of forgiveness and the rare political courage to trust a former opponent. After the two finished their private conversation and shook hands, Sabath endorsed Wilson that same afternoon. The word went out in headlines in the nation's largest newspapers. What those headlines did not reveal, however, were the valuable promises Sabath had extracted from Wilson to help immigrants—those who, like Sabath himself, would come to the nation's shores with little, in search of the American Dream.

Over the eight years of their ensuing political partnership, while Wilson was in the White House, Sabath kept closely in touch with the president to ensure those promises were kept—even in the face of a wave of unpopularity for those views. And for a time, at least, their efforts protected those who sought refuge in America. That partnership happened, and Wilson gained the election endorsement he needed from the man known as "the immigrants' representative," because Adolph Sabath had the foresight and political skill to recognize when to set aside his anger and make a new friend of a former adversary.

Sabath's story could happen only in America. A small boy from a tiny, impoverished town in Bohemia (now in the Czech Republic), he would become among the first Czech Americans to serve in the House, feted and cajoled for support by a future president, and would go on to serve longer in the US Congress than any member before him. Sabath worked with eight presidents, from Teddy Roosevelt to Harry Truman, and for many years served as chairman of the Rules Committee, at that time the second most powerful position in the House. His legislative accomplishments for immigrants, working people, children, and the elderly would easily fill a book of their own, among them the enactment of important federal statutes on child labor and pensions, and his key role in developing the social safety net with President Franklin D. Roosevelt's New Deal. But along with those accomplishments, he also won the admiration and affection of his legislative allies and opponents alike, as a powerful advocate who was unfailingly gentle, and who, unlike some other chairmen, did not use his power in an arbitrary or self-serving way, but rather, to help make good law. When he died in 1952, two days after being reelected by a 2-to-1 margin to a twenty-fourth consecutive term in the House, a long parade of House members eulogized him, calling him a personal friend or mentor, including many who had been his longtime political opponents.

As President Harry Truman would later observe of Sabath, "in him the forgotten man always found a champion."

Adolph Joachim Sabath was born April 4, 1866, into the only Jewish family in Záboří, Bohemia. His mother, Babette, had twelve chil-

dren with his father, Joachim, a butcher. At age thirteen, after scant
education, Adolph apprenticed as a clerk in a dry goods store in a
town about ten miles away, where he worked fourteen hours a day
and, in the evening, cared for the blind brother-in-law of the shop's
owner. The brother-in-law had been to America, and at night, as the
light gave way to the darkness, the man who could no longer see
would regale Adolph with colorful tales of his travels and the promise
of America. Adolph was transfixed. These stories inspired Adolph,
who saved his money for two years until, in 1881, he had forty dollars
for the passage to the United States. After a long journey across the
Atlantic, he arrived in Chicago—at that time, the second largest city
in the country and one of the largest cities in the world—and began
staying with a cousin.

He only had $2.15 left in his pocket. And he was fifteen years old.

His first few years in America were anything but easy. He was fired
after a brief stint in a wood-planing mill for being too small for the
work, and got a job instead as a shop clerk selling shoes and household
goods. But by the time he was twenty-one, he had worked his way
up to be the store's manager and had become an American citizen.
He also had accumulated enough savings to start a real estate business with a partner. As more Bohemians arrived in Chicago, Sabath
acquired tracts from insurance companies and subdivided them to sell
to the newcomers, helping build the Pilsen neighborhood, named for
a Czech city, on Chicago's South Side. Sabath did well in his business
and earned enough money to bring to America his parents and ten
siblings.

While he worked, Sabath also attended night school, studying business and then law, which he originally chose to pursue to save on legal
fees in his land transactions. He passed the bar in 1891. Sabath also
helped start various civic organizations in the Czech community in
Chicago, such as the Pilsen Youth Club, a singing club, the Czech-
American Club, and the Democratic Political Club. He served on
a ward political committee and helped the first Czech alderman get
elected. At twenty-nine, he had become a leading figure in the eastern
European immigrant communities in Chicago, and the governor of Illinois appointed him a justice of the peace and later a magistrate for
criminal cases.

In 1896, Sabath attended the Democratic National Convention for the first time, and on the way to the Chicago Colosseum experienced a stroke of good luck. Riding a streetcar, Sabath noticed a famous congressman across from him. He quickly shifted his seat to talk to him— he would later say he had thought, "One of the greatest honors that could come to a young immigrant in America was to be able to sit beside and talk to a member of Congress." The congressman was William Jennings Bryan, the most famous orator of his age, who would become a leading figure of the progressive movement, transforming the Democratic Party from its conservative roots in the nineteenth century to become the more liberal of the two major political parties. Bryan was only six years older than Sabath.

The two struck up a lasting friendship.

That day on the streetcar, Sabath asked Bryan who he thought would get the presidential nomination at the convention. Bryan responded that he thought he would—if he could just get the floor to speak.

And get the floor he did. That night, speaking about the party platform, Bryan gave a speech considered by many historians among the greatest in American politics, calling for an end to the gold standard that progressives believed had contributed to economic hardship for farmers and the working class, and ending with the cry, "We will answer their demand for a gold standard by saying to them: 'You shall not press down upon the brow of labor this crown of thorns; you shall not crucify mankind upon a cross of gold.' " The speech electrified the convention and made Bryan the Democratic nominee. He remained the leader of the party as its nominee for president again in 1900 and 1908, although he never won the presidency.

The streetcar meeting with Bryan determined the future course of Sabath's life, as he related many years later over lunch with a colleague twenty-five years his junior. On that day, he said, he had witnessed "[o]ne of the greatest demonstrations of free democracy in action that could come to any nation in the world." The experience convinced him to dedicate the remainder of his career to public service.

Bryan himself would be a significant help. Sabath supported him, and Bryan helped Sabath along the way. In 1906, Sabath had become popular enough in his immigrant-dominated district to defeat an incumbent Republican for a seat in the Congress. Bryan saw to it he received desirable committee assignments, including the Committee on Immigration. Sabath's courtesy also earned him another powerful friend. Members of Congress in those days received assigned desks, which were selected by lottery. Sabath, seeing he had been given a coveted aisle seat near the front, insisted on trading with a more experienced member, Champ Clark, who he knew would need the favored position more to help lead his caucus. Clark became a friend and mentor, as he advanced to become minority leader, Speaker of the House, and a front-runner for the Democratic presidential nomination.

Soon after he was elected, Sabath used his position to create opportunities for immigrants within the party and to recruit ethnically diverse slates of candidates for election. But he truly made his name with his first speech on the floor of the House, in January 1908.

At the time, the body was considering the proposed expansion of an immigration station in Philadelphia, a discussion that had descended into a heated debate about the value of immigrants and whether to limit them. A leader on the pro-immigration side suggested Sabath weigh in with his own comments. Sitting in the chamber, he listened intently as his colleagues argued vociferously, streams of words interrupted only by the heavy thud of the Speaker's gavel as he sought to retain order. Sabath was focused on every word of the debate, but at first resisted the temptation to jump into the fray. After only a month on the floor, he felt he was simply too new to the Congress to engage.

That changed quickly.

Two members from Iowa and Alabama began making remarks he simply could not ignore, charging that most immigrants were "undesirables," and that they would not become loyal Americans. One member declared it would be better to "burn down" the immigration station than expand it.

Sabath, his hands sweaty and his eyes fixed on his colleagues, felt compelled to speak, as nervous as he was to stand before the House. "I dragged myself to the well," he later recalled. "I seen before me thousands of great giants, members of Congress. Between you and me, I never in a Turkish bath perspired more."

As he rose from the floor, he began by first responding directly to the two members who had disparaged immigrants, scolding them for their careless attacks. And he pulled no punches.

"For twenty-seven years of my life I have lived and worked in Chicago, in the very midst of these people to whom the gentlemen have referred as undesirable citizens," he declared. "I come in contact with these people every day of my life. I have lived among them; they are my people, *and I am one of them.*"

Thunderous applause interrupted Sabath, but he continued.

"I know them as no other man here knows them, and I have watched their brave struggles to adapt themselves to the conditions of this country. I have seen them come to America with their faces lighted with hope at the prospect of living in a land of freedom and liberty, and I have seen them struggle long and bravely, and sometimes against overwhelming odds, to realize those hopes."

Sabath was interrupted by applause six times in the course of his speech. As he held up immigrants for their strength and devotion to America, their hard work doing jobs others often scorned, and their positive economic impact, which he enumerated with a blizzard of statistics, loud applause echoed, from the chamber to the gallery.

Nearing his conclusion, Sabath paused and took a deep breath. "Mr. Chairman," Sabath explained plainly, "my district in Chicago is peopled by representatives of nearly every nation in the world. It is peopled by . . . [those] whose struggles for liberty and freedom date back to periods before the western world had a place in the dreams of men. It is peopled by men and women from the countries of Europe, who, oppressed in their own lands, long looked forward to American citizenship that they might for themselves and children enjoy that freedom and that liberty which they had heard and dreamed. . . . Let us build this building at Philadelphia, to give these worthy foreigners a welcome when they come, and to show them that our country ever extends the warm hand of sympathy and fellowship to the oppressed people of the earth."

Long, sustained applause carried Sabath back to his seat. The bill passed, and immigrant voters heard about what Sabath had said. From then on, his assistant recalled, immigrants all over the country regarded Sabath as their representative in Congress, regardless of where in the nation they lived.

Immigration had become a burning political issue. The previous year, 1907, the highest number of immigrants in US history arrived, almost 1.3 million, with the largest portion coming from Italy and Eastern Europe. That contrasted to the wave of immigration that had peaked thirty years earlier, when most came from Great Britain, Ireland, Scandinavia, and Germany. (Immigration from Europe remained essentially unlimited, although the 1882 Chinese Exclusion Act outlawed nearly all Chinese immigration.) The flood of new people into New York and Philadelphia produced crowding in tenements, exploitation in sweatshops, and a backlash and call for restrictions. Some anti-immigration politicians in both parties maintained that the former group of immigrants had been superior, and that those coming from southern and eastern Europe—who also included a much larger share of Catholic and Jewish immigrants—were hurting America and should be limited.

A strong statement of that view came from a noted intellectual writing a sweeping history of the United States, who was not yet considered a political figure at all. In his five-volume *A History of the American People*, published in 1902, the author, a professor, took conservative positions against labor unions and regulation of business and decried the changing flow of immigration, using terrible words he would later state that he had come to regret. After praising immigrants from northern Europe, he wrote that, "Now there came multitudes of men of the lowest class from the south of Italy and men of the meaner sort out of Hungary and Poland, men out of the ranks where there was neither skill nor energy nor any initiative of quick intelligence; and they came in numbers which increased year to year."

That author was Woodrow Wilson.

Wilson, a Democrat, would later leave academia behind as he transitioned to politics, and in 1910, won election as governor of New Jersey. And in less than a decade, he had evolved politically to become progressive on many issues. In his first year as governor, he passed a package of legislation protecting workers, regulating utilities, and cracking down on corruption and the state's political machine. The national attention he received made him a potential contender for the presidency, and he worked behind the scenes to find allies, including courting William Jennings Bryan to come to his side as he sought the Democratic nomination for president. But his stiff, haughty demeanor had made enemies, too. When the newspaper magnate William Randolph Hearst offered his support in 1911, Wilson said, "Tell Mr. Hearst to go to hell."

That reaction may have been principled—Hearst was, by many accounts, unscrupulous—but it pushed Hearst to support Wilson's main opponent, and Sabath's dear friend, Champ Clark. Wilson had also created the very weapon that Hearst would use to attempt to destroy him: his derogatory writings about eastern and southern European immigrants. Hearst published the passage widely, especially focusing on areas with large immigrant populations. Then, he published news of angry rebuttals from groups representing people of Polish, Hungarian, or Italian ancestry.

Wilson had a serious political problem on his hands. As a progressive, he needed those votes. And so, he wrote to these Americans virtually every day of the campaign, traveling the country as he tried to explain himself to immigrant clubs and foreign language newspaper editors by claiming that his words had been misconstrued and taken out of context. He had little success. Most immigrant groups remained firmly against him, with some even passing resolutions of denunciation. And his tortured explanations did nothing to allay the immigrant groups' fears that, if elected president, he would support wholesale restrictions on immigration.

His campaign was in real trouble.

Wilson considered Illinois, then the third-largest state, as key to winning the nomination. He campaigned hard there, speaking fifteen times from the back of a train, and holding several mass rallies in Chicago, including one of Polish Americans whom he again tried to convince that he would, indeed, support immigration for those who wanted to become Americans. Clark didn't go to Illinois at all but won the state's presidential primary anyway, by a more than 2-to-1 margin. As chair of the Cook County Central Committee, Sabath prepared to go to the national convention in Baltimore and gladly help cast Illinois's votes for Clark. On the eve of the convention, Clark had twice as many committed delegates as Wilson, who admitted in private that he had little chance to win.

It was in that context, and with his presidential aspirations on the line, that Wilson waited anxiously at the Governor's Summer Cottage in Sea Girt. His supporters would manage his affairs at the convention in Baltimore, which would prove to be one of the most hotly contested and convoluted in US history. Although Wilson had instructed no deals should be made on his behalf, his aides made many, even reportedly giving away the vice presidential spot on the ticket in exchange for delegate votes without Wilson's knowledge.

In the credentials committee, Wilson's supporters managed to discredit Illinois's legitimate delegation—of which Sabath was a member—and instead, installed a delegation led by Illinois political boss Roger Sullivan, an enemy of Bryan and opponent of Clark. Nonetheless, from the first ballot, Clark still led the voting, and by the tenth ballot, had a commanding majority—although still short of the two-thirds majority needed under party rules to pick a nominee.

Wilson was ready to give up. Bryan, however, had a plan. He hoped the convention would deadlock and nominate him as a compromise candidate, giving him a fourth chance to become president. To make that happen, with Clark appearing close to a win, Bryan helped Wilson with his still-potent political power and the strength of oratory to win the crowd. The balloting got closer and closer through the twentieth, thirtieth, and even fortieth ballot. Then, on the forty-third ballot, Roger Sullivan threw Illinois to Wilson—despite the state's strong primary vote for Clark. It was the decisive move. And it resulted in Wilson's win on the forty-sixth ballot.

Wilson, finally, had secured the nomination. But the danger of it being a pyrrhic victory was real. The party he now led was bitterly divided after a process of selection that had been highly questionable. And key Democratic voters and constituencies remained deeply alienated from him over his writings on immigration.

To sew the party back together, delegations trooped to the big house in Sea Girt, with its broad veranda, in the July heat, to pay their respects. Cook County sent a group, but Sabath refused to go. Then, on a hot day in the nation's capital, Clark, as both Speaker of the House and the loser to Wilson, made a grand gesture, adjourning the House to bring most of the Democratic caucus with him to Sea Girt. And this time, Sabath agreed to go along—but with the intent of telling Wilson he would not have his support.

The newspapers recorded the spectacle of almost a third of the Congress traveling to the Jersey shore on a special train and walking up Wilson's front lawn, where he came down from the porch to meet the delegation. It was the first time in history Congress had adjourned for such a trip. Champ Clark interrupted the receiving line to make a magnanimous speech at Wilson's side and handed him a book of the Congress members' signatures. The congressmen cheered and gave the newspapers many statements of support.

All but Sabath.

After a big group picture, they broke up into knots of conversation. And it was then that Wilson drew Sabath away for a private talk in the garden. As Sabath would later remember it, he was ushered into a pavilion with Wilson for a drink, and Wilson asked him the reasons for his opposition. After some discussion, Sabath finally said, "You have written a book which has done injustice to immigrants."

"My dear Judge," Sabath recalled Wilson saying, "I wrote that book not as a candidate but as a historian. By itself that phrase may look bad, but read the context. Read the entire book." And then, lifting the book in question, Wilson said, "Here, I'll read it."

Wilson then read aloud. He spoke at length of his views on immigration and labor. Sabath responded in kind. And while history does not record everything Wilson promised, many believe he assured Sabath that he would not support restrictions on legal immigration. Some other decisions subsequently went Sabath's way as well, which surely had their beginnings in that pavilion, including Wilson's repudiating Roger Sullivan, which prevented him from winning a seat in the US Senate from Illinois—despite the fact he had, in effect, given Wilson the presidential nomination.

Whatever commitments were made, when the two men emerged from their one-on-one in the garden, Sabath made a statement to the press that received wide attention, partly because it was so unexpected.

The *Washington Post* reported that "Representative Sabath, of Illinois, who came here prepared to say that he wasn't going to support Gov. Wilson if he found the governor entertained race prejudices, had a long and earnest talk with him. 'He's fair and broad enough for me,' Sabath said afterward." The article went on to recount, in detail, Sabath's explanation of Wilson's account of his oft-quoted anti-immigrant passage, including Wilson's apparent claim that when he referred to people of a "lower class," he had "meant men of no particular nation," and that he believed "healthy immigration was a good thing and should be encouraged."

The next month, Sabath gave a speech to Congress on Wilson's beliefs regarding immigration. He added pages of evidence to support it in the *Congressional Record*, with all the thoroughness and reasoning of a legal brief. Writing to constituents and editors of foreign-language newspapers, Sabath explained his views on Wilson's negative quotation and related his own decision to support him, asking for votes for the nominee and each time recounting his private meeting at Sea Girt. "Notwithstanding there were present on that day about 150 Democratic Members of Congress, when I stated to Mr. Wilson my mission, he gave me nearly one hour of his time, because of his desire to be put right before the foreign-born citizens and the American people at large on this question," Sabath wrote to the editor of *Bohemian Country Life,* in Omaha, Nebraska. "Feeling satisfied that Gov. Wilson is not prejudiced against foreign-born citizens or against immigration, I have decided not only to give him my vote, but also to support him to the best of my ability. I hope that all those who have heretofore believed in me and approved of my views and humble effort in their behalf will approve of my views in this matter and will bend every effort to secure his election, as I believe it is our duty to show the American people that we will not be misled by the efforts of Mr. Wilson's opponents to poison our minds against him."

One cannot say for certain how much difference Sabath's efforts made in Wilson's landslide election that fall. The largest factor in Wilson's victory was a split in the Republican Party, which led former President Teddy Roosevelt to enter the race as a third-party candidate, leaving William Howard Taft, the incumbent, to finish third. But one can easily evaluate Sabath's strategic judgment at that moment when he met with Wilson, as he controlled his anger and indignation and established the backing of the future president for his cause of the support of immigrants. Sabath's statements appear honest—he apparently did believe Wilson would stand by him on immigration—but there is also clear evidence of Sabath's political savvy, in that he extracted his revenge on his Illinois rival, Roger Sullivan, while simultaneously convincing Wilson to commit to some diplomatic appointments. Sabath was very much aware of what he was doing, both in his openness and willingness to listen, and in his incisive use of the power he had in that moment.

"I'll say this," Sabath later recalled. "Every promise he made me he carried out."

It didn't take long for a test of Sabath's relationship with the new president. Twice in the first year of his term, in October and November of 1913, Sabath received information that Wilson would support an immigration restriction bill if it came to his desk. Each time, he went to the White House to meet privately with the president. Both times, he came back satisfied. The anti-immigration movement (which was bipartisan) had gained strength with the public and in Congress. Near the end of Taft's term, the Congress had passed a bill that would require immigrants to prove their literacy, in any language, to gain entry into the United States. The bill's intent, according to several of its sponsors, was to reduce immigration from the poorer, southern and eastern parts of Europe. President Taft had vetoed the bill, as had President Grover Cleveland before him. But it would come back. And the only real chance of stopping it would be another presidential veto.

In December 1913, Alabama Democrat John L. Burnett introduced an immigration bill with a variety of restrictions, the most important of which was again a literacy test. In debate, Burnett assured the House that the test in question "would not keep out the splendid German people that come to this country, the magnificent Scandinavians," or the English, Irish, Welsh, Scottish, Bohemian, or French, for that matter. But, he said, it would block half of those from southern Italy, whom he characterized as "too ignorant" to avoid following "dangerous anarchists," and adding, "That is the class at which this bill is leveled. It would keep out about thirty percent of the Poles, about forty percent of the Greeks, some sixty or seventy percent of Turks." One of Burnett's stated reasons for reducing those nationalities' numbers was also his belief that it would preserve jobs for Americans—and the American Federation of Labor had, critically, endorsed the bill—but his desire to continue allowing northern Europeans, the previous wave of immigrants Wilson had praised in his book, was because he believed them inherently superior. Of southern Italians, Burnett asserted, "Gentlemen, they are the descendants of those who came chained to the chariot wheels of the ancient Romans and came behind their conquering eagles as their slaves. They are those who came from the blood of the Saracens, Arabs, Moors, and Africans who are across the Mediterranean."

Once again, it was time for Sabath to speak up for immigrants across the country.

During the debate on Burnett's bill, Sabath rose decisively from his chair, and responded directly and firmly. "The supporters of this measure," Sabath began, "will tell you that by adopting the literacy test we will keep out a great portion of those coming from southern Europe, and that we will therefore secure more desirable immigration." However, Sabath declared, "Mr. Chairman, literacy is not a test of character, of honesty, industry, or integrity. There are several European countries that make it impossible for their subjects to receive an education, but because of this fact are we to shut our doors in the faces of these people when they seek to enter this country in order that they may attain that which they have been deprived of in their native land?"

The chamber was silent as Sabath posed the question.

"To assume such an attitude," Sabath told his colleagues, "would be to place our stamp of approval upon the despicable practices of these foreign countries."

Sabath responded to attacks on behalf of all immigrants, although he noted that he had few of the targeted ethnicities or nationalities in his own district. Like Burnett, he repeated a list, talking about the immigrants in his hometown of Chicago. "There are within its borders hundreds of thousands of Germans, Irish, Bohemians, Poles, Jews, Italians, Scandinavians, Norwegians, Slovenians, Lithuanians, and those of other nationalities," Sabath explained. "People whom . . . the gentleman from Alabama [Mr. Burnett] has seen to designate as 'undesirables.' These people have demonstrated time and time again that they are honest, industrious, law-abiding, and virtuous, and that they make very desirable citizens. . . . And now our city, with eighty percent of its people of foreign birth or foreign parentage, is the wonder of the age. It is the center of education, of invention, of industry, of art, of music, and of everything that contributes to the progress and elevation of the human race. Gentlemen, I proudly point to it as an example of what the immigrants have done for our country."

In his major speech against the bill, Sabath knocked down Burnett's arguments one by one, and deftly parried challenges that came from the other side. To counter the contention that the immigrants of the past were somehow more desirable—the British, Irish, and Germans— he read a quote by an anti-immigration group from 1819, almost one hundred years before, that expressed the exact same fears and disdain about them. Sabath argued that the opposition to immigrants at the time had largely come from places that didn't have any, while the cities where most immigrants lived generally supported immigration. And as Sabath continued his remarks, he implored his colleagues to consider the empirical data underpinning his argument about immigrants and the job market, quoting statistics that, he contended, showed during the period of heavy immigration that wages in various trades had gone up while hours went down.

Democratic Representative Frank Buchanan of Illinois, an iron worker, interrupted, demanding, "Does not the gentleman know that that increase in wages has been largely due to organized labor?"

"Yes, it has," Sabath said. "And if it had not been for the foreign element, we would not have organized labor in this country."

The House applauded. And Sabath went on. One by one, he listed the labor leaders who were immigrants, including Samuel Gompers, the founder and president of the AFL; most of the federation's executive board; and even the US Secretary of Labor William B. Wilson.

Another member interrupted, incredulous, and demanded to know if Sabath was implying Secretary Wilson would have been excluded from America if the bill had been law.

"I do not know whether he would or would not," Sabath admitted. "The chances are that he might have been, because I do not know what his financial condition was when he came over. I know that I would have been embarrassed and that I could not have landed if the law that you propose now had been in force in 1882. I did not possess twenty-five dollars, nor did I possess, perhaps, some of the other qualifications that some of these gentlemen now desire these immigrants to possess."

The House roared again in applause. And it didn't stop until Sabath ended his speech, to a stirring and powerful conclusion.

The next day, the *Washington Post* carried a front-page article about his admission that he had been poor and illiterate when he arrived, while also predicting he would lose the issue in Congress. The headline said it all: "Fight of Sabath Futile."

Even as Sabath led the opposition to the bill, a test vote showed him that it would certainly pass. His hope was for a veto by President Wilson, and enough support in the House to sustain that veto—even while Democrats in favor of the bill were predicting he would sign it. Wilson was Sabath's most important audience for his speeches, and his relationship with the president his most important asset to stop the bill, as it assured Sabath that he had Wilson's ear.

Knowing Wilson's veto would be crucial, Sabath sent him messages through his speeches on the House floor. During the final day of debate, as the vote approached, he praised Wilson as "[t]he greatest president this country has ever known" and read a series of statements Wilson had made in favor of immigration—which Sabath had helped extract from him—including Wilson's assertion, "It would be inconsistent with our historical character as a Nation if we did not offer a very hearty welcome to every honest man and woman who comes to this country to seek a permanent home and a new opportunity."

The bill passed the House, but it lingered a year in the Senate, as World War I began in Europe and drove a new tide of nativism in the United States. When it finally came to a vote, only seven senators opposed the bill. The political stakes were high for Wilson, as he contemplated the bill on his desk. Samuel Gompers brought the entire executive committee of the AFL to the White House to lobby him for his signature. Immigrant groups weighed in with their opposition. On January 22, 1915, Wilson sat down in the East Room of the White House to hear the two sides debate the bill and persuade him one way or the other on whether he should sign it. Leaders of the two sides, including Sabath, sat at a small round table, facing the president, with five hundred guests behind them, representing civic groups of many kinds. Wilson listened quietly but attentively for three hours of impassioned speeches made for his benefit. Sabath and his allies, during their half of the time, called upon priests and Jewish leaders, professors, newspaper editors, and immigrant societies. Much of the testimony was persuasive, some less so. As the hearing concluded, Wilson didn't reveal what he would do. And then, one week later, the announcement was made.

President Wilson had vetoed the bill.

His veto message used words similar to those Sabath had quoted him saying in the debate on the bill a year earlier. "This bill embodies a radical departure from the traditional and long-established policy of this country, a policy in which our people have conceived the very character of their government to be expressed, the very mission and spirit of the nation," Wilson declared. As to the literacy test, he said, "Those who come seeking opportunity are not to be admitted unless they already had one of the chief opportunities they seek—the opportunity of education. The object of such provision is restriction, not selection."

Scholars still debate today if Wilson was sincere. Had the man of such derogatory views truly changed his outlook? He remained steadfastly and appallingly prejudiced against African Americans and Asian Americans, and his administration segregated the federal workforce. Did he believe the votes of those who opposed the bill would be more important than the strong public opinion in favor of it? Or did he simply hold to the promises he had made to Sabath and others? The answers to those questions are unknown. We do know, however, that Wilson never again wavered from his opposition to the literacy test or other measures to restrict immigration from Europe.

Supporters of the measure were confident they could override the veto because the bill had originally passed with more than the two-thirds margin needed in each chamber. But they underestimated Sabath.

He immediately began sending out urgent telegrams, bringing back to Washington all members who supported immigration. At the same time, Democratic Party leaders began considering the price they might pay with immigrant voters in the 1916 election if they received blame for allowing the bill to become law—as they likely would, since a Democrat sponsored the bill and Democrats controlled both houses of Congress. They quietly began pushing their members to support the president.

Once again, Sabath led the fight on the floor of the House, allotting time to each member on his side before going last, with a speech to address each of the points the opposition had raised. He quoted Wilson's veto message and his own speech from before the 1912 election, in which he had praised Wilson and said he trusted his promises to immigrants. And he finished off to applause with a grand finale.

"The gentleman from Alabama is fearful of our future citizenship. If he would take the trouble to visit the homes of these people whom he dubs the scum of the earth and undesirable citizens I feel confident that he would not stand on the floor of this House and slander these hardworking, sincere, and law-abiding people. . . . Due to immigration, our country is the wonder of civilization. Its population is made up of all the peoples of the earth. We have all races, all religions, all nationalities. They have come to us from all quarters of the globe, and we have the best. Only the courageous hearts and adventurous spirits, who had the courage to face away from their native country and the homes of their birth, their kindred and friends, to face out to an unknown land, where the language they spoke was not understood, with nothing to beckon them on but the beacon light of human liberty, are the ones who have sought to make this country their home."

Burnett, of Alabama, followed. He also quoted Wilson, reading from his *History of the American People* about the undesirability of eastern and southern Europeans and how their arrival was straining American resources. And, like Sabath, he too brought down the House in cheers. After a full day of debate, when the vote finally came, just enough Democrats switched their positions to support the president and barely uphold his veto. The margin was just four votes. Indeed, the tally was close enough that the Speaker called for it to be checked twice.

The immigration fight, however, was far from over.

Public opinion continued to trend against immigration during World War I. In 1916, Burnett's bill passed once more. Yet again, Wilson vetoed it.

Sabath fought to sustain the veto, delivering one of his most impassioned speeches, upholding the accomplishments and contributions of Jewish people in America. But his efforts, this time, proved unsuccessful. Congress overrode the veto. And the immigration restrictions, including the literacy test, became law.

Within a few years, the test proved less effective at weeding out immigrants from the countries Congress had disfavored, as those nations' education systems improved. In 1921, the Congress passed a bill that specifically limited the number of immigrants from eastern and southern Europe by creating annual quotas based on the nationality of people already in the US as of 1890. The nation had decided, decisively, to strictly limit immigration and impose preferences for immigrants from some nations over others. The laws would be amended from time to time. But the policy would not substantively change for over forty years, until 1965.

Sabath's battles on the immigration bills are considered by some as his greatest hours as an orator and legislative leader. But they were only the opening innings in his nearly half century in the Congress. As chairman of the Rules Committee, his fingerprints and influence can be found on many major pieces of domestic legislation that have stood the test of time, from the World War I era all the way through President Franklin Roosevelt's New Deal. He also was an avid participant in foreign policy. For ten years, he worked to help establish the nation of Israel, and after World War II, used his strong relationships with President Franklin Roosevelt and President Truman to encourage diplomatic decisions in support of the country.

Decades earlier, during the Wilson administration, Sabath had worked for the creation of the nation of Czechoslovakia (which preceded the current Czech and Slovak republics). In 1918, when he received word that Wilson was considering negotiating a separate World War I peace treaty with the Austro-Hungarian Empire—which encompassed the Czech homeland—he went to the White House three times to convince Wilson not to do so, seeking to persuade him that such a treaty would deny independence for Czechoslovakia, Poland, and the Baltic states. He finally was successful by telling President Wilson that if he withdrew from the negotiations and declared support for independence movements, revolutions would break out that would take Austria-Hungary out of the war. Wilson followed that advice. The revolutions erupted, just as Sabath had predicted, and Poland and Czechoslovakia gained independence. Sabath later arranged for a meeting between the president and a leader of the Czech independence movement, which led to the United States recognizing Czechoslovakia as a nation.

Three decades later, in 1947, Sabath received a letter, relayed by the State Department, which contained a certificate of honorary citizenship from his old village of Záboří. It read, "As a brave fighter for the ideals of democracy he deserved credit for the liberation of our dear country through spreading the Czechoslovak idea abroad and through organizing assistance in America. He gave expression to social feelings by the erection of a home for the poor citizens of his native village." It turned out, as Sabath explained to a reporter, that he had built an old people's home in Záboří, in honor of his mother.

Sabath was known for his kindness. One magazine journalist faulted him for it. Writing in 1946, when Sabath was eighty years old, John R. Beal reported that, as chairman of the Rules Committee, "Sabath's personal inclination is to be kind, polite, gentlemanly, while the post calls for qualities of toughness and stubbornness." Beal added that "Despite his sympathy for the little fellow, which is genuine, he never had learned the trick of using the perquisites of long service to do anything very effective to implement it."

History tells us something different.

The historical record suggests Sabath was both kind *and* effective— such was certainly the case when he disarmed his adversaries in debate with the disclosure that their immigration legislation would have prevented his own arrival to America, as well as when he convinced President Wilson to keep his promises and veto both bills. And perhaps the same can be said of when he sat in the future president's garden pavilion in 1912, using his leverage to win the promises that Wilson would later keep. He had been deeply effective, and yet, despite his considerable power, remained deeply human, beloved among his colleagues, as they demonstrated in their heartfelt eulogies and the loving anecdotes they told on the House floor after his death in 1952.

They described a fierce and energetic advocate for the underdog. As Rules chairman for twelve years, Sabath had been the second most powerful member in the body, but nonetheless helped many freshmen Congressmen find their legs and formed strong friendships with his strongest Republican adversaries, treating everyone with fairness and courtesy while constantly performing small acts of charity and assistance for his colleagues. He charmed them with his still-thick accent and warm smile. A member remembered fondly when, on his eighty-fifth birthday, Sabath related that he had received a phone call from his brother, Joseph Sabath: "Twice he came to me on the floor and said, 'Joe telephoned me; Joe, my brother.' The heart of Adolph Sabath was as tender as his mind was vibrant." Joseph by then had spent fifty years on the bench as a highly respected Chicago judge—a career made possible because Adolph had earned the money to bring him from the old country.

"His career will always stand as an exemplary and shining symbol of the opportunities for all under our democratic system in this land of free men," a colleague said in eulogy. "Adolph Sabath, in fact, epitomized in the political and legislative fields the contribution which the foreign-born have made, and their descendants are making today, in the building of the greatness of the United States, and in its achievement of world leadership. He was a fighter for the causes in which he deeply believed and vigorously espoused. Yet, I venture to say, that even among those with whom he differed strongly, there is none who does not mourn his passing. His friendships knew no party or faction limitations . . ."

"He was a man. Take him for all and all, we shall not look upon his like again."

5

Oscar Stanton De Priest

* * * * * * * * *

I say further, ladies and gentlemen of the Congress, that America never will be what it was intended to be until every citizen in America has his just rights under the Constitution.

—OSCAR STANTON DE PRIEST

It was a chilly Tuesday morning in the nation's capital, January 23, 1934. Morris Lewis, a private secretary for an Illinois Republican congressman, was hungry. Sharply dressed in a traditional three-piece suit befitting the times, pocket square and all, Morris began the long walk through the maze of hallways towards the House dining room. He had asked his son, who also worked on Capitol Hill as a clerk, to join him that day for lunch. Together, they walked toward the restaurant. The aroma of fresh soups and lunch dishes was as striking as the gleaming diamond checkered marble floor. Lewis knew the restaurant well—he had eaten there many times before. This day, however, would be unlike the others. For as Lewis opened the ornate doors and entered the room, the cashier bluntly told him that he was not welcome.

Lewis was Black. And while he frequently ate in the section of the House restaurant called the grill, which was open to the public (rather than in the basement space near the kitchen, where African Americans were normally relegated), the restaurant's policy had apparently changed. He asked to speak to the manager, as other patrons quietly watched the scene unfold. When the manager finally appeared, Lewis explained that he and his son "were American citizens" and they "refused to be insulted like that." The manager demurred. And he told Lewis that if he objected to the policy, he should take it up with Lindsay Warren, a Democratic congressman from North Carolina, who chaired the House Accounts Committee and had apparently given the order.

Lewis decided to raise it with his boss. He, too, was African American. A three-term Representative from Chicago, his election a few years earlier had made American history. The restaurant manager surely assumed that the matter would simply go away. Warren must have assumed the same.

But they were both wrong. For they didn't know Oscar Stanton De Priest.

When De Priest was sworn into the Congress on April 15, 1929, he became the first African American Congressman ever elected from the state of Illinois, and the only one, at that time, in the entire House of Representatives. None had been elected to the Congress in nearly thirty years—in fact, he was the first to be sworn in during the twentieth century. He would face angry and overt discrimination as soon as he arrived on Capitol Hill. But he soldiered on. And his lonely fights for all Americans to be treated equally in the seat of their government would become his lasting mark on history. His efforts would draw criticism from many quarters—including not only his opponents, but his own supporters as well—and would contribute, at least in part, to the end of his political career.

Long before his election to the Congress, among De Priest's earliest memories as a child was seeing a White man killed by a mob—the man, who was about to be lynched, briefly escaped, only to be shot down right in front of his home. The next day De Priest and the other children found the dark bloodstains on the concrete. When he was born, in the agricultural city of Florence in northwest Alabama, in March 1871, his parents had been free from slavery for just six years, living in a wooden cabin and scraping by. His mother, Mary, was a laundress and his father, Alexander, a small man in stature, hauled cargo in a cart from the river or rails and did a little farming as well.

In those years of Reconstruction, Alexander was intensely interested in politics and faced down threats to stick with the Republican Party. His friend, James Rapier, also from Florence, was one of the remarkable Black Congressmen of that era, serving alongside Joseph Rainey and Josiah Walls. Alexander De Priest saved his life. One day, after overhearing a group of men planning to kidnap Rapier, De Priest found him at his own home, where the family turned off the lights and Rapier and De Priest hid among some trees, while a mob of men walked through the town checking each house, including theirs.

Those terrifying events convinced the De Priest family to leave.

They moved to Kansas when Oscar was seven years old. And the next ten years of his life continued to teach him the toughness to survive. In the town where the family ultimately settled, De Priest and his five siblings were often picked on. Oscar fought back, and quickly gained a reputation as a fighter. He fought other boys when they made racist comments while in his presence, not realizing, apparently, because of his light skin, that Oscar was African American. "He was sandy haired, long legged, barefoot with rolled pantaloons, light complexion and blue eyes," recalled a contemporary. And an "opprobrious reference to his race was a sure signal for a fight—a real fist fight."

De Priest ran away at seventeen and landed in Chicago, one of America's biggest cities. He eventually went to work on his own as a contractor and decorator, and later, began a real estate business. He had arrived at the start of the Great Migration, as many African Americans sought more freedom and opportunities in northern cities. As neighborhoods expanded, De Priest gained control of buildings on their leading edge and re-leased apartments to the new arrivals for higher rents. Investing his profits in real estate and the stock market made him a rich man. But even pursuing his business required fearless persistence, as his apartments were repeatedly bombed to frighten away the new residents.

De Priest got involved in politics while he was still hauling his ladder on the streets of Chicago to and from remodeling jobs. One evening, a friend came by his home and asked De Priest to join him for a meeting at a building nearby. As he recalled many years later, "I had nothing to do, so I went." De Priest would discover soon after arriving that the gathering was a "precinct meeting" for the local Republican party to elect precinct captains.

As he sat in the back, with people shuffling around the room, plotting amongst each other in hushed voices, De Priest analyzed the scene before him.

He proved to be a quick learner.

"The vote was twenty–twenty for rival candidates," he explained, "and I saw right away that a deal could be made. So, I went to one of the candidates and said, 'Now you're a man who ought to be captain, I'll give you two additional votes if you'll make me secretary.'"

The man refused his entreaties.

And so, De Priest improvised. "I went to his rival and made the same proposition; he accepted. I was made secretary. I kept at it because it was recreation to me. I always like a good fight. The chance, the suspense, interests me."

Chicago politics in those days involved competing factions and machines. Political bosses built support from their neighborhoods by "taking care" of loyal voters as part of a team, helping people secure jobs and attending to their problems. That system of patronage and back-scratching included criminals at times, such as the infamous Al Capone, as well as church leaders and legitimate businessmen. De Priest entered the byzantine tangle of alliances and dealmaking with gusto and skill, and in 1904, won a surprise nomination and election to be a Cook County commissioner, ahead of other leaders with both more experience and greater oratorial skills. De Priest had impressed one mentor in particular with his organizational skill—Martin Madden, the president of the large Western Stone Company, who had previously been an alderman. Madden needed De Priest's support as a precinct leader for his nomination to Congress. De Priest managed the situation by moving the date of the district convention to before that of the state convention where Madden needed his votes, forcing Madden to support *him* before he would have to support Madden.

By most accounts, De Priest performed well in office. He was reelected, and in 1915, was elected Chicago's first Black alderman, a position more powerful in Illinois at that time than a seat in the legislature. He introduced a civil rights ordinance, which did not pass, but his main work in local government was to secure jobs and contracts for African Americans who had been excluded from the patronage system. Indeed, he was known for confronting and cursing out important officials who wouldn't give his supporters a fair chance. He became so popular that crowds were said to have followed him in the street.

Having achieved that success, however, De Priest remained an alderman only two years before his political career seemed to come to an abrupt end. In 1917, he was indicted by a state's attorney, a political foe, for conspiracy and bribery, charges that alleged he protected gangsters running gambling houses. The famous lawyer Clarence Darrow defended him in court, and De Priest was acquitted. Nonetheless, Republican party bosses forced him to drop out of his reelection campaign.

Afterward, he lost his party positions and connections. His political career appeared to be over.

De Priest, however, was nothing if not a fighter.

Faced with daunting odds, he organized. Unable to get back into the political system after his acquittal, De Priest went into South Side Chicago neighborhoods to create an organization one person at a time, realizing that, as a political actor without his own base of support, he had made himself dependent on others and vulnerable to their judgments. He called his group the People's Movement. Working with ministers, businessmen, clubs, and ordinary residents—anyone with sway on the community's voters—he persuaded them to stick with him as he navigated his way back to power. And stick with him they did, even as De Priest jumped from one faction to another and worked for candidates from either party. With the People's Movement behind him, he could walk into any smoke-filled room with a group of loyal voters at his back. They, in turn, knew he would fight for their interests.

The other key to his future success happened both unexpectedly and tragically. It was the third unbearably hot day in late July 1919, when conflict over an informally segregated swimming beach boiled over. A Black teen drifting in the water near a White area was hit with a rock and drowned. A police officer refused to arrest the man who had thrown the rock. An angry crowd gathered and fighting soon broke out. That spark blew up into a full-scale race riot that spread across the city, with spontaneous fighting and organized attacks that lasted a week. The violence ended only when troops arrived and a big rainstorm doused the city. By then, thirty-eight people had died, more than five hundred had been injured, and more than a thousand families had lost their homes—the great majority of whom were Black.

De Priest emerged as a hero to many in the African American community in Chicago for his efforts to stop the violence. With other leaders, he called for calm, but he also waded into the midst of the fighting to protect the vulnerable. He stood up to an angry crowd of dozens to protect a middle-aged White woman who had shot an African American man. And after it became too dangerous for African Americans to go outside, he armed himself with pistols and drove twice daily to bring food to his neighborhood so families could eat. A soldier just returned from World War I recounted watching De Priest "put on a

policeman's cap and uniform and drive a patrol wagon into the stockyard to bring out the Negroes who were trapped inside during the
riot . . . again and again, he went into the stockyard, bringing Negroes
out with him in the patrol wagon until finally he had rescued all of
them" from the mob.

His actions had made him famous. And his political fortunes immediately improved.

De Priest soon became a delegate to the Republican National Convention, a ward chair, and a key part of the machine supporting Chicago's mayor, "Big Bill" Thompson. When his old ally, Representative
Martin Madden, suddenly died, shortly after winning the 1928 primary
for reelection, De Priest was away on vacation. But he acted quickly,
hoping his party position could give him the nomination as a replacement candidate. He immediately sent telegrams requesting support to
Thompson and to members of the district committee that had the legal
power to pick a new nominee—a committee made up of the five ward
chairs, of which he was one. Besides De Priest, members of the committee included gambling associates of Al Capone and a bootlegger who
would be assassinated in a mob-related murder two years later. All were
part of Thompson's organization and would likely do as he dictated.
The newspapers headlined speculation about whom Thompson would
pick, with excitement rising, from far beyond Chicago, that he would
choose an African American for the majority Black district.

De Priest sped back to the city to meet the mayor in person.

Thompson was popular and well-known in the Black community.
Moreover, he had relied on African American votes. And De Priest had
helped deliver them.

When De Priest arrived back in Chicago, he went straight to City
Hall. As he walked into the mayor's stately office, Thompson, tower-
ing as De Priest lumbered toward him, said simply, "You know, Oscar,
I'm for you." The loud and gregarious Thompson later said to a polit-
ical rally, "There came some Judas from Washington and said to me,
'We don't want a Negro Congressman. You're the man that can keep
a Negro out of Congress.' I said, 'If I'm the one man who can keep a
Negro out of Congress, then, by God, there'll be one there.'"

De Priest now had the Republican nomination. But a series of barriers remained before he could make history. A lawsuit from another

candidate challenged his nomination. And then, once again, he was indicted, this time by an attorney general from a rival political faction,
with nebulous allegations harkening back to his trial a decade earlier.
De Priest said he was told the charges would be dropped if he quit his
campaign. Another Black candidate jumped in the race, as an independent, saying he was against "leadership of the gangster, gambler, grafter
type." Meanwhile, fliers appeared at voters' homes urging White Republicans to cross over and support the Democratic candidate.

Day after day, De Priest kept campaigning.

On election night, when the polls finally closed, it was clear his past
organizing and popularity had paid off. He had just barely won a plu-
rality of votes. But any euphoria from his victory was short-lived. Concerns immediately arose that Congress would not seat him as a member
while he was under indictment. The criminal case had not yet advanced,
and De Priest's lawyers repeatedly demanded the state proceed to trial.
With less than a week left before De Priest was due to take the oath of
office in Washington, the prosecutor admitted he didn't have evidence
to go forward. Once again, De Priest demanded a trial. And at a Sat-
urday court hearing—less than two days before the Monday swearing
in—the judge dismissed the case.

Of course, another threat remained. Under the rules of the House,
any sitting member could object to the swearing in of a new member. And many southern Democrats were known to oppose De Priest's
pending membership in the House. During the swearing-in ceremony,
as states were called in alphabetical order, some of them would gain the
ability to act as members of the House before the Illinois delegation,
giving them a chance to potentially prevent him from taking his oath
of office.

Communicating with allies through a back channel, De Priest got
to work. Over the weekend, the widow of a late Illinois senator had
contacted her friend, Alice Roosevelt Longworth, former President
Teddy Roosevelt's daughter and the wife of then–Speaker of the House
Nicholas Longworth. And when Monday dawned, Speaker Longworth
had a plan.

As the House prepared to gavel into session, the bald and mus-
tached Longworth, cane in hand, marched up the stairs to the marble
rostrum and Speaker's chair. The House floor and gallery stood still, as

representatives-elect and visitors awaited his remarks. Without prior warning, he declared to all, "The Chair has decided to practice an innovation in the manner of administering the oath of office to Members." He continued, "The Chair has observed that under our general practice, where groups are sworn in separately, the remainder of the House is apt to be in pretty complete disorder . . . [which] does not . . . contribute to the dignity of this most important ceremony."

Then came the *coup de grâce*.

"The Chair thinks that it will more comport with the dignity and solemnity of this ceremony," Speaker Longworth explained, "if he administers the oath to all Members of the body at once." And with that, every member-elect raised his or her right hand and became a Member of Congress simultaneously, including De Priest.

No members had time to object.

Longworth, who died just a few years later, couldn't have anticipated the durability of his decision. But the House has been sworn in that same way ever since.

Because Longworth's gambit had worked, De Priest had officially broken a racial barrier that had stood for three decades. A knot of colleagues gathered around him with congratulations. "Now that I am elected, I will represent all people, both Black and White. I will not be a 'Black' congressman," De Priest declared. But an ominous silence had fallen over the section of the House occupied by southern Democrats. The battle was far from over.

In the first weeks of his service, De Priest faced insulting displays of discrimination from several of his colleagues. Some refused to eat in his presence in the House dining room, instead going to the Senate dining room. When he brought a group of guests to dine that included both races, he was reprimanded for a "very embarrassing" breach of etiquette. A Mississippi member with greater seniority complained on the floor of the House that De Priest had been offered an office that he wanted, saying, "I am entitled to this office over this Negro, and I am going to have it." When De Priest selected another office, his next-door neighbor, from North Carolina, telegraphed his staff to move out immediately, turn in the key, and remove his name from the door.

Further, while African Americans nationally had celebrated De Priest's victory, most people still were uncertain as to what kind of congressman he would be. Some critics in the African American community saw him as a self-serving product of corrupt ward politics and pointed out that he sometimes had supported White politicians over Black challengers, as he did when he had backed his sponsor and predecessor, Madden. Others saw his victory as a purely symbolic one and assumed he would stay quietly in the background, with one writer describing him as "a lonely figure" isolated in the back row at President Herbert Hoover's inauguration in March 1929.

What none of De Priest's critics could dispute, however, was that he was a patriot. Indeed, among his first acts was to order ten thousand copies of the Declaration of Independence and the Constitution to give to his constituents. He also was an ardent anticommunist, warning of "its spread in the urban areas experiencing the acute effects of the Great Depression."

Supporters and critics alike understood him to be an activist as well. De Priest introduced antilynching bills and legislation to enforce the Fourteenth Amendment by transferring criminal cases to federal courts when a defendant could not receive a fair trial in a state or local court. He successfully amended legislation creating the Civilian Conservation Corps to prohibit discrimination. And later, he refused to vote to appropriate money to enforce the Eighteenth Amendment, which outlawed the sale of alcohol, until the Congress also spent money to guarantee equal protection under the law.

And then, there was the tea party incident.

In June 1929, the First Lady of the United States, Lou Henry Hoover, invited De Priest's wife, Jessie, to a traditional gathering for afternoon tea at the White House with congressional spouses. The invitation ignited a national firestorm. Many southern newspapers and politicians objected to Jessie's attendance at the tea and made their outrage known. When the press looked to De Priest for a response, he chose to amplify the controversy rather than backing down. He announced a "Black and Tan Musicale" to raise $200,000 for the National Association for the Advancement of Colored People (NAACP), to which he invited every congressional Republican (except two who had discriminated against him) and used the attendant publicity to call for equality for African Americans.

The reaction to his actions caused a political storm—which he surely anticipated. Legislatures in Texas, Mississippi, and Florida passed resolutions denouncing and personally censuring First Lady Hoover, while northern newspapers, clubs, and politicians came to her defense with editorials, letters, and resolutions of their own.

Two weeks after the musicale, De Priest spoke to an NAACP gathering of two thousand people in Cleveland, Ohio, with another thousand people outside who couldn't get into the hall. They cheered wildly as he ridiculed as cowards those who had attacked his wife and the First Lady over a cup of tea. Shouting over the applause, he declared, "This is my country and your country. I've been elected to Congress the same as any other congressman, and I'm going to have the rights of every other congressman—no more and no less—if it's in the congressional barber shop or at a White House tea." As the audience roared, he continued, "I want to thank the Democrats of the South for one thing—they were so barbaric they drove my parents to the North. If it hadn't been for that, I wouldn't be in Congress today. I've been Jim Crowed, segregated, persecuted, and I think I know how best the Negro can put a stop to being imposed upon. It is through the ballot, through organization, through fighting eternally for his rights."

De Priest kept the uproar alive through the summer as he continued forcefully speaking about it and generating headlines. He had exposed the ugliness of discrimination and demonstrated the power of his fearless refusal to go along. An Arkansas representative who saw him as a threat told a hometown newspaper that the First Lady's real sin had been to give De Priest a platform, "[p]ushing himself forward at every opportunity," and he added, "Southern Democrats do not like his presence in the House of Representatives and the privileges he has taken."

De Priest would continue to push against segregation on Capitol Hill as a potent and visible symbol of discrimination African Americans faced every day—even as that fight would eventually lead to his political demise. His activism filled his congressional office with mail from all over the country, including constant invitations to speak. He traveled widely, addressing large audiences and handing out his copies of the Declaration of Independence and the Constitution. He had never been known as an orator and was sometimes criticized for poor grammar and indistinct pronunciation. But De Priest spoke loudly, in simple, direct language that anyone could understand. And his audiences loved it.

He identified with them, frequently saying, "I come from the common herd." Citizens filled halls to overflowing to hear him, with cheers, enthusiastic applause, and standing ovations. When he spoke in Harlem, thousands were unable to get into the historic Bethel AME Church. Inside, men whistled and women waved their handkerchiefs. De Priest urged them, "Learn to stand on your own feet, if you want race leadership." In Providence, Rhode Island, he similarly told his audience, "The only way you will ever do anything or get anywhere is by organizing and standing together." According to one admirer who saw De Priest speak, "He doesn't need to say anything. All he needs to do is stand in front so the people can see him. He looks like a fighter."

De Priest also spoke in the Deep South, urging Black residents to demand their rights. Where they had voting rights, he told them to work from within the dominant Democratic Party rather than with his own Republicans, because that would give them a greater chance of building power. These appearances called for constant, physical courage. The Ku Klux Klan burned him in effigy before a speech in Birmingham, Alabama. He was warned to stay away from a Florida appearance because his life would be in danger. He went anyway. In Memphis, Tennessee, he received a letter signed by the Klan threatening him and demanding he leave town. De Priest turned the letter over to the FBI. The agency's files show that its director, J. Edgar Hoover, dismissed it (although he monitored De Priest's own activities long after he left office). In following elections, southern Democrats would hold up De Priest as a bogeyman to stir up fear that could turn out voters.

De Priest didn't back down. "[He] is courageous, independent and resourceful, and therefore easily the outstanding man of the race," wrote the *Washington Tribune,* a Black newspaper. "To the race, Congressman De Priest has become the national idol, inspiring, and to some extent uniting the race. He is in the position to render a great service . . . [and has] given the Negro new hope, new courage, new inspiration."

De Priest waged many political battles. But perhaps none more controversial than his fateful decision to challenge segregation on Capitol Hill itself.

He had worked with his secretary, Morris Lewis, his trusted friend and advisor, for nearly forty years. And when he received word from Lewis on a Tuesday afternoon in January of 1934 that he had been denied entry to the House restaurant, he was livid. Before Representative Warren—whom the manager had told Lewis to contact—could even be reached, De Priest decided to make the issue into a cause. Seated angrily in his office in the House Office building, he called in the Capitol press corps, who could tell he was furious. "I am going to see to it that Negroes are going to eat in the grill," he declared to the reporters, "or we can close it."

That same evening, Warren, a North Carolina Democrat, released a written statement saying the grill "[h]as never served colored employees or visitors, nor will it, so long as I have anything to do with the restaurant." Later, he admitted more truthfully that he hadn't known Lewis and other Black staff and visitors were using the grill, and once he learned of it, ordered it stopped to avoid a precedent that would allow all African Americans to eat there.

The next afternoon, the national press was gathered in the House gallery, ready for verbal fireworks that would surely ensue. They would be disappointed, however.

Hoping to head off an immediate floor fight, the Speaker of the House, Henry Rainey, an Illinois Democrat, had called De Priest into his office. Rainey told De Priest that he could introduce a resolution on the issue without objection—if he would simply hold back from making a fiery speech. De Priest agreed. He would strategically bide his time, for now, but the resolution he submitted made it clear he would not shrink from using the national stage to advance this symbolic fight. The resolution recounted the contributions of African Americans, praising their bravery in war and loyalty to the nation and their intended protection from discrimination by the Fourteenth and Fifteenth Amendments to the Constitution. And it charged that Warren lacked authority to refuse service to those loyal Americans, demanding an investigation by a five-member committee to be appointed by the Speaker.

The battle was joined, with extensive national newspaper coverage, reminiscent of the tea party incident years before, but this time with De Priest using the power of his seat in the Congress to directly attack Jim Crow segregation. Commentators saw the fight as a proxy for resistance to the indignity of segregation that African Americans faced every day, with separate bathrooms and water fountains, and exclusion from lunch counters, hotels, beaches, housing, transportation, and many other public accommodations. Civil rights leader Channing Tobias made clear that the stakes were high. "If the national Congress will not protect the secretary of a congressman in eating his lunch in the Capitol building, then we have little hope as a racial group of securing just treatment by private business concerns," he declared. The *Baltimore Afro-American* predicted the resolution could have wider impact, "as the Waterloo in the battle against Jim Crow." Others were more cautious, however, asking why De Priest hadn't made his stand earlier and in a situation with greater chances of success.

Democrats held a three-quarter majority in the House at the time, and a Democrat from Alabama chaired the Rules Committee, where he had the power to hold back De Priest's resolution to keep it from reaching the floor. And that is exactly what he did.

After waiting nearly a month, De Priest had had enough. He decided to file a "discharge petition."

It was a bold and significant step.

The petition was neither long nor complex. On little more than a single piece of paper, it declared, with De Priest's signature, his attempt to discharge the Rules Committee from consideration of his "Resolution to prevent discrimination." But the simplicity and brevity of the petition certainly belied the potential impact of this single piece of paper. For if the petition—an obscure legislative tool—was successful, it would enable his stymied resolution to bypass the committee entirely and be voted on directly on the House floor.

The odds of success for his discharge petition were extremely low. Under House rules at the time, a petition to overrule a committee chair and bring a matter to the floor required hand signatures from a third of all members. Put another way, he would need to gather the signatures of one hundred forty-five of his colleagues from across the country. Making matters even more difficult, he'd have to do so despite his own political party having only one hundred seventeen members in the House. That appeared next to impossible.

De Priest, once again, got to work.

One can imagine De Priest buttonholing his colleagues, one by one—some in the hallways, others at committee hearings, and perhaps more on the House floor—wherever he could, as he worked to gather the requisite number of signatures. Some signed their names in blue ink.

Others signed in black. Some signed eagerly. Others did so reluctantly. And many refused to sign the petition at all.

Fortunately, he also had help. For opponents of segregation, the drive to gain signatures on the petition invigorated the cause. African American newspapers urged their readers to contact their congressmen and ask them to sign the petition. To add pressure, African Americans began requesting service in segregated restaurants in the Capitol, using direct action that anticipated the sit-ins of the Civil Rights movement a generation later. A sociologist was forcibly removed from a restaurant in the Senate office building. A professor from Howard University entered the House grill with a founder of the NAACP. They were served, but with evident hostility. Another professor who came in a mixed-race party was asked if he was a foreigner—as dignitaries from African countries were sometimes permitted to use the grill—and when he said he was American, was asked to leave. Next a group of Howard students came to the restaurant but were refused. A scuffle ensued and District of Columbia police arrested one of the students and threatened the others with arrest. Southern Democrats attacked the students as "hoodlums" and "communists," and the university considered expelling them, but Howard professors took up their cause. Each of these events generated more headlines.

And the number of signatures on De Priest's petition kept growing.

By the spring, news coverage had climaxed. On the morning of March 21, De Priest made his way to the House chambers, as he had been given the opportunity to address his colleagues on the issue. The speaking time would be short. He had been allocated a mere ten minutes to speak during a debate on a legislative appropriations bill. And his petition had only ninety-three signatures so far.

De Priest hoped against hope that he could persuade his colleagues to give him the fifty-two more that he needed. The stakes could not be higher.

Standing roughly six feet tall, De Priest looked even taller due to the styling of his sandy hair, which appeared ivory white. Sporting a fashionable bowtie, with his speech in hand, he cut an imposing figure as he made his way to the floor. The speech would be his greatest in the Congress. It included few soaring phrases or much elaborate rhetoric. But the strength, clarity, and sense of humor he projected to the House held the audience spellbound.

He began by explaining the genesis of the restaurant conflict and his procedural arguments. He wisely focused on Warren as his only opponent, and posed his request as limited to an investigation of the situation. "I am going to ask every justice-loving member in this House," De Priest declared to his colleagues, "to sign that petition, as that seems to be the only way it can be threshed out on the floor of the House." But soon he moved on from technical procedures to the heart of the matter.

Much more was at stake than the rules of the House alone.

"The restaurant of the Capitol is run for the benefit of the American people, and every American, whether he be Black or White, Jew or Gentile, Protestant or Catholic, under our constitutional form of Government, is entitled to equal opportunities," De Priest boldly professed, as he gestured his arms toward his colleagues on both sides of the aisle. "If we allow segregation and the denial of constitutional rights under the dome of the Capitol," De Priest exclaimed, "where in God's name will we get them?"

He continued, "I appreciate the conditions that pertain in the territory where [Warren] comes from, and nobody knows that better than I do. But North Carolina is not the United States of America. It is but a part of it, a one-forty-eighth part. Then I expect, too, as long as I am a member of this House, to contend for every right and every privilege every other American citizen enjoys; and if I did not, I would not be worthy of the trust reposed in me by my constituents who have sent me here."

De Priest's colleagues erupted in sustained, loud applause. A Texas Democrat, Thomas Blanton, rose from his chair and began to speak out as he tried to interrupt De Priest. He failed. And De Priest went on.

"I say to the members of this House . . . that this is the most dangerous precedent that could be established in American Government. If we allow this challenge to go without correcting it, it will set an example where people will say Congress itself approves of segregation; Congress itself approves of denying a tenth of our population equal rights and opportunity; why should not the rest of the American people do likewise?" He then brought up the courage of Black soldiers in defending America and their loyalty to the United States, adding, "I say further, ladies and gentlemen of the Congress, that America never will be what it was intended to be until every citizen in America has his just rights under the Constitution."

Applause again interrupted the speech. Some members stood, clapping vigorously as De Priest held the chambers captive. Again, Blanton interjected, this time with De Priest's acquiescence.

"Our colleague from Illinois does go in that restaurant whenever he wishes," Blanton wryly observed in his deep, Texas accent, "and he takes his colored friends with him whenever he wishes to do so."

Representatives and visitors alike surely pondered how De Priest would respond.

"I am not asking for privileges for Oscar De Priest or proper treatment for him down there, because I will take care of that," he declared. "But I am asking for those people who have no voice in this Congress, just like you, Mr. Blanton, would do if some of your constituents came here from Texas and were refused to be served in that restaurant." Then came the decisive blow. "You [Blanton] would raise more hell than anybody I know of about it!"

The House roared with boisterous laughter and applause.

"I have been here long enough to know just what you would do, and I would vote with you on raising that hell. I would say that you were right, and that your constituents had a right to have the same treatment that I want for mine."

At that, De Priest's time to speak had expired. But De Priest was not finished making his case to the House. Nor was the House finished hearing from him. The power of his remarks had earned him double his time.

The Republican floor leader gave him ten more minutes.

De Priest went on, explaining the circumstances of his assistant being refused service, and then discussing the other African Americans who tried to eat in the grill. "One man was asked if he was a foreigner. If he had said 'yes,' he would have been served. Has the time come when American citizens cannot be served, and aliens can? . . . At least we are entitled to the same treatment as every other American citizen, and we will be satisfied with nothing less than that."

Like Blanton, another Democratic member asked De Priest to yield the floor. It was Joseph Gavagan, from New York. De Priest acceded, not knowing what the Democratic representative had in store. This time, however, it was to inform De Priest that Gavagan was collecting signatures *for him* while he spoke. The shock of such an announcement struck the chambers like a lightning bolt. Thundering applause shook the House once more.

De Priest's time ended for a second time. Again, the leader extended it.

"I hope when I leave this Congress I shall leave with the respect of the Members; but if securing their respect means sacrificing my race, that respect I do not seek any longer," De Priest declared, continuing over the applause, "I am sorry I have to devote my time trying to watch the needs of the American Negro. I wish I could devote my time, like you gentlemen devote your time, trying to watch the interests of all the American people instead of just twelve million of them."

De Priest's time expired a final time. He was finished.

When he had started speaking, only ninety-three of his colleagues had signed his petition. As he walked back to his seat and sat down, the petition had one hundred thirty-five.

The speech had worked.

And he was now short only ten more signatures.

Two days later, Warren gave his rebuttal. Before he began, an Alabama member, the Rules Committee Chair, asked for a call of the House, forcing members to be present (although De Priest himself did not appear). When everyone was in their seats, Warren began. First, he underlined his own legal authority to run the restaurant. He spoke about the profits the restaurant made and complained that ten days of protests had cut into its receipts. He called the protestors "toughs" and "hoodlums," blaming De Priest for their demonstrations. And he offered little in defense of segregating the restaurant, claiming it had been segregated for a long time and he was simply "carrying out the policies and rules that have been in force ever since this restaurant was established, and before I came here."

Warren's less than persuasive speech did him no good. When he was done, ten more members signed De Priest's petition. It had received the one hundred forty-five signatures needed for the resolution to come to the floor despite the opposition of the powerful Rules Committee chair.

De Priest had won.

The unusual and dramatic battle in getting the resolution out of committee was over. And when the resolution made its way to the floor, it passed by a sizable margin.

But the resolution's call for an investigation by a five-member committee would, ultimately, prove insufficient to end segregation in the Capitol. Speaker Rainey, who favored the existing restaurant arrangement, picked three Democrats for the committee. De Priest picked two Republicans. After holding hearings, the committee split on party lines, with the Democratic majority siding with Warren, without ever addressing the basic issue of segregation. The two White Republicans De Priest had chosen issued a blistering minority report citing the Fourteenth Amendment, which they said required everyone to be treated equally in the government restaurant. But the issue went no further.

In the end, nothing had changed.

Some Black leaders perceived the whole episode as a step backward, damaging their cause by creating expectations but yielding only disappointment. They blamed De Priest. In the reelection he faced soon thereafter, the restaurant controversy became a liability, as his opponent accused him of focusing on what he contended were the wrong problems. At a time of extreme economic hardship, De Priest, who had strong fiscally conservative views, had voted against New Deal relief. And campaigning in his district back on the South Side of Chicago, De Priest for the first time faced an African American Democrat, Arthur Mitchell, as his opponent. Mitchell strongly supported the New Deal and declared to voters that he did not "plan to spend my time fighting out the question of whether a Negro may eat his lunch at the Capitol or whether he may be shaved at the House barber shop. What I am interested in is helping this president of ours feed the hungry and clothe the naked and provide work for the idle of every race and creed."

In November 1934, Mitchell won the election in an upset that shocked Chicago. The battle over the House restaurant had, it seemed, proven to be De Priest's Waterloo.

Historians aren't precisely sure when the House dining room was finally desegregated. It may not have been formally opened to all until a Supreme Court decision in 1952 struck down any discrimination in public accommodations within the District of Columbia. But in any event, it was long after De Priest's career had ended.

Still, any fair appraisal of De Priest's tenure must look deeper than that one restaurant on Capitol Hill. His assertive spirit and political skill broke a major barrier to African Americans' serving in Congress. His powerful voice and his outspoken, unapologetic demands for equality inspired many. And in his fight to desegregate the grill, he had faced down the Congress itself.

He had fought the good fight—not for himself, but for his countrymen, and his country.

After leaving Congress, De Priest stayed active in the Republican Party. He returned to the real estate business and served on the Chicago City Council, working for equal opportunity in employment. He lived a long life, dying in 1951 at age eighty. And he continued handing out copies of the Constitution and Declaration of Independence until his final days. In fact, the family that eventually moved into Oscar and Jessie De Priest's home after they departed Washington found literally hundreds of copies of both sacred documents left in the house.

A patriot to the end.

6

Margaret Chase Smith

★ ★ ★ ★ ★ ★ ★ ★ ★

Margaret Chase Smith
2nd District Maine
1943

Elected June 1940 Skowhegan

I lost all the battles except the last one.

— MARGARET CHASE SMITH

In the spring of 1950, fear of Senator Joseph McCarthy of Wisconsin cast a pall over much of the Capitol. Some senators refused dinner invitations because McCarthy could name almost anyone a communist or fellow traveler. And after that happened, merely having eaten a meal at the same table with one of the accused could be enough for guilt by association. McCarthy would often stand on the Senate floor—where he was immune from legal accountability—and hold up sheets of paper he claimed contained evidence of subversion by important government officials. The reputations and careers of many would be destroyed by little more than his finger-pointing and shoddy props.

Republican Senator Margaret Chase Smith of Maine, like many others, at first took McCarthy's showy revelations at face value. But, in her characteristically practical way, she was determined to ascertain for herself the veracity of his allegations. One day on the Senate floor, she stepped toward McCarthy's desk, two rows behind her own, and asked to read the documents he had held up in his hand during his speeches. What she learned was beyond startling.

She could see no proof of his charges.

As McCarthy continued to annihilate his opponents with his unsubstantiated allegations over the coming months, remaining silent became all the more untenable to Smith. And so, she secretly began preparing a speech of her own. It would become known as one of the greatest speeches ever delivered in the history of the United States Senate.

Few would have expected Smith to be the only senator brave enough to directly challenge McCarthy. She had been in the Senate for only a year, remaining mostly quiet as a junior member. And during her four terms in the House of Representatives, she had rarely spoken on the floor.

Those who underestimated Smith, however, would be proven wrong.

Years earlier, during her service in the People's House, Smith had gained a national reputation for her work with the Navy during World War II. And it was there where she took on perhaps the most difficult fight of her career—leading the charge, against the opposition of powerful leaders and her own mentor, to include women as regular members of the military. Her effort would be opposed and criticized by many. But as a rural, small-town representative, with a common-sense style of communicating and a practical knack for building political partnerships, she would ultimately prevail. She was never one to avoid waging a battle for what she believed was the right cause. Now, she would do so again.

Working long hours with her lifelong aide, William Lewis Jr., Smith crafted a document denouncing McCarthy's tactics. She called it simply "A Declaration of Conscience." And she quietly approached other Republican senators who could be trusted to keep her secret, asking them to be cosigners. Six agreed to do so. As Smith would later note, all but one would eventually abandon her in the backlash after she delivered the speech.

On the first day of June, with her speech in hand, and her aide Lewis pre-positioned with copies of the declaration to distribute to the press corps after she began talking, Smith boarded the underground train connecting senate offices with the Capitol.

It was time.

Of all the senators heading to the Capitol that day, McCarthy himself boarded the train at the same time. And as fate would have it, he sat down next to her.

The train slowly departed towards the Senate chambers.

McCarthy, glancing over at Smith, quizzically asked her why she looked so serious. Smith answered honestly. She was about to give a speech, she explained—a speech that *he* would not like.

"Is it about me?" he asked, with a smile.

She replied, "Yes, but I'm not going to mention your name."

In response, McCarthy threatened Smith. He suggested he could keep her from getting support to be nominated as vice president of the United States, which some had speculated could one day soon be in the cards for Smith.

The threat, however, fell flat. A few minutes later, Smith walked into the stately Senate chambers to deliver her remarks.

Her language was simple. It was direct. And it was powerful.

"The United States Senate has long enjoyed worldwide respect as the greatest deliberative body in the world," Smith declared, as the tension of the moment held senators on both sides of the aisle silent and spellbound. "But recently that deliberative character has too often been debased to the level of a forum of hate and character assassination sheltered by the shield of congressional immunity . . . I do not like the way the Senate has been made a rendezvous for vilification, for selfish political gain at the sacrifice of individual reputations and national unity."

As Smith called for the body to remember American principles of free speech and fairness, she did not mince words. It was time, she stated plainly, for her party to disavow "[t]he four horsemen of calumny—fear, ignorance, bigotry, and smear." The eyes of the reporters were transfixed on McCarthy, sitting a mere three feet away, as he turned pale and grim. He rapidly left the chamber as Smith finished her speech.

As senators gathered around to congratulate her, it was clear Smith's speech would become among the most famous of the century in the Senate. The next day, her words led newspapers nationally. The moment became the most noted legacy of Smith's historic, thirty-two-year congressional career, in which she also was the first woman elected by Maine to the House and to the Senate, the first to serve in both chambers, and the first to have her name put in nomination for president by a major political party. But on that summer day in 1950, Smith's political future remained far from clear. McCarthy's reign of fear would last four more years, during which he destroyed other colleagues who tried to challenge him. He also tried to destroy Smith, with political intrigue, character assassination, and a campaign to defeat her for reelection. To this day, some contend that one factor in his final political demise was her ability to survive it all, demonstrating to other senators that McCarthy was not invincible, before they gathered their own courage to censure him in 1954.

Smith's courage, at least, had already been demonstrated. Three years before her Declaration of Conscience, in October 1947, she had been returning from Europe as the leader of a House subcommittee, after a five-week inspection of the postwar American occupation zone.

Flying high over the Atlantic Ocean, their four-engine aircraft lost power in one engine and another engine began sputtering. The plane was 800 miles and four hours away from the nearest land, Portugal's Azores archipelago. The passengers and crew put on inflatable life jackets and prepared to ditch in the water, panic rising in the faces of the two dozen aboard the big troop transport plane. A military aide later recalled, however, that Representative Margaret Chase Smith, the only woman on board, remained cooler than anyone else. She pulled out a box of harmonicas she had purchased in Switzerland to give away to children and handed them out to her colleagues on the plane for an impromptu songfest. The plane landed safely.

Smith was a courageous person and a historic legislator. And it was arguably during Smith's service in the House, which has been far less publicized than her time in the Senate, that she made her most historic impact.

But it is, perhaps, best to start at the beginning.

Margaret Chase was born December 14, 1897, in the small town of Skowhegan, Maine, the eldest daughter of a barber and a traditional homemaker. After high school she worked at various jobs of increasing responsibility and became involved in local politics, before meeting Clyde Smith, a successful and rising state politician who courted her by taking her along on campaign trips to meet voters in Maine's rural communities. They married in 1930 and continued as full partners in politics. For voters, her face became as familiar as his, and, when he was elected to Congress in 1936, she took a role in his office that gave her all the duties of a member except for voting and attending committee meetings, as she later recalled.

In 1940, when Clyde had a series of heart attacks, the political flame of their relationship kept burning, despite his collapsing health. On the day he died, he gave Margaret advice on how to win his seat and, once elected, how to handle other politicians. He dictated a press release from his bed, asking voters to select her as his replacement. The next day it ran alongside his obituary in the *Portland Press Herald.*

Smith easily won the special election to fill out her husband's mostly completed term, but faced much more competition for the next full term, with a primary election scheduled in June 1940, only a week after she was first sworn in. The political landscape was complex. Clyde had not focused on foreign affairs during his service in Congress, but now, World War II had begun, and Hitler's tanks were rolling into France. At the time, many in the Republican Party generally supported keeping America isolated from the conflict and opposed President Franklin Roosevelt's war preparations, including his Lend-Lease program to provide weapons to the allies, a US military buildup, and activation of the draft. Chase, however, had long supported improving the United States Naval Forces, a popular issue in Maine with its coastline and shipyards, and she supported Lend-Lease and the draft as well—positions that made her an outsider in her party.

Her primary opponents derisively declared that voters should not elect a woman to Congress while war ravaged Europe. Smith, however, had built popularity over her years of campaigning with Clyde. Her pro-defense position was also popular in Maine for economic reasons. And, she had the support of an army of women volunteers all over the state, some calling themselves the "Mrs. Smith Goes to Washington Club," after a recent Jimmy Stewart movie.

She won the primary with an overwhelming majority. And when her general election opponent made the same mistake as her primary opponents, attacking her for being female, she trounced him, too. Over time, Smith would become a Maine political institution—a practical, independent representative whom Mainers could relate to, with easy reelections. She would describe her own life as "simple but useful."

On December 7, 1941, when Japan attacked Pearl Harbor, Smith's support of Roosevelt was vindicated, as the entire Congress and the country rallied around the president in the declaration of war and total mobilization. And in the very next session of Congress, she won a coveted and important seat on the Naval Affairs Committee. The key moment came when she interviewed with the committee's autocratic chair, Georgia Democrat Carl Vinson, who called himself "the Admiral" and referred to freshmen members on his committee as "ensigns." She impressed him with her prescience about the need to augment the Navy and her respectful demeanor. While Vinson expected the so-called ensigns on his committee to speak as little as possible, Smith would continue to make a lasting impression on him and others through her careful preparation, perceptive questioning, and polite refusal to be put off by military brass and corporate heads who didn't want to answer.

In time, Vinson came to regard himself as her mentor. And when she recommended creation of a subcommittee to investigate the negative impacts of the wartime economic boom in coastal communities, Vinson quickly agreed and appointed her to be a member, making her the first woman to be sent on an inspection trip.

The unprecedented surge of war production and ships preparing for sea filled port towns with sailors and defense workers and overwhelmed restaurants, shops, and hotels, with lines constantly in front of businesses. Shortages of housing forced "hot-bunk" sharing of beds, with shift workers rotating through the sheets of a single cot, which rented on San Francisco's waterfront for $1 a night. Many workers slept in cars or outdoors. Restaurants commonly ran out of food. An epidemic of sexually transmitted diseases ripped through the fleets, generating fevered interest in the press. In several cities, some unaccompanied women walking the streets were detained for invasive and humiliating testing, followed by months of forced isolation if they were found to be infected. Norfolk, Virginia, and other communities around the harbor of Hampton Roads—where scores of large warships were rapidly built—became a focus of moral concern after several magazine exposés described the outrageous red-light districts, as well as the flood of people overwhelming all public services, even the sewer systems.

Smith's committee flew into the maelstrom—and a rare Virginia snowstorm—on Monday, March 22, 1943, for a week of tours and hearings, determined to study and solve the problems. Each evening, after work, the seven subcommittee members dined together. But after dinner, the men would excuse themselves for other entertainment, leaving Smith—who didn't drink alcohol, smoke, or play cards—behind as they disappeared into the night. Instead, she went for walks with a lieutenant the navy had assigned to the subcommittee staff. Bill Lewis was practical, political, and intensely dedicated, like her. During the subcommittee's meetings, he sat next to Smith at the end of the table— the spot she was assigned as the member with the least seniority—and passed her notes with questions she could potentially ask. Lewis became her lifelong aide, personal companion, and housemate, although they never married.

In Norfolk, Smith asked Lewis to set up clandestine outings so she could see for herself the city's infamous nightclubs, wearing a disguise so she would not be recognized. On Friday of that week, he arranged for her to visit the jail, so she could meet women languishing for weeks after being picked up by the vice squad. A cell for twenty-five contained ninety-one women, with few beds, no sheets, and nowhere even to sit. Many of the women had been wrongly swept up in indiscriminate raids for merely being out in the street by themselves, including one who had been trying to find her husband, who was a sailor, when she was improperly arrested. "They were just children, comparatively. One was only fourteen years old," Smith told a reporter. "Most of them seemed to be farm girls from poor homes, and every one of them certainly deserved a better chance."

Smith worked to alleviate the hardships she had seen. She also defended workers in weapons factories, opposing a bill advanced by her committee colleague, friend, and future president, Texan Lyndon B. Johnson, which would have taken away draft deferments for plant workers who were absent too frequently. And she made the perceptive point that in congested port cities with shortages of food and transportation, rampant food-borne illness, and medical care lacking, workers deserved more support, not punishment for missing work.

She provided critical strong support for the Lanham Act, which was intended to fund day care facilities for sixty-five thousand children of working parents—a step toward helping, but far less than was needed when the War Manpower Commission was calling, at the time, for another six hundred thousand women to join in wartime production. Joined by five other female members of the House, Smith spoke to the Appropriations Committee, which seemed supportive. But several of her colleagues—including some in her own party—denounced any federal spending for child care. The debate soon degenerated into odious and discriminatory statements. Clare Hoffman, a male Republican from Michigan, charged the money wouldn't be needed "if some of these women, instead of going into beer parlors, would go home and take care of their children." John Taber, a New York Republican, made a motion on the floor of the House to cut the funding in half. Smith stood up in opposition to that amendment, the first time she had spoken on the floor in her four years in Congress, to tell her colleagues about the suffering she had seen while traveling with her subcommittee.

"Women are coming into industry in increasing numbers. They are trying to do their part in the shipyards and the aircraft plants. But in addition to this, women are obliged to maintain their homes and keep their children and their husbands fed and clothed," she said.

She explained that her subcommittee had personally seen women, done with work for the day, waiting hours to buy food or see a doctor.

"We found children roaming the streets and some even locked in automobiles, not only because their war-working parents were absent from home but also because of the lack of child-care facilities and schools. This is an emergency. We have waited altogether too long to meet it. We should anticipate these things and be ready for them. We cannot expect these women to come into industry and take the place of men unless we help them."

Within half an hour, the amendment to cut the funding failed by only five votes. The full appropriation was approved.

After the impact and publicity of the subcommittee's work, Vinson sent Smith on the first congressional inspection tour of the war in the Pacific. She crisscrossed the ocean 25,000 miles by ship over three weeks. The subcommittee members visited Saipan, which recently had been liberated. They joined the Pacific Theater commander Admiral Chester Nimitz on the bridge of an aircraft carrier while the crew practiced operations for battle. Smith's fame grew with press coverage of the trip, especially after she was pictured nationally with Nimitz in a gun emplacement.

Smith investigated conditions faced by service members across the ocean, vividly describing the bleak existence of thousands of brave troops exposed to the sun on a small, treeless island, and the insecurity endured by female nurses who would not be treated in their own hospitals if they fell ill or got injured. When she arrived back home, she used her newly elevated political status to educate the public on the service members' needs and how to support them, and made recommendations for improvements to the Pentagon, many of which were adopted.

Women in the military were her special concern. In addition to employing nurses, each of the services addressed its shortage of enlistees by bringing in corps of women for non-combat duties such as clerical work, air traffic control, or pilot training. Members of the Women's Army Corps were called the WACs, and the Navy's Women Accepted for Volunteer Emergency Service were the WAVES. During the war, the

US had 100,000 WAVES in uniform. Smith visited nurses and WAVES on duty during the war and attended their training center, eating and sleeping with the inductees, going to classes, and even joining in their physical training, which included a parachute jump. Convinced of their abilities and usefulness for defense, she passed legislation, supported by the Navy, to enable women to rise further in the military.

With the end of World War II, soldiers and sailors went home, but the world had changed. The new, fateful contest of the Cold War began. Smith supported the Marshall Plan to rebuild Europe and was staunchly committed to increasing military expenditures to match the Soviet Union's. She also believed women should still have a role in the defense of the country. And she worked to retain gains women had made toward equality during the years when the nation had called upon them to aid in its defense.

Many others vehemently disagreed. Members like Vinson, the powerful committee chairman and Smith's mentor in Congress, wanted women to return to their prewar roles. The military still required the assistance of some women, both for day-to-day work and to act as a core for female units that could be called up in case of a national emergency. But Vinson would not consider legislation allowing women to be a regular part of the military in peacetime. The Pentagon worked around the problem by treating women as reserves—but, unlike male reserves, who were used only in emergencies, the women were called up for indefinite periods of service for routine jobs.

Smith objected.

As she would explain eloquently in committee proceedings and the heated legislative debates to follow, reserve status denied women the chance to build a career. She believed it was unfair to utilize women in the military in the same capacity as men without the same benefits of military membership.

The legislative battle would last three long years. It would lead to Smith turning against the very same committee that had been the base of her largest accomplishments, and require confronting members of her own political party. And, ultimately, it would end with Smith challenging Vinson, her mentor and committee chairman.

Many of her colleagues—in both political parties—rejected her effort outright. Committee chairman Vinson's sexist dismissal of her concern was, "When a woman gets a bee in her bonnet, she worries over it just like a baby." Smith, however, had nearly the entire military establishment on her side. In 1947, General Dwight Eisenhower, then the Army Chief of Staff, asked Congress to pass a bill to approve regular, permanent status for women in the military. The bill was needed soon, as the wartime authority for women's service would expire shortly. Eisenhower and Admiral Nimitz, the Navy Chief of Operations, testified in committee that the armed forces needed women's help to prosecute the dawning Cold War. General Douglas MacArthur also sent a telegram of support. As Eisenhower put it, "Due to the critical shortage of trained infantrymen, we have recently permitted all combat men presently holding military desk jobs to be reassigned to the infantry. We need replacements for these soldiers; WACs are the most logical source of replacement."

The bill encountered little opposition in the Senate, passing in July 1947. But that was not the case in the House.

The bill immediately ran into trouble in the House Armed Services Committee, where Vinson, after the intervening election, remained influential as the ranking minority member (with the unification of the services, the House's Navy and Army committees had been unified as well). In subcommittee, Republican members—Vinson's "crew"—questioned whether General MacArthur's telegram was even legitimate or if he had been ordered to send it. They suggested there was no reason women couldn't perform noncombat jobs as civilians and asked why disabled men couldn't be utilized instead of women. A Pennsylvania Republican, James Van Zandt, who had visited Pacific units staffed with WACs during the war, objected to women being sent beyond the territorial United States, stating that "[s]eeing an American girl running around with her hair full of dust and not having a bath for several days and in fatigue clothes doesn't satisfy the eye of the American who is accustomed to seeing his American girl dressed and clean at all times."

The bill languished for eight months. Then, Vinson and the Republication chair of the committee, W. G. "Ham" Andrews, held a confidential session with other senior committee members. And during that private meeting, a final deal was struck: they would agree to an amendment to delete regular military status for women, who would continue as reservists.

After learning of the decision, an outraged Smith fired off a sharp letter to Andrews, alleging that Navy officers had attended the executive session and undercut the military's own bill with unfounded concerns about women serving in the armed forces. And then, she sent the letter to the press. In Smith's historic papers, one can see a note with advice from Bill Lewis that suggests she knew the identity of the officers who had attended the secret meeting, but did not intend to disclose them. The Navy's legislative liaison, Captain Ira Nunn, called on Smith at her office to deny any Navy officers had sought to sink the bill. But a deal had clearly been struck. And when the bill went to the full committee, it went with the amendment deleting regular status for women.

Smith could not attend the meeting for the final committee vote, but she sent her proxy. And in it, she made clear the point she had been making all along: that while she would support women having full status in the military, she would not support continuing to utilize them as reservists, which took advantage of their skills but denied them the opportunity for a military career. If they were needed, they should be respected with status like men; if they were not needed, they should not be utilized as reserves. To some, her position was a risky one. Many women serving in the military as reservists were already bombarding Smith's office with requests that she go along with the amended bill, as some preferred to at least keep reserve status rather than being barred from the military at all. And that meant Smith stood alone—literally—without allies even among some of those she was advocating for.

The committee voted 26–1 to advance the bill, extending for another year women's status as reservists.

Smith was the only person to vote against it.

A few days later, Captain Nunn visited Smith again, this time to inform her that the bill had been placed on the House's Consent Calendar. The Consent Calendar was a list of noncontroversial bills that would be passed with no opportunity for debate or amendment, a system for passing routine matters efficiently. It was not, however, normally used for important bills such as this, especially one that contradicted a version already passed by the Senate. Nunn told Smith that he supposed she would not object to it after the committee's overwhelming vote.

He was wrong.

Smith's colleagues on the Armed Services Committee may have

hoped to slip the bill by her without her knowledge, as she wouldn't normally have reviewed the content of the Consent Calendar. They may have been afraid of the debate she would raise. And, they may very well have succeeded if Nunn hadn't come to meet her with remarks that she interpreted as a veiled warning not to object.

But his warning didn't work. Smith knew she had the power to re-move the bill from the Consent Calendar and force a debate. And she was determined to do so.

"It was surprising defiance of normal parliamentary procedure to put a controversial bill on the Consent Calendar," Smith later recalled. "Fortunately, there was one rule which prevented their getting away with it. Any bill called up on the Consent Calendar can be blocked by one objection. In other words, bills on the Consent Calendar must be passed unanimously. They must have felt that in the final crunch, I wouldn't dare to object."

Smith was seated in the House on the day when the Consent Cal-endar came up. "Members of the Armed Services Committee kept a steady eye on me, some of them coming up to me to plead or argue, a few almost threatening reprisals," she later wrote.

But, when the time came, Smith rose and said, "I object."

Paul Shafer, a Michigan Republican and the subcommittee chair who had amended the bill, jumped to his feet to challenge her.

"Mr. Speaker, it is difficult to understand the gentlewoman's objec-tion," Shafer bellowed indignantly. He pointed out that the bill would actually keep women in the military by enabling them to continue serving in the reserves. "She [Smith] has always been a great friend of women in service. Her objection may mean the ultimate defeat of this legislation which was reported favorably to the House by the Armed Services Committee. Should there be adverse action as the result of the gentlewoman's objection, she must assume full responsibility."

The speaker intoned: "Is there objection to the present consider-ation of the bill?"

And again, Smith's voice alone rang out in its challenge, as she firmly repeated "I object."

Later that day, she reinforced her position in the record, pointing out that the committee was free to bring the bill forward for an open debate on the floor. "This legislation does not give women any security in their military service because it discriminates against women," she declared. "I am convinced this is extremely unwise legislation. I am further convinced that it is better to have no legislation at all than to have legislation of this type. I am, therefore, unalterably opposed to it and I objected."

Newspapers across the nation quickly took up the controversy. Two days later, John McCormack of Massachusetts, the Democratic whip (who would later become Speaker of the House), rose on the floor to defend Smith and criticize the scheme attempted by the Armed Services Committee to slip the bill through. As he astutely explained, passing the bill on the Consent Calendar would have prevented the House from even considering the Senate version.

"For anyone to undertake to prevent this bill coming up under the rule of the House, so that the House can pass upon either the Senate bill or the House substitute, would be a grave mistake. The gentlewoman from Maine did the right thing, in my opinion," he said. "I admire her. When the gentleman from Michigan undertook to place the responsibility upon her, he should have taken a little look at the gentlewoman's chin, and he would know that he could not bluff her, because the gentlewoman from Maine is not the type that can be bluffed very easily from my observation of her during the years that both of us have served in this body."

Committee Chair Andrews did bring the bill forward for debate on the floor. And he warned Smith that she wouldn't get more than four votes for her amendment to allow women to serve. Meanwhile, the committee assigned its counsel to draft an amendment for Smith to offer, restoring regular status for women. But the draft arrived at the very last minute. Even worse, it was indecipherable. The counsel who drafted it, as it turned out, was an appointee of Republican Dewey Short of Missouri—one of the strongest opponents of women serving in the military.

Smith quickly improvised. She called on Bill Lewis to immediately draft simple language to achieve what she wanted. And he completed the draft just in time.

With the pages of the fresh document in hand, Smith strode to the House floor.

The time for a final battle on the issue was nigh.

As she later recalled, the outcome suddenly stood in doubt. More members were coming to her side than anyone had expected. Her party's leadership in the House put out an urgent call to bring stalwarts to the floor who would vote to uphold the committee. Smith only spoke a few sentences in support of her amendment. As she stood on the House floor, glancing at her colleagues, she began simply.

"I am not going to talk long about this amendment because the issue is very simple and clear."

The chamber stood still.

"The heads of our armed services," Smith explained, "have vigorously stated they have a permanent need for women in regular status in their Regular Establishments. The Senate granted their request. The House Armed Services Committee refused to grant the request and gives only a reserve status. Either the Members of the House accept the statement of the military heads as to their needs, as the Senate did, or they do not."

Smith supporters rose to add their own arguments. Some lauded the distinguished service of women in the war and called for the justice of treating them equally. Others argued it would be political good sense to do something positive for a group that comprised roughly half the voting public. Opponents, for their part, raised various imaginary fears, including that the amendment would impose additional costs on the military, even though testimony in committee had demonstrated that expenditures associated with women in the armed forces would be lower than those for their male counterparts (as under the customs of that time, their dependents could not be supported by the military).

Representative Dewey Short claimed that many lower officers and enlisted men in the Navy did not want women serving with them. Growing testy as the debate proceeded, he took a direct swipe at Smith, saying, "Hell hath no fury like a woman scorned." Then, referring back to the private executive session when the committee leadership had made their decision, he said, "There are several aspects to this bill that I do not care to discuss here publicly. We discussed them in detail and rather intimately in our committee . . . [and] were told that because of certain biological differences in the sexes when they reach the age of menopause or go through the change of life, with the physical disabilities or illnesses that result, the cost of the program would be stupendous if not prohibitive. Those are a few of the fundamental and essential facts, unpleasant as they might be, which we must as legislators wisely and soberly consider."

Smith was furious. Indeed, she was angry enough to quote Short's entire monologue in her autobiography, decades later. But in the moment, she did not respond, knowing that Short had, unbeknownst to many, just inadvertently tipped his hand in a way that would provide her a powerful tool to win the issue. For he had confirmed exactly what Captain Nunn had so carefully denied before—that the Naval officers *had* met, in secret, with the subcommittee, to give them reasons not to allow women to have equal status, despite the policy directive of the civilian leader, Defense Secretary James Forrestal, as well as General Eisenhower and Admiral Nimitz.

As the debate continued, two of Smith's allies leapt to her defense, challenging Short for insulting the women who had served in World War II and for his veiled suggestion that he had secret information that would influence the House if he disclosed it. Shafer, speaking for the Armed Services Committee, countered that the debate was inappropriate on a question the committee had agreed upon nearly unanimously.

In other words, the time for party discipline was now.

The vote was called soon thereafter. And when the initial tally was completed, it was clear Smith's amendment had been defeated. It lost by twelve votes. With more time for a second count, she lost two votes and the other side gained twelve more.

Smith was undeterred.

She decided to next move an amendment to stop the military from utilizing women in the reserves in everyday duty entirely. Put another way, the women's reserve would become like that for men—to be activated only in the case of emergency. It was a daring motion. Her amendment would have forced dismissal of eight thousand women from military service who wanted to remain in the military.

Chairman Andrews rose to make that point abundantly clear, highlighting that, in his view, Smith would hurt the same women that she and her allies had been trying to help. But Smith was unyielding. "Reservists are not accorded equal treatment with Regulars," Smith explained to her colleagues. "In other words, you are using women just as you would Regulars without giving them Regular status and instead placing them under the misnomer of Reserve."

The amendment failed, as Smith surely knew it would. But the battle was not over. "Getting permanent Regular status for women in the services had literally become a crusade with her," Lewis later recalled. The Senate and House had passed different versions of the bill—the Senate bringing women into the military on an equal basis with men, and the House keeping them as active reservists. A conference committee would resolve the differences. And Smith's floor fight had weakened the hand of those who opposed equal treatment for women by showing that the House was not unified.

Smith's final move, however, would not be in the House chamber. Instead, she would use her influence with the Pentagon. For in her eight years in the House, that was where she had won most of her victories—not on the floor, but rather, in the offices of the administration. And often, without a trace.

Smith had learned how to effectively work behind the scenes during her first term. In the summer of 1942, wartime shortages of oil and rubber had hit Maine hard, making fuel and tires so scarce that some residents couldn't get to work, including those needed at the shipyard in Portland to build Liberty ships. Smith believed that railcars of fuel headed north were being waylaid in Boston, denying Maine its rations. She decided to investigate by asking for a private meeting with Interior Secretary Harold Ickes, President Roosevelt's right-hand man.

"I was nervous," she later recalled. "He was so powerful and had a reputation for being difficult." But the secretary had spent summers in Bar Harbor, and he and Smith made a personal connection. After swearing her to total secrecy, he promised to get the tank cars delivered to Maine. True to his promise, they soon started arriving, easing the fuel shortage. Smith kept her promise, as well, and told no one. How or why the crisis had been averted was generally unknown until decades later, when a historian interviewed Smith and she revealed Ickes's intervention. Speaking in 1984, she said, "Getting that oil showed me how to operate in Congress."

Smith often cultivated relationships to get things done, developing influence to quietly address problems she saw for Americans in uniform and working on the home front. In her committee work during the war, she sponsored three bills that didn't pass, but were nonetheless implemented by executive decisions within the Pentagon. One helped families facing the draft. Another enabled women to work in defense plants at the same age as men. And Smith's efforts also led to military base hospitals providing maternal and infant care for dependents, which immediately benefited hundreds of thousands of mothers and babies each year.

Her most important inside connection, however, was James Forrestal, the powerful and wealthy Wall Street financier who became undersecretary of the Navy in 1940, and whose staff in that office included her future aide, Bill Lewis. Forrestal's energetic leadership received much of the credit for the Navy's amazing expansion during the war, as it increased from 1,100 ships to 50,000. He rose to become secretary of the Navy in 1944, and then, secretary of defense in 1947 when President Truman unified the services. While Smith worked closely with Forrestal to attain her goals on the Naval Affairs Committee, she also befriended his wife, Jo Forrestal, a New York socialite and former magazine columnist, who also used her public profile to support Smith's efforts and advocate for the WAVES. In the summer of 1943, Jo visited Smith in Maine, and during the course of the trip, Smith purportedly learned of Jo's alcoholism and mental illness, which included paranoia and hallucinations. Quickly realizing the depth of the illness, Smith confidentially cared for Jo personally at her home over the course of a vacation. Secretary Forrestal was profoundly grateful for the care. He gave Smith a piano, which remained in her living room in Skowhegan for the next fifty years.

Forrestal would ultimately prove to be Smith's high card in the political hand she had been playing with her adversaries on the House Armed Services Committee. Still angry from the debate on the House floor, she wrote to him the very next day, quoting all of Dewey Short's degrading remarks and charging that Pentagon representatives had created the problem by opposing women's regular status in the executive session—subverting the work of civilian leaders and the top brass. Found in Smith's papers, the rough draft of her letter reveals how truly angry she was. She had marked it up with a pen, placing blame directly on the legislative liaison (Captain Nunn) for this "duplicity," and, in her heavy script, adding a final sentence reminding the secretary that the bill was now in conference and "I believe that immediate action and reply on your part is imperative."

Forrestal complied. He weighed in heavily with the conference committee, insisting on regular status for women. And in a conciliatory letter to Smith, he insisted that all Navy officers had supported that position all along. The next month, the House-Senate conference committee adopted the version of the bill advanced by the Senate and by Smith, with minor differences.

The Women's Armed Services Integration Act finally became law with President Truman's signature on July 12, 1948.

As Smith would later say, "I lost all the battles except the last one."

By the time that battle was over, however, Smith was already well into her new challenge, running for Maine's open seat in the United States Senate. In the primary election in June, she faced three challengers, including the incumbent governor, who was endorsed by the Republican Party. Once again, she ran with little financial support, but with an army of women volunteers and a busy travel schedule to visit voters in person, who usually greeted her as Margaret, as if she were an old friend. She won the primary with more votes than all her opponents combined. In the general election, she received 71 percent of the vote.

Smith's courage had paid off with extraordinary loyalty from Maine voters. It would continue to do so in election after election over the next twenty years. In total, she was reelected to the Senate three times. And in between, she launched an unprecedented presidential campaign. Following her own unique script, the campaign was run on a shoestring budget, reliant on volunteers and personal stump speeches rather than advertising, and winning her twenty-seven delegates at the Republican National Convention in 1964.

But as the Book of Ecclesiastes tells us, "For everything there is a season."

In 1972, Smith lost her reelection in Maine—for the first and last time. By then, in the later years of the Vietnam War, her views on use of military force appeared, to many, out of step with the times. At the age of seventy-four, her time in government service had come to an end.

Smith faced daunting obstacles throughout her career. But through it all, she maintained a fidelity to her conscience that is all too rare in the political arena. Firm in her belief that she could prevail in the weighty legislative battles that she waged, she repeatedly faced down opponents and critics—including those in her *own* party—many of whom doubted her at every turn. For as she once said, "When people keep telling you, you can't do a thing, you kind of like to try."

7

Henry B. Gonzalez

★ ★ ★ ★ ★ ★ ★ ★ ★

Every one of us can make a difference. Every one of us should. Whether we make a difference or not, depends on just one thing—the courage to be true to ourselves, the faith to try.

—HENRY B. GONZALEZ

On a late evening in the fall of 1988, British American journalist Christopher Hitchens found himself walking the stately, marble halls of the US Capitol. He was there to give a visitor a tour of the building, which had closed hours earlier. As they ambled by the ornate rooms and imposing statues of great American patriots, some lionized and others long forgotten, they peeked into the historic House chamber. The chamber was nearly empty, save for one lonely representative. The heavy wrinkles around the older man's penetrating eyes revealed his age, but not his energy. Dressed in a loud, electric-blue suit, he orated loudly and enthusiastically to darkened rows of vacant seats, prophesizing about a looming financial crisis, the passion of his voice piercing the otherwise silent chamber.

Hitchens recognized the man immediately.

He would recall later that the representative had, in some quarters, become a laughingstock in Washington. Some derisively called him a "crackpot" and "loose cannon." Others labeled him a "conspiracy theorist" or worse. News articles at the time openly mocked his clothing and his causes. And that evening, without even listening to what he had to say, Hitchens assumed, as others did, that anyone who would use the privilege of "special orders" at the end of the legislative day in the House, giving long, complex speeches that no one wanted to hear, must be at least a bit eccentric. That the conspiracies he warned of must be ungrounded theories.

He was wrong. And less than two years later, Hitchens, and much of the country, would reach a very different conclusion.

Henry B. Gonzalez was not like most representatives. And the dark warnings from his lonely speeches during much of the 1980s turned out to be prescient. Hundreds of financial institutions were collapsing, costing the United States Treasury hundreds of billions of dollars. Gonzalez's revelations soon tattered the reputations of five famous US senators, four of them members of his Democratic Party. Rather than being praised for being right, Gonzalez would be attacked for having the courage to challenge the actions of his colleagues. And for his willingness to administer the bitter medicine of truth and reform, members of his own party would repeatedly try to strip him of power.

Gonzalez had made an art of public speaking, beginning in his days in the Texas State Senate, in the 1950s. Elected in 1961 to represent San Antonio in the House, he became the first Hispanic American ever elected to Congress from Texas. State journalists called him the city's most respected political figure, despite his outsider reputation in Washington. And the qualities that made Gonzalez a misfit in the eyes of many in Washington made him a leader in the eyes of many of his constituents, who lovingly called him Henry B. and returned him to office with overwhelming support, term after term. They applauded his unwillingness to profit from his service; he turned down fees for giving speeches or serving on boards, refused campaign contributions from the industries he helped oversee, and devoted himself to the truth, even when it led to uncomfortable places and exclusion from the insiders' club. He spent time sitting at a card table in front of his district office to meet anyone who wanted to chat, but wouldn't attend evening lobbyist receptions or political fund-raisers in Washington, preferring to stay home alone in his small Capitol Hill apartment, reading books and government documents.

In 1988, almost no one was on hand in the House chambers as Gonzalez delivered his nearly weekly speeches. But C-SPAN cameras captured the scene well.

As he moved to the lectern on the floor of the House, week after week, the light faded to darkness along the back row of seats. Only one other figure was typically visible, a typist at Gonzalez's side, recording his words for the *Congressional Record*. And the only other person in the chamber was the Speaker Pro Tem, behind him on the dais, out of sight, a member doing the duty of presiding into the quiet evening. Gonzalez—his voice rich and deep, bearing an almost imperceptible accent from his upbringing speaking Spanish—was nothing if not confident. His words flowed with ease and grace, the product of an extraordinarily well-read mind, as he extemporaneously commanded quotes from the classics and statistics he gleaned from reports and research materials.

Elsewhere, the presidential campaign was in full swing. Massachusetts Governor Michael Dukakis had just clinched the Democratic nomination, challenging Vice President George H. W. Bush to succeed President Ronald Reagan. And neither party wanted to talk about the looming financial crisis that Gonzalez has been warning of for years, which was undeniably coming to a head.

Savings and loan associations, which were originally chartered to hold traditional savings accounts and lend that money for home mortgages, were deregulated, over Gonzalez's opposition, in 1980 and 1982. Many of them went on a binge of speculative investments with depositors' money soon thereafter. By 1986, that house of cards began to fall, initially in Texas, Gonzalez's home state, when a drop in oil prices slowed the local economy.

The contagion gradually spread across the country.

The Federal Deposit Insurance Corporation (FDIC), the federal insurance program that guarantees deposits up to $100,000, drifted toward insolvency. Then, the danger spread to the banking industry itself. Still, few politicians wanted to acknowledge the substantial bill that would soon be coming due.

And so Gonzalez raised this danger on his own.

President Thomas Jefferson once wisely remarked, "When right, I shall be thought wrong by those whose positions will not command a view of the whole ground." Gonzalez saw the whole ground. And he was determined to share what he saw with the American people. Speaking weekly, he warned the country about the billions of dollars being added to the ultimate cost of the problem because of the government's continuing inaction.

On July 28, 1988, as he almost always did, he titled his speech, "My Advice to the Privileged Orders" and pointed once again to the folly of ignoring the problem.

"[I am] more than ever troubled by what appears to be the psychology among the people in power, the regulators as well as the administrative branch of our government, and perhaps even to some extent reflected in our own deliberations in an election year, and that is that we can whistle past the graveyard until November, believing that things should hold together until November," said Gonzalez, declaiming into the empty darkness. "Mr. Speaker, I am worried about the depositors. I am worried about the average little wage earner, that home owner, that family that depends on the fixed income but who manages to save a little, puts it in these institutions with the assurance that their deposits, if they are not over one hundred thousand dollars, are protected. I think we have got to face reality as much as we like to say otherwise, and that is that they are exposed and that sooner or later this Congress is going to have to move in and save this crumbled institutional situation."

The next year, after the election, Gonzalez himself attained the power to do something about it. He had risen through seniority to take the chair of the Committee on Banking, Finance and Urban Affairs. And it was there that he assumed the responsibility to save the depositors.

His actions would produce a firestorm.

Investigating Lincoln Savings and Loan Association, in California, and its owner, Charles Keating, Gonzalez uncovered evidence of improper attention from five senators, who held off regulators looking into his teetering and ultimately fraudulent financial institution. Gonzalez never flinched, despite the fact that four of the five senators were from his own political party and his work threatened to ruin them, their presidential chances, and his own party's hold on the Senate.

The spectacle amazed Washington observers. "It's unbelievable," one banking expert at the Brookings Institution told the *Washington Post* at the time. "I can't think in my lifetime where a House committee has gone after senators . . . He doesn't calculate political consequences. When he smells something bad, he goes after it." And that, he certainly did.

Gonzalez's journey to the People's House was a difficult one. His parents were political exiles from Mexico and had hoped to return there, even after Henry was born in 1916, but they never did. An avid student of American history and the Constitution at an early age, he learned to speak English during the first grade in San Antonio and spent his days at the local library, reading history, literature, and classic texts in English. To eliminate his accent and improve his public speaking voice, he practiced with pebbles in his mouth in front of a mirror, after learning from his reading that the Greek orator Demosthenes had done the same. At home he read widely in Spanish, as well, devouring books brought home by his father, Leonides, who was editor of a Spanish-language daily newspaper.

A constant stream of Mexican politicians and intellectuals came through the house. Henry grew up listening to debates that lasted deep into the night. Only after Leonides was an old man, when Henry was serving in office himself, did he disclose the story of his family's past. Their ancestors had come from Spain in 1532 and discovered a silver mine in Durango. There, they founded a town. Leonides would, centuries later, become its mayor and patron; he was still mining silver in 1910, when he was dispossessed by revolutionaries and narrowly escaped a firing squad. Not much later, Henry had been born in Texas.

Other than his remarkable, self-taught education and a powerful sense of his own identity, Gonzalez started out with little. Working his way through college during the Depression, he frequently went hungry and ultimately had to drop out. He finally received a bachelor of law degree but was presented with a blank diploma because of unpaid tuition bills. He never practiced law but served as a youth probation officer in San Antonio, a job that showed him how government could improve individual lives, and tested his physical courage and the boxing skills he learned in college—facing down a teen who tried to shoot him and another teen armed with a knife. Later, he worked in a public housing agency.

An entertaining storyteller and humorist, Gonzalez soon gained popularity through a series of civic roles and businesses. When he ran for San Antonio City Council in 1953, a local newspaper called him "[a] young man with a razor-sharp wit and a wide smile," who had been "catching the public eye for some time." He was the council's first Hispanic member. The job paid only a small stipend, however, and Gonzalez worked so hard for his constituents that he had little time for his translation business, leaving him broke with a fast-growing family at home (he and his wife Bertha ultimately had eight children). Borrowing from relatives got him through, and on the council, Gonzalez passed San Antonio's antidiscrimination law, telling colleagues how he and his own family had been refused entry to a public park and swimming pool. Walking home from one of those council meetings, he was shot at in the street.

Gonzalez won election to the Texas State Senate in 1956, becoming its first Hispanic member there, as well. Some senators were shocked by his presence and openly referred to him as "a lousy Mexican." He ignored them. And he tried to build respect by quietly introducing a series of bills for his district.

Still, civil rights issues were inescapable.

When Gonzalez arrived, the legislature was already embroiled in a backlash to the US Supreme Court's ruling desegregating public schools, *Brown v. Board of Education*. The governor and majority of legislators sought to nullify the ruling with a package of ten new state laws, including measures to let local schools segregate and one barring any member of the NAACP from holding public employment. Gonzalez strategized with another senator to filibuster the bills. When the legislation arrived on the Senate floor, his Lebanese American colleague, Abraham Kazan, spoke for fifteen hours, assisted by long questions from Gonzalez. And when Kazan sat down, Gonzalez took over.

He spoke for twenty-two hours—longer than anyone before in Texas history.

A reporter for the *Texas Observer* watched in awe as Gonzalez spoke for hour after hour. "A tall Latin man in a light blue suit and white shoes and yellow handkerchief was pacing around his desk on the Senate floor. It was eight o'clock in the morning," Ronnie Dugger told his readers at the time. Gonzalez was recounting the history of Texas, including the contributions of Mexicans and African Americans. "My own forebears in Mexico bore arms against Santa Anna!" Gonzalez exclaimed. "There were three revolutions against Santa Anna—Texas was only one of its manifestations. Did you know that Negroes helped settle Texas? That a Negro died at the Alamo?"

Dugger's report continued, "The angry, crystal-voiced man stopped in his pacing and raised his arms to plead, 'I seek to register the plaintive cry, the hurt feelings, the silent, the dumb protest of the inarticulate.' For twenty-two hours he held the floor, an eloquent, an erudite, a genuine and a passionate man; and any whose minds he didn't enter had slammed the doors and buried the keys."

Many years later, as publisher of his paper, Dugger still could not forget that moment. "It was an epiphany for a political reporter," he said. "He was quoting [George] Santayana and [John] Locke and I listened to him all night."

Gonzalez had no hope of defeating the ten desegregation bills. But, in the course of the filibuster, he attracted the attention of the state—with banner headlines in every newspaper—and then, the nation. *Time* magazine reported, "Time and again he warned his colleagues of the ultimate perils of segregation: 'It may be some can chloroform their conscience. But if we fear long enough, we hate, and if we hate long enough, we fight. . . . The assault on the inward dignity of man which our society protects, has been made. And this . . . is an assault on the very idea of America, which began as a new land of hope.' "

He had made a name for himself—not only as a man of stamina and commitment but also as a knowledgeable speaker and advocate. Fort Worth columnist Molly Ivins noted many years later that Gonzalez's accomplishment had been unique. It required more than the endurance to speak continuously for twenty-two hours. Gonzalez had also needed a mind with enough learning to fill that time with thoughts about history, the law, and the constitution. She said hardly anyone had that much knowledge. "They just don't know enough to talk that long," Ivins wrote, "in addition to the extraordinary passion for justice that animated the whole."

When he was done, Gonzalez had attracted enough attention to his cause that only two of the ten bills passed the state senate.

After the filibuster, and for the rest of his life, Gonzalez was known as the most powerful and popular politician in San Antonio. His name became known across the country. He soon ran for higher office, first for governor, and then for senator. But he fell short on both occasions.

And then, fate intervened.

In 1960, he was recruited by John F. Kennedy to campaign on his behalf for president. They had first met nearly a decade before, in 1951, and began regular correspondence after meeting at a campaign event several years later. In 1959, the senator's brother and aide, Robert Kennedy, visited Gonzalez to strategize on Texas politics for the coming presidential election. The State of Texas would be key. The Kennedys soon made Gonzalez cochair of a Hispanic campaign committee called

Viva Kennedy. The position took him to eleven states and all over Texas as he stumped with Robert and the campaign. John F. Kennedy won the election in November to become the thirty-fifth President of the United States.

The young president-elect was only forty-three years old. Gonzalez was forty-four.

On the Sunday before his inauguration, President Kennedy called Gonzalez to thank him and offer him an ambassadorship. Gonzalez declined.

Instead, he filed to run for Congress in a special election, to fill a seat vacated by a Kennedy appointment. That race, coming so soon after Kennedy's inauguration, became a national test of his popularity. Former president Eisenhower campaigned in San Antonio for Gonzalez's Republican opponent, while Vice President Lyndon Johnson, a Texan, visited to campaign for Gonzalez. The president wrote an endorsement for Gonzalez, focusing on his courage.

Gonzalez won handily. And he was never seriously challenged again.

His fateful relationship with the Kennedys continued as a key connection in his life. In November 1963, in Dallas, Texas, he was riding in part of the presidential motorcade when an assassin shot President Kennedy. He later stood next to First Lady Jacqueline Kennedy at a local hospital when, still caked in blood, she kissed the president's lifeless body for the last time and put her ring on his finger. Gonzalez's very first of many rides on Air Force One was accompanying Kennedy's body back to Washington, as Lyndon Johnson was sworn in as president. Gonzalez remained close to President Johnson, working with him and advising him on economic issues, which were Gonzalez's strongest interest.

How did a congressman with such popularity, powerful friends and rhetorical skills come to be known in Washington DC as an "eccentric" and a "crackpot"?

The evidence suggests it was Washington that changed, not Gonzalez. His unwillingness to compromise on principle, regardless of the consequences, especially when defending the constitutional powers of the Congress, made his voice an increasingly lonely one. A turning point may have come in 1964, when Gonzalez and other members of Congress heard a then-rare sound, the bell calling for a roll-call vote.

As members rushed to the floor, the chair of the Foreign Affairs Committee explained the vote would be on a resolution responding to news they had learned in that morning's headlines: a confrontation between a US Navy ship and a North Vietnamese vessel in the Tonkin Gulf. Gonzalez read the document, which struck him as a wide-ranging, back-door declaration of war. Leaders assured him it would do no more than offer the president moral support. He wavered.

As Gonzalez later recalled, "I still hesitated, and I did not vote until after two of the three roll calls had been read. Finally, because I would have been the only one voting in any way other than 'aye,' I succumbed to what I hope I have not since then and will not again succumb—to the fear of ridicule for not supporting the president. The rest is history. That resolution was the basis for an enlargement of the war effort on the part of the United States that led to the most divisive period in our society since the Civil War."

Gonzalez blamed himself most, however, not for voting in support of the war, but for, in his view, helping erode the power of Congress, which American history had taught him was intended to be the primary branch of government. Indeed, it was for that same reason he would later cast the lone vote against the Twenty-fifth Amendment to the Constitution, on presidential succession, and oppose deficit reduction laws with automatic spending levels, which he contended would infringe on the legislative power of the purse.

His longest crusade was to defend the power of the Congress to declare war. Determined never to repeat the mistake he believed he had made when he supported the Tonkin Gulf Resolution, Gonzalez in 1967 submitted an amendment to enforce a limitation on the draft, allowing conscripted servicemen to serve overseas only when Congress had formally declared war under Article I of the Constitution. He could not find enough support to even bring the amendment into debate. As the war lost popularity, he submitted the amendment again in 1971. Again, he lost—but this time, with 151 votes on his side.

"If the president has unlimited foreign as well as domestic powers, what remains to prevent the development of a police state?" Gonzalez demanded. "What remains to keep the government from assuming all power in the name of one man? The answer is that Congress must share the power. The president may not like this, but if we want this government to survive, that is the way it has to be. When the flexibility and suppleness of the Constitution are gone and power is no longer divided, the revolution will be over, and the king will be restored to his throne."

As military actions not expressly authorized by Congress became more frequent in the 1980s and early 1990s—in Lebanon, Grenada, Nicaragua, and Kuwait—Gonzalez became more strident in his opposition, and even advanced impeachment motions against multiple presidents for decisions he considered unconstitutional. In response, he received death threats, and some of his strongest supporters from San Antonio denounced him. His stands won him the title the Don Quixote of the House, which Gonzalez relished, but some colleagues simply called him "a flake" for making speeches to empty chambers that no one would hear and about causes they believed he could never win.

Gonzalez made no effort to ingratiate himself into Washington's social life or insider circles. Some colleagues found him prickly and quick to take offense, as when, at age seventy, he punched a man in a restaurant who taunted him as "a communist." (Although, in that case, Gonzalez claimed he had not lost his temper: "If I had acted out of passion, that fellow would still not be able to eat chalupas," he said.) Besides his wit, he became noted from the beginning of his service for refusing financial support or outside income, and never moved his family to Washington, explaining when he was first elected in 1961 that he simply couldn't afford it. Thirty years later, as he oversaw legislation worth hundreds of billions of dollars for the banking system, his campaign accounts remained tiny, and his personal financial disclosure remained virtually the same every year, listing a modest two-story brick house in San Antonio and a $2,500 bank account. Often outspent by political opponents, he told his supporters, "You can drink his beer and eat his tamales, but when you go to the polls, vote for Gonzalez!" Even after three decades, he returned to his family in San Antonio every weekend, and lived in a $641-a-month efficiency apartment in Washington—his office adorned, according to one enterprising reporter, with "an aging-bachelor look, with opened jars of peanut butter and honey and mismatched coffee mugs."

His crusades were quixotic, but some proved correct more often than his critics liked to admit. In the 1970s, he alleged in his speeches that, contrary to original investigations, some type of conspiracy had been

entangled with the assassination of President Kennedy—allegations
that were later validated, at least in part, by the select committee that
he had successfully argued for the House to empanel (he initially served
as chair but resigned amid clashes with top committee staff). He was
mocked relentlessly for his repeated criticisms of the Federal Reserve
Board, but a General Accounting Office report and *Wall Street Journal*
article would ultimately validate his charges. And he also persistently
charged that the murder of a federal judge in San Antonio in 1979 was
the work of organized crime. Three years later, when federal convic-
tions proved him correct, then-FBI Director William Webster publicly
thanked Gonzalez for "keeping the issue alive."

All of those causes, and battles, were significant. And some were
more difficult than others. But such difficulties paled in comparison to
what would become the biggest fight of his career. For the next battle
would require Gonzalez to take on towering members of his own party.
It would require moral courage all too uncommon in the halls of power.

And it would end with Gonzalez fighting for his own political survival.

As in his defense of the Constitution, a principle guided him in the
savings and loan crisis. At the core of his philosophy since arriving in
Congress, he believed in creating fairer economic conditions for ordinary Americans, and that families of middle and lower income—like
his own—needed stable interest rates and access to credit in local banks
to buy homes and build small businesses. That need drove his politics
during most of his career—not the civil rights issues that had made him
famous early on. Indeed, Gonzalez often rejected being known primar-
ily as a Mexican American congressman and at times pulled back from
causes related to his ancestry, sometimes angering Latino activists by
his lack of support. Early in his career, in 1964, when President Johnson
asked Gonzalez for names of Mexican Americans in Texas to appoint
to offices—in thanks for his reelection victory in that year—Gonzalez
told him, "If I know of a good person, I'll be glad to give you his name,
and if that person happens to be Mexican American, so much the better." He worked, instead, for the benefit of every ordinary family—to
improve housing, make loans affordable, and give security in routine
banking. And he deeply disapproved of Wall Street speculation and
high-flying finances.

To pursue his unpretentious goals, Gonzalez set out to gain power slowly in the financial world, putting in decades of dogged service on the fifty-member Banking Committee, gradually working his way up in seniority. In 1980, he became chair of the Subcommittee on Housing, overcoming Democrats who opposed him because of his unconventional ways. At the time, the Reagan administration was rolling back some of the nation's social safety net programs and pushing forward with deregulation of financial institutions. It was not an easy time to work on public housing policy. The administration supported allowing S&Ls into many more risky kinds of investments, and in fact, had the help of the Democratic Chair of the Banking Committee, Fernand St Germain, a Rhode Island Democrat.

Opponents accused St Germain of benefitting from the law himself. While he was chairman in the 1980s, newspaper exposés revealed he had purportedly received loans to amass real estate holdings and a chain of International House of Pancakes restaurants, as well as building a vast campaign account contributed by the institutions he oversaw. In 1986, one of the Democrats who had tried to deny Gonzalez his subcommittee chair pushed him to try to oust St Germain. Gonzalez refused, saying he supported following the regular order—and adding, wryly, that he would fight like "Davey Crockett at the Alamo" if Democrats didn't follow seniority when it was his turn to be chair.

All the while, Gonzalez continued delivering his lonely special-order speeches, calling attention to the gathering storm of S&L failures and the insolvency of the federal deposit insurance program. He had been speaking about the danger to the S&Ls since the 1970s. Back then, spiking interest rates had made the S&L business model a faulty one, as traditional thirty-year home mortgages on their books lost value and savers abandoned accounts paying low regulated interest rates. St Germain's legislation had tried to address the problem by allowing S&Ls to pay higher interest and to invest deposits more aggressively, at the same time increasing federal insurance to encourage customers to deposit more money.

But higher risk brought larger losses.

Insolvent S&Ls, called "zombies" by some, attempted to dig out with even riskier bets, attracting more deposits by offering very high interest so they could invest that money in ever more speculative ventures. Typically, that extended the losing streak. The longer the insolvent institutions stayed open, the larger their losses became, and the more money the Federal Deposit Insurance fund would, ultimately, be responsible to repay. By 1983, the cost of paying off depositor losses at failed savings and loan institutions already amounted to $25 billion. And the fund to cover those losses?

It contained only $6 billion.

By ignoring the problem—and Gonzalez's speeches—congressional leaders avoided taking a political hit for their costly mistake. But while they waited, the cost for taxpayers continued to grow, ultimately reaching $124 billion. As Gonzalez spoke to the empty House, he was predicting that outcome, blaming both parties for "whistling past the graveyard."

Then, in 1988, with the crisis at its apex, Rhode Island voters retired St Germain. Gonzalez's turn to lead the Banking panel would finally arrive with the start of the new Congress the next January.

His fellow Democrats, however, had their doubts. Many banking lobbyists worked feverishly to block his rise to the chair. But the challenge fizzled in the face of Gonzalez's threat to fight like Davey Crockett. Indeed, his Democratic colleague from Austin, Texas, J. J. Pickle, made clear that the threat was not an idle one, stating, "Henry will charge hell with only a bucket of water and think nothing of it."

The bucket of water was unnecessary. Gonzalez ascended to the chairmanship.

At first, colleagues were pleasantly surprised by his leadership. Despite his history of fiery speeches and lonely crusades, he led the committee with courtly, polite manners and openness to all points of view, yet kept the work moving forward at the pace needed to pass major legislation addressing the emergency. A banking trade journal called his committee "a model." Two Republican members said the new chair was "kind and generous" and that he ran the committee in "a fair, bipartisan way." And Republican Jim Leach of Iowa said, "If there were such a thing as chairman of the year, Henry would be uncontested winner."

By August of his very first year as chairman, Gonzalez's solution to the S&L crisis had already become law. It was a rapid victory for complex legislation that set up a new insurance system and regulatory agency, while creating a corporation to close insolvent institutions—more than one thousand in all—and pay back all depositors for the full amount of their federal insurance. His open process at the committee had worked. The bill passed with support from both parties and the administration, and eventually, successfully cleaned up the disaster.

Gonzalez rapidly moved on to reforming the banking deposit insurance system, as well. And, that same year, he started work on another significant, wide-ranging bill, to reform the nation's housing finance system. It, too, included ideas from the Republican administration and minority members. And it passed the very next year.

No similar legislation had made it through Congress in seventeen years.

Gonzalez had carefully, and successfully, constructed legislative solutions to the financial crises that faced the nation. He had done so on a bipartisan basis. And he did it in his first year as chair. But his work was not complete.

There had to be accountability, too.

Gonzalez had long been interested in investigating the roots of the S&L crisis, beginning his probe even before formally receiving his gavel in 1989. He initially expected to spotlight what he believed to be lax regulation and questionable decisions by the outgoing Republican administration. But his investigation would, unexpectedly, lead back to a much more uncomfortable place for some—to prominent members of Gonzalez's own party.

The subject of the investigation was one of the largest and most damaging collapses of the era, at Lincoln Savings and Loan of California. Besides racking up billions in federally insured losses, the bank had also convinced elderly customers who intended to put money in insured accounts to instead buy its own high-risk bonds, which became worthless when the institution's owner declared bankruptcy. More than twenty-three thousand people lost their money. Some lost their entire life savings. And yet, all that activity had been allowed to continue long after Lincoln was already broke and targeted for takeover by regulators.

As it turned out, the professional regulators had been overruled by a political appointee, who decided to leave Lincoln open and operating for more than two years as it built up more losses, committed more fraud, and destroyed more families' finances. And the evidence suggested that several Democratic members of the Senate might have played an improper role.

Rather than backing off the investigation—as many politicians on both sides of the aisle undoubtedly would have done—Gonzalez did the opposite. He immediately intensified his investigation and quickly ran into what he called "a ripple of opposition" or "indirect pressure" as he closed in on the facts.

"Many members from his side of the aisle are trying to whitewash what happened," a Republican committee member, Toby Roth of Wisconsin, told the *Washington Post*. "But he has the stick-to-it-iveness of an English bulldog. He's a genuine old-fashioned public servant." The *Post* quoted unnamed Democratic Party leaders who were afraid Gonzalez could ruin the prospects of a future presidential contender. "Party types are monitoring this very closely," the anonymous official said. "He's cowboying this one, which is very much his style and what everyone was worried about when he became chairman." In October, when Gonzalez asked the committee to issue subpoenas to bring the professional S&L regulators in front of the committee to testify, some members resisted. He won approval of the subpoenas with only twenty-six votes, just enough on the fifty-member committee.

On October 26, 1989, a group of regulators from the San Francisco office of the Federal Home Loan Bank sat before Gonzalez's committee as he opened a series of explosive hearings. All seats were full in the large committee room in the Rayburn House Office Building. Photographers crouched on the floor along the front of the dais, facing the witnesses, their cameras bursting into a squall of clicks and flashes as Gonzalez asked the men seated at the table to stand and raise their right hands.

He introduced the hearing by explaining what was known so far: that these examiners had found ample evidence to take over Lincoln two years before, in 1987, which would have stopped its financial bleeding and defrauding of investors. Instead, the head of the regulatory agency had mysteriously canceled that action and pulled them out of Lincoln's offices. As they spoke, the men's voices carried an edge of frustration and indignation, even as they formally documented their recollections with letters and factual details. The agency's former general counsel,

William K. Black, said its staff had constantly worried about Congressional interference in their work. With the case against Lincoln solidly established, they had been suddenly called off, and the institution allowed to go on attracting customers' deposits and investments.

"Clearly we were shot in the back," he said, "as we battled to protect the taxpayer."

"The little examiner, existing on his monthly paycheck, reads the message from on top very quickly and very accurately," Gonzalez said. "The decision to pull the regulators out of Lincoln sent a blast of cold wind throughout the entire regulatory system coast to coast. Riding on that wind was the message, 'Go slow. The people at the top won't support you when the big guys complain.' It's a highly dangerous message that could cost the nation and the financial industry heavily."

But who exactly were those "big guys"?

Two weeks later, Edwin Gray, the former chairman of the board of the regulator, the Federal Home Loan Bank Board, sat in front of the committee to explain the pressure and how he had tried to resist it before he left the agency. Seated at the microphone, he was the picture of respectable credibility, a classic banker in his dark blue suit, horn-rimmed glasses, and a touch of gray in his thinning hair. As he began his statement, he congratulated Gonzalez for his political courage. And what he had to say blew open the scandal some Democrats had hoped to avoid.

First, Gray explained how Lincoln's owner, Charles Keating, had used the bank like an investment fund, making few home mortgages while plunging depositors' money into risky, high-return ventures. That strategy allowed him to make big bets with potential losses covered by the deposit insurance fund. "True venture capitalists take risks—big risks—on their own money," Gray said. "Keating's idea, apparently, of venture capitalism was to take risks on money backed by the taxpayers, and the taxpayers lost." Gray had tried to rein in the practice with regulations preventing direct investments by S&Ls, but he came under intense pressure from Keating and was repeatedly undercut by the Reagan administration. "I sometimes felt like I was a sheriff without a gun," Gray explained.

In March 1987, Gray testified, Keating's pressure campaign widened, when Gray received a request from the chair of the Senate Banking Committee, Democratic Senator Donald Riegle of Michigan, to talk about Lincoln with a group of senators in the office of Senate Democrat Dennis DeConcini of Arizona. Three other senators were on hand for the meeting on April 2, 1987: Democrat John Glenn of Ohio, Democrat Alan Cranston of California, and Republican John McCain of Arizona.

Gray testified that several of the senators told him that Lincoln would improve its lending if he would relax regulation on investing. "It was a quid pro quo," Gray said. A week after that meeting, all five senators were on hand for another meeting in DeConcini's office, which lasted two hours, as they pushed four bank board examiners to back off from their probe of Lincoln. The senators allowed no staff witnesses to attend.

In the firestorm of publicity around Gonzalez's hearings, the press nicknamed the senators the Keating Five. Keating had given the senators a combined $1.3 million in contributions for their various political campaigns, as well as other gifts. In a subsequent Senate Select Committee on Ethics investigation, the senators received varying levels of penalties for different levels of involvement. Senator Cranston of California, who received the most money, and had kept fighting for Lincoln almost until it closed, was formally reprimanded by the Senate. Only two of the senators were able to recover their political careers through the next election. Keating himself served four and a half years in prison.

But they would not be the only ones who would face consequences. Gonzalez would, too.

For him, the repercussions would come from within his own party. He had declined to call the five senators as witnesses before his committee, saying, "Only once before, back in 1850, did a member of the House issue a subpoena of the Senate, and it's still over there a-moldering away." But while Gonzalez's committee focused on the reform legislation to strengthen the financial system and reduce corruption, the Senate ethics committee investigation soon launched in earnest. And party members were furious that Gonzalez had damaged Democratic senators when he could have, in their view, focused more on the role of the Reagan White House.

As the end of Gonzalez's first term as chair neared, in 1990, his angry colleagues quietly made their move. Bruce Vento, a Minnesota Democrat, who was seventh in seniority on the committee, planned a coup to place himself in the chair instead. Secretly strategizing through the autumn, he developed allies with various complaints within the House Democratic Caucus, before announcing his challenge in a letter on the eve of the caucus meeting in December, when chairs would be elected.

Vento's letter to the secretary of the caucus didn't attack Gonzalez directly for investigating the Democratic senators.

But the subtext was clear.

He suggested Gonzalez had been too bipartisan and critical of party members. In the housing bill, for example, he had dropped a provision advanced by Vento in favor of one the Bush administration had wanted, as a way to reach compromise and pass the legislation. In his letter, Vento explained, "The current chairman has unjustifiably singled out Democratic colleagues for criticism; has structured hearings without any apparent sense of consequence or purpose; he has treated the sub-committee and their chairs as irrelevant; and finally, he has defied the rules of the Democratic Caucus by campaigning against a Democratic candidate by praising the ranking Republican of the committee in a television ad."

The ad, in particular, became a key part of the attack. Gonzalez explained that he had agreed to record a statement for ranking member Chalmers Wylie, of Ohio, to defend against a Republican primary opponent, who had falsely charged that Wylie had been responsible for the S&L crisis. The chair of the liberal-leaning Democratic Study Group wrote to the Speaker asking for an investigation of Gonzalez's support of the Republican—although Gonzalez was known as one of the most liberal members of the House. A newspaper reporter said a member of the group had tried to convince him to write about the controversy. Gonzalez also received a threatening phone call on the issue. The ad never ran. And Gonzalez, for his part, said simply, "I don't owe Wylie anything, politically or anything else, other than testifying to his co-operation, his earnest sincerity and his truthfulness. I admire him very much."

Of course, the ad wasn't the real issue. According to a journalist quoting one unnamed source "close to the matter," it was simply "a vehicle to bring a challenge for many other things, particularly the over-sight hearings on . . . Lincoln, where the Democrats were hit hardest."

The caucus met in December. The day had come for members to

render judgment on the chair of the Banking Committee. The meeting would be behind closed doors.

As he entered the room, Gonzalez wasn't sure if he'd prevail.

But he knew, win or lose, his integrity would be intact.

Nominations were made. Speeches were delivered. Some applauded. Others did not. And finally, votes were cast. The tally was announced soon thereafter.

The challenge had failed, on a vote of 163 to 87.

Vento had called the vote a rebuke that would discipline Gonzalez. Gonzalez, in turn, called Vento a "snake," adding, "I think that was a pretty damn good vote considering the circumstances—no time to defend, no time to approach anybody, no time to contact new members who might have been very much confused. The only bad taste is the method used. It was a failed blitzkrieg, a stab in the dark, in the back, an attempted legislative mugging that failed."

But criticism against Gonzalez and pressure for him to leave the chair didn't let up. Another challenge circulated, remaining under cover leading up to the congressional organization meetings of 1992. Critical articles quoting unnamed sources charged that Gonzalez was ineffective and did not collaborate—despite passing landmark, bipartisan legislation and a total of seventy-one bills as chair. Meanwhile, many banks and their lobbyists complained openly and contributed millions of dollars to the campaigns of other members of the committee. They wanted loosened banking rules that Gonzalez would not support, and they hoped for a new chairman who would be more accommodating. Democratic representative Barney Frank from Massachusetts defended the chairman, telling one reporter, "Henry is very smart, very disciplined," while adding, he "can be difficult."

Again, however, Gonzalez overcame expectations, passing a major overhaul of the federal deposit insurance system for banks and fending off another financial crisis in that industry. And, ultimately, Vento never challenged Gonzalez's leadership in the caucus that year.

Two years later, in 1994, as Gonzalez neared the end of his third term as banking chair, speculation again rose to a new peak that he would lose the position. But he was also beginning to receive public vindication for his courage and honesty. That September, as the election neared, the John F. Kennedy Library Foundation bestowed on him the Profile in Courage Award, named for Kennedy's book, and led by Senator Edward Kennedy, who in his remarks recalled his brother's endorsement of Gonzalez thirty-three years earlier, during his first run for Congress. Journalists writing about Gonzalez had noted that in many homes of his older constituents, President Kennedy's picture still hung on the wall, with Gonzalez's picture hanging beside it.

"My brother knew political courage when he saw it, and ever since then, Henry Gonzalez has justified that description. Courage fits him like a glove," Senator Kennedy told the morning audience, which was full of Gonzalez's extended family. "From the day he took his seat in the House of Representatives, Congressman Gonzalez has been a Congressional original—fearless in serving the long-suffering people and families of his district, fearless in challenging entrenched interest groups, fearless in standing up for those who are pressed down by injustice and prejudice."

Gonzalez rose to accept, nodding to the applause and admiring the silver ship's lantern engraved with his recognition, a replica of a lantern on the USS *Constitution*. He spoke in a deep, calm voice, reflecting the humble honor he felt. And in a spellbinding talk, he told his own story of learning courage, beginning with his arrival in first grade in San Antonio, when he couldn't understand a word of the teacher's English, and, later, growing to understand what political courage could accomplish for others. As Gonzalez explained:

"Once I got into politics, I learned this very early: people will respond to you if they can believe what you say. People will trust you if you keep your word. People will respect you if you respect yourself. If you lay out the problem accurately and if you propose a reasonable solution, people will give you a chance, notwithstanding your heritage or race. Some would never vote for the Irish Kennedy or the Mexican Gonzalez; and some would only vote for us because he was Irish and I am Mexican; but most would decide the issues on the merits, and us on our ability . . . He and I came from different worlds, but we traveled a common path, we shared the same goals. We believed in the same things. Here was a man of absolute, undeniable physical courage; here was a man of grace, and charm and wit; and here was a man who called on himself, and all of us, to be better, to do better, to see farther. For me to receive any recognition in his name is a greater honor than I could have ever dreamed."

There were few dry eyes in the room as Gonzalez concluded his remarks. Looking out at the audience before him, he said, "In my time I have had the honor to be vilified for standing up against segregation. I have had the privilege of being a thorn in the side of unprincipled privilege, and the great joy of being demonized by entrenched special interests. I have had the special pride of seeing hard jobs completed: the great civil rights laws; the cleanup of corruption in the savings and loan industry; the enactment of federal laws that help educate the poor, care for the sick, eradicate disease, and house the people."

It was a fitting honor, particularly at the twilight of his career. For Gonzalez's years of power would soon come to an end.

In November 1994, a Republican landslide changed control of the House and ended his run as Banking chair. He became ranking member, but was, by some accounts, simply not as effective in the new role. "I think we had a very good six years under Henry," said Barney Frank, "but the transition from chairman to ranking member was personally very tough for him." And by the end of that term, in 1996, an effort arose once more to remove him from his position and make a less senior Democrat the ranking member. Again, Vento campaigned hard to take the spot. Another member, and the next Democrat in line in seniority after Gonzalez, John LaFalce of New York, also advanced his name, deemed by some a pro-industry voice that the banks preferred. Even some longtime Gonzalez supporters said it was time for him to step aside. The Democratic Steering and Policy Committee voted 22–19 to recommend that the full caucus strip him of his post.

But Gonzalez gathered friends and allies. Jesse Jackson Jr., who had just been elected to represent Chicago, campaigned for Gonzalez to remain ranking member, writing to colleagues that "his record is characterized by an unwavering commitment to equality of opportunity, economic development, civil rights and social justice for all Americans." Chairs of the Black and Hispanic caucuses also wrote a joint letter of support. Joseph Kennedy II, of Massachusetts, the son of Robert Kennedy and heir to John Kennedy's congressional seat, also came to Gonzalez's defense. Kennedy said the Democratic minority on the Banking committee, of which he was a member, had been effective against the Republicans, even if Gonzalez's powers had declined. "What are we going to do, take away a ranking membership from a guy who is a folk hero among Democrats?" Kennedy asked. "This guy defines the Democratic Party's values."

When the caucus meeting convened, in November 1996, Gonzalez was the last of the three candidates to speak. Perhaps his opponents hadn't counted on the power of his voice and his extraordinary mind. But they should have. After all, he had been enthralling audiences with his oratory for more than forty years. Now, he would do so again. The speech, delivered behind closed doors in the caucus meeting, became famous and would be discussed by those who heard it for years afterward, its text widely quoted.

"For those of you who do not know me, I am Henry B. Gonzalez of Texas. I am a Democrat without prefix, suffix, apology, or any other kind of modification," he began, although surely aware that everyone in the room knew exactly who he was.

He praised the younger representatives, especially Kennedy and Jackson, and he listed his many accomplishments on the committee and its success. Then he went directly, and shockingly, to the point, saying, "Today, I know that the Steering Committee has endorsed someone else to be ranking member. I do not know why. What I do know is that it is wrong, based on the record. It is unfair. How can I acquiesce in a thing that ignores my record of honorable and successful leadership? How can I be silent in the face of such an injustice? I cannot. I will not cower, I cannot retreat, and I will defend myself. All I can do is appeal to you. I appeal to your sense of justice and fairness."

He then changed tone, lowering his voice briefly to recall the beginning of his service, thirty-five years earlier.

"My colleagues, when I came here, I was something of a curiosity, being the only so-called ethnic minority member in my delegation. I was accepted as a peer—but that was not to say I was welcomed. And I stand before you today, accepted, but seen by some as an inconvenient and unwelcome obstacle.

"They cannot say that I have failed," he continued, but "only that they fear I will."

His colleagues spellbound, Gonzalez continued.

"How many times have I heard that?" he asked his colleagues. "In every step of my career I have been told: 'It is impossible, don't even try.' When I first ran for office, my own mother begged me not to, because it just wasn't done: 'You'll make the Americans angry,' she said. But my mother also said, 'First, respect yourself.' And so, I ran, because it was the right and honest thing to do. Still, everyone said I couldn't be elected to my local city council. They said I couldn't be elected to the Texas Senate. They said I couldn't be elected to this House. They said I couldn't run a subcommittee. They said I couldn't run a committee. And now some say I couldn't run a minority. But I did all of those things: I did them well, and I did them better than anyone ever dreamed possible."

Members of caucus jumped to their feet and interrupted Gonzalez with extended applause. But he wasn't finished. He roared onward in his deep, smooth voice.

"Some say, you can't do it, don't even try. But I say to you, I have served with honor and integrity and success. I have never failed myself, and I have never failed you. And so I appeal to you: do the right thing. Do the fair thing. I rest on my record, and I ask for your support. I appeal to your sense of justice: one last term as ranking member, and I will not disappoint you."

The members again jumped to their feet, applauding so loudly that, outside the doors of the closed meeting, they could be heard down the halls of the Longworth House Office Building. Voting commenced immediately. And the impact of Gonzalez's words was immediately apparent.

Gonzalez got 82 votes, LaFalce 62, and Vento 47.

He had won the first round.

Rather than go to a second ballot, LaFalce recognized his colleagues had become uncomfortable with the process. He withdrew.

As LaFalce said later, "Henry was so good, I almost voted for him."

Gonzalez was overwhelmed by emotion after the vote, as friends gathered to congratulate him. He had surprised even himself with the strength of his speech. "My gosh, the spirit moved me," he said.

Alas, that final term lasted only six months before he fell ill during a House session and was taken to a hospital by ambulance. His heart had been damaged by an infection. Returning in the fall, he announced his retirement. In the next general election, his son Charlie won the seat, which he would hold until his retirement in 2013.

Tributes poured in as Henry B. prepared to leave. Only the nation's bankers were happy to see him go, as one of their trade journals reported. Jim Leach, the Iowa Republican who would replace Gonzalez for sixteen years as Banking chair—and with whom Gonzalez had repeatedly clashed—praised him. "Few members of Congress have had a more distinguished congressional career in this century than Henry Gonzalez," said Leach. "I know of none more honorable."

Gonzalez died of the heart ailment less than a year after leaving office, in November 2000. His funeral in San Antonio filled the historic San Fernando Cathedral, with more people watching on video monitors in the city council chambers. Crowds of thousands filled the steps and the Main Plaza outside, lining the four-mile route to the cemetery. An extraordinary series of political leaders paid their respects. But back in Washington, Gonzalez had an even more fitting memorial: a special order, of the kind he had used so many times before to give his speeches, this time well attended by colleagues, and taking place in the morning, not late at night. His son, Charlie, now serving in his seat, poetically noted how appropriate it was. "This special order, something that was so dear to Dad," Charlie Gonzalez said. "He truly believed this was the greatest institution on the face of the earth, and I'm convinced that he was right."

Steny Hoyer, a Maryland Democrat who would later become House Majority Leader, said it plainly. "This is the people's House. We are proud of that. No person in history better represented an advocate for the people than Henry B. Gonzalez of Texas."

*Leadership does not mean putting the ear to the ground to fol-
low public opinion, but to have the vision of what is necessary
and the courage to make it possible.*

—SHIRLEY CHISHOLM

On May 15, 1972, Representative Shirley Chisholm received chilling news. It was an otherwise pleasant spring day in Detroit, Michigan, and Chisholm, who represented a portion of Brooklyn in the House of Representatives, was far from home. As she shook voters' hands at a community children's home, her historic campaign to become president of the United States was in full swing. And then a sheriff's deputy came to her side to share a shocking development.

Her opponent had been shot.

Chisholm immediately thought of dropping out of the race. Rushing to the local airport in a car with her staff, deeply disturbed by the political violence that had become so pervasive in her country, she kept repeating to herself, "We're all animals." Alabama Governor George Wallace had been shot five times by a gunman at a rally outside a shopping center in Maryland. He had been riding high, harnessing the backlash against desegregation and racial progress to win presidential primaries. That day in Maryland he had inveighed against politicians in Washington, DC, and the "senseless and asinine" busing of children to desegregate schools before wading down into the crowd, where a man shouted for his attention and then fired multiple bullets into Wallace. A nation traumatized by a decade of political assassinations anxiously waited to learn more.

Chisholm knew she could be in danger. News initially arrived in the car that the assailants were African American (a false report, as it turned out). Chisholm was among the most outspoken and controversial African American leaders in the country, and the first Black woman ever to serve in the People's House. Others shared her concern. Among President Richard Nixon's first actions during the crisis was to assign a Secret Service detail to protect Chisholm.

"I was so shaken and confused, if it was someone Black, I was going right back to New York," she recalled a year later. "If there ever was a moment when I was ready to withdraw from the campaign, this was it. If a Black was the assassin, who knows what ugly retaliation against Blacks might follow the shooting? Who would be the prime target but me?"

If anyone had ever doubted Shirley Chisholm's courage, her decision to go on campaigning despite the fear of assassination was further proof. She had already overcome seemingly insurmountable obstacles to rise in politics, and had done so the hard way, with a brash, uncompromising voice and a direct attack against the established political system. Since first running for the House in 1968, the year both Martin Luther King Jr. and Robert Kennedy were killed, she had received a steady stream of threatening phone calls and letters and had often observed suspicious figures watching her house in Brooklyn. For protection, she had relied on her private investigator husband, Conrad, and had kept a private schedule. But she didn't shy from her mission. In her presidential campaign, she went into the deep South, speaking from the courthouse steps in Marianna, Florida, where thirty-four years earlier the infamous lynching of Claude Neal had spawned a sustained riot against the town's Black community. Surveying the crowd and staring at the faces of many who were old enough to remember those events — some in tears, and others with raised fists — Chisholm spoke of unity and the need to bring together men and women, of all races, in equality and common cause. Later that evening, Wallace would speak in the very same town, with the opposite message.

But Chisholm's most extraordinary act of political courage was certainly yet to come.

As soon as she had heard that Wallace was ready to accept visitors, three weeks after the shooting, she left her office in Washington, DC, by car, joined by a congressional staffer and her new Secret Service detail, to travel to Holy Cross Hospital in Silver Spring, Maryland, where Wallace was recovering.

Chisholm was determined to pay a healing visit to the man whom Reverend Martin Luther King Jr. had once called "the most dangerous racist in America."

Wallace had survived the shooting and a five-hour operation to remove a bullet. But one bullet remained lodged next to his spine. His legs were paralyzed, and he would never walk again. His convalescence would be difficult.

Chisholm arrived at the hospital unannounced. As she made her way to Wallace's room, she found him propped up weakly in bed, tubes running into his nose and his arms.

Wallace looked at her in utter surprise. "Shirley Chisholm, what are you doing here? You shouldn't be here," he said.

Politically, he was right.

Chisholm, however, was not there for political purposes. True, she and Wallace had gained mutual respect on the campaign trail, a fact that most observers at that time could not comprehend. But she had come as an act of basic humanity. And because, she believed, it was the right thing to do.

Many of her supporters vehemently disagreed.

The media carried news of her visit widely. And as the country learned of her shocking visit to Wallace's hospital room, the backlash was immediate and fierce. Much of the country simply could not understand why Chisholm, a widely respected symbol of African American political success, would offer comfort to one of the nation's most notorious racial separatists. Some of her strongest supporters quickly turned against her in the heat of the revelation. When she returned home to Brooklyn, her constituents expressed a level of rage that made her seriously fear losing reelection to her seat in Congress.

But Chisholm didn't apologize. And neither would she back down.

Instead, she explained to all who would listen what she believed was right. Back in Brooklyn, she soon attended a raucous community meeting, the room filled with angry faces. Some constituents were confused and upset. Others were furious. As she stood up, barely five feet tall, impeccably dressed in a bright, modish suit, she delivered her views in a strong, distinctive, clearly enunciated voice, as blunt and direct as a hammer. She would give her honest reasons for showing sympathy to her adversary and then let her neighbors decide.

Chisholm was an icon, and in the fifty years since, has grown into a legend, personifying the courage and self-assuredness that her day demanded of a person who insisted on taking their share of power in society. She established that image herself, and it was an accurate one, with her slogan emblazoned on the side of the cars and sound trucks that campaigned for her on the bustling streets of Brooklyn: Fighting Shirley Chisholm: Unbought and Unbossed. But Chisholm was also more than a fighter, as her compassionate visit to Wallace demonstrated. She was a woman of principle who saw good in every person and believed equality would benefit all. And she had the courage to speak and act on her beliefs, regardless of the consequences.

A few years before her death in 2005, Chisholm said, "I want history to remember me, not that I was the first Black woman to be elected to the Congress, not as the first Black woman to have made a bid for the presidency of the United States, but as a Black woman who lived in the twentieth century and who dared to be herself. I want to be remembered as a catalyst for change in America."

Where did that daring come from?

Chisholm suggested that she was born brave, writing an autobiography penned before she finished her first term in Congress. Describing herself before age three, she wrote, "I learned to walk and talk very early. By the time I was two and a half, not bigger than a mite . . . I was already dominating other children around me—with my mouth. I lectured them and ordered them around. Even Mother was almost afraid of me."

Partly because Shirley and her two younger sisters were too much to handle for their parents, who were struggling to survive as recent immigrants in Brooklyn, they were sent to their mother's childhood home in Barbados, to live on a farm with their grandparents. Chisholm credited her upbringing there for her outlook on life. In the late 1920s and early 1930s, schooling was rigorous and strict, church attendance frequent, farm chores required, and behavioral expectations high. Chisholm recalled learning her work ethic and sense of dignity from her beloved grandmother, a stately, powerfully voiced woman, who made her stand and recite her homework every night, saying, "Child, you got to stand up straight, let the world see you coming"—perhaps the reason she stood ramrod erect her whole life. Her grandmother was, Chisholm later wrote, "One of the few persons whose authority I would never dare to defy, or even question." Chisholm felt loved in her joyous life on the farm and island, where the barefoot girls roamed free and swam in the ocean.

She gained virtually no awareness of racial discrimination as a child in Barbados. Not until her parents brought the girls back to Brooklyn, seven years later, did she first encounter racial slurs and overt discrimination. Adapting to city life after her idyllic childhood in Barbados was difficult for Chisholm, and for her family. Her mother, Ruby St. Hill, worked as a seamstress. Her father, Charles, a self-taught intellectual, grew thick calluses laboring in a burlap bag factory, where he worked until the day he died. They devoted themselves to advancing their daughters. Ruby ensured the girls worked hard in school, took them to church three times every Sunday, and kept them away from the social world, especially the gifted Shirley, who attended an elite public high school. Charles, an avid reader and follower of Black political movements, brought home male associates of his for evening philosophical and political discussions. Shirley, as his favorite, was expected to contribute as they debated late into the night. It was during those discussions that she came to believe in working within the system, with faith in the unrealized potential of America's founding ideals. But she also knew persuasion and patience would never be enough. Among her favorite quotes was one by Frederick Douglass: "Power concedes nothing without a struggle."

Chisholm's success in high school brought her college scholarships to elite private schools, including Vassar and Oberlin. But her parents persuaded her that, even with tuition waived, her living expenses would be too much. And so, she attended the free, public Brooklyn College and stayed at home. She would later conclude that the choice set her course in life. For instead of being potentially diverted from the cause of justice by attaining middle-class comfort, she spent her time with other students like herself, deepening her understanding of racial issues, poverty, and the societal gaps on full display in the community. She volunteered for several community organizations and formed a sorority, as African American students were not allowed in campus social clubs. She had always excelled in debate, having won a citywide competition at the early age of fourteen (Eleanor Roosevelt gave her the prize and encouraged her), but didn't dream of public service until an exchange with her favorite professor and mentor, Louis Warsoff, whom Chisholm called "one of the first White men whom I ever really knew and trusted." After a big debate win, he said, "You ought to go into politics." Chisholm shot back that he was naïve to think a Black woman could be elected to anything. But he gently countered, "You really have deep feelings about that, haven't you?"

A seed grew in Chisholm's mind. From then on, she would ponder how she could use her own life to fulfill the goal of political participation.

After graduating from college in 1946, Chisholm chose the only career open to her, education, working at a Harlem child care center while earning a master's degree in children's education at Columbia University. At the same time, she dove into the politics of the New York machine system. And eventually, the key to her rise would come from taking over the political organization of her Bedford-Stuyvesant neighborhood—a process that would take fifteen long years.

At the time, New York's political clubs controlled the dominant Democratic Party by offering services to poor people in need. At evening meetings, residents could come in to meet a lawyer or receive assistance with a government agency in exchange for their support of the club and its candidates. In the late 1940s, when Chisholm became active, none of the clubs or candidates were African American. In fact, New York City had no Black elected officials at the city, state, or national levels, and few women, who typically served in clerical roles at the neighborhood level of the political clubs, where they set up fund-raisers and managed administrative tasks but had no decision-making authority.

Chisholm was determined to change that. She worked in many community organizations while pushing up against the leaders of the club in her district. She learned her first lesson about working within the system when she was assigned to organize a fund-raiser with several other women, decorating cigar boxes for the center of each table to gather raffle tickets and cash. After winning praise for her crafting skills, she asked the other women why the men had provided no budget to put on the party. At a subsequent meeting, the women—mostly wives of committee members—rebelled, demanding funds to support their effort. After that, the women spoke up on other issues. The committee suspected Chisholm was behind the revolt, and in an attempt to co-opt her divergent voice, they made her a member of the committee and a third vice president.

It didn't work.

Chisholm, undeterred, kept raising difficult issues, pointing out problems, and demanding change, informed by what she learned at meetings of the NAACP and in her many other community organizations. Then, one day, she received a letter from the committee informing her that she was no longer a member.

"The experience contained lessons that were valuable over and over," Chisholm later recalled. "Political organizations are formed to keep the powerful in power. Their first rule is, 'Don't rock the boat.' . . . Power is all anyone wants, and if he has a promise of it as a reward for being good, he'll be good. Anyone who does not play by those rules is incomprehensible to most politicians."

Chisholm intended her own career as an antidote to that cynicism, starting at the bottom and using her own speech and conduct as her tools. With other activists, she helped start a competing political club in her assembly district, called the Unity Democratic Club, which included Black, Puerto Rican, and White neighbors. They recruited volunteers, canvassed neighborhoods, and convinced celebrities, including Eleanor Roosevelt and Harry Belafonte, to headline rallies. It took time, but in 1962, the club's slate won and took over party control of the district, relegating the old club to oblivion. In 1964, when the district's seat in the state assembly opened up, Chisholm claimed the club's endorsement, as the most qualified candidate, and as one who had paid her dues in her many years of compiling voter lists, carrying petitions, ringing doorbells, making phone calls, stuffing envelopes, and taking voters to the polls.

"I had done it all to help other people get elected. The other people who got elected were men, of course, because that was the way in politics. This had to change someday, and I was resolved that it was going to start changing right then," she later wrote.

Chisholm won the race for a seat in the state assembly. And she completed her political education in four years in Albany, creating a popular profile—and big reelection margins—as an independent mind, defiant to party bosses, and yet capable of passing important legislation. She created a program to help disadvantaged students attend college, increased state funding for public education and day care centers, and passed bills to end discrimination against pregnant schoolteachers and provide unemployment insurance to domestic workers. She was lonely at times but didn't sacrifice her conscience, something she contended that her colleagues did with regularity when told how to vote by their leaders. She voted as she saw fit.

"Maybe I am just lucky, but being a maverick hasn't kept me from being an effective legislator," she wrote, while still in the midst of her political career. "One reason may be that there is a lot more to a party than its leadership."

She ran for Congress in 1968. The redistricting process had culminated in the creation of a majority African American district centered on her Bedford-Stuyvesant neighborhood. And Chisholm believed she could win. Other strong Black candidates also entered the primary, but she prevailed. After she won the first round, a famous national civil rights leader, James Farmer, was recruited to run against her on the Republican and Liberal Party ballot lines in the general election. It would be a difficult race.

Without much money and facing powerful political forces opposed to her, Chisholm told a *New York Times* reporter, "I am the people's politician. If the day should ever come when the people can't save me, I'll know I'm finished. That's when I'll go back to being a professional educator."

Chisholm researched the voter rolls in the new district and realized far more women than men were registered. And as her opponent's campaign reportedly leaned on gender stereotypes, she became confident that such antics would actually help her, not him. "The women are fierce about Shirley," said her husband, Conrad, as the couple sat with the *Times* reporter. "She can pick up the phone and call two hundred women and they'll be here in an hour. And she gives them nothing more than a 'thank you' and a buffet supper."

"It stings the professional boys," Shirley interjected. "All I have to say is, 'We gotta go to war.'"

As the campaign neared a climax, Chisholm rode the streets with a fleet of dozens of cars and her flagship sound truck, pulling up to the Breevort Houses, a public housing project in the heart of Bedford-Stuyvesant where thirteen hulking buildings stood in rows. Her armada had been roaming Brooklyn for weeks, with as many as fifty cars on weekends, all plastered with her Unbought and Unbossed slogan, and stopping wherever people gathered. At this stop, Chisholm climbed atop the sound truck while volunteers jumped out of the cars and fanned out into the gathering crowd with sacks of campaign materials—a biography and list of legislative accomplishments, as well as reusable shopping bags with her slogan, pens, and handkerchiefs. They passed out as many as two thousand of the packages at each stop. Chisholm took the microphone, her sharply pronounced words booming out from the speakers, across the asphalt, and bouncing back from the bare brick of the building walls beyond, as she announced, "Ladies and gentlemen of the Breevort Houses, this is fighting Shirley Chisholm coming through!"

To the reporter she later explained, "I have a theory about campaigning. You have to let them *feel* you." And that they certainly did.

Chisholm won her race. Her victory made her a national celebrity overnight.

At the Capitol, media deluged her office, and she was constantly greeted by passersby. But Chisholm was miserable, as she admitted only many years later. Some of her colleagues made sexist remarks, while others would not sit near her in the House dining room because of her race—a Georgia representative, she recalled, moved to an empty table, and openly gave her that specific reason. She maintained her dignity when she could. On the floor of the House, a member who was normally positioned near her pulled out a handkerchief and coughed whenever Chisholm walked by, which she didn't understand until a helpful colleague explained that the member was spitting toward her, into his handkerchief, each time she passed. Chisholm responded by copying him. The next day, wearing a dress with big pockets, she pulled out a handkerchief just as he was about to perform his insulting routine and spat in synchrony, at the same moment he did. She said, "Yes sir, beat you to it today."

A more serious slight came when Wilber Mills of Arkansas, the all-powerful chair of the Ways and Means Committee, assigned Chisholm to sit on the rural development and forestry subcommittees of the Agriculture Committee. Although she could address food issues on Agriculture, the two subcommittees were irrelevant to her district—and Mills knew it. Chisholm appealed to the Speaker of the House, John McCormack, who politely told her to "[b]e a good soldier." Congress in those days was organized almost entirely based on seniority. Newcomers, like Chisholm, were expected to keep quiet and go along with the system in order to eventually gain power within the established structure. And objecting was considered political suicide.

Chisholm would take the risk.

Ignoring her colleagues' warnings, she bulled forward with her demand to change committees, incurring the anger of the important chairmen above her. When they refused to make the change, she took her final option, to speak up at a caucus meeting where all Democrats would formally vote to approve the organizational arrangements. A friendly colleague explained how to make her case, but also predicted she would not be able to get the floor, as tradition held that senior members would always be called upon first.

Almost two hundred fifty Democratic members of Congress gathered in the closed meeting for the caucus vote. And each time Chisholm rose to speak, men more senior to her would jump up and get recognized first. After this happened several times, she saw some smiling and nudging each other. The fix was clearly in. And so, after half a dozen times, she left her seat and walked down to the well, directly in front of Mills, at the dais.

The meeting came to a halt.

Mills conferred in whispers with the House Majority Leader, Carl Albert of Oklahoma, seated next to him. Finally, he turned to Chisholm and intoned gravely, "For what purpose is the gentlewoman from New York standing in the well?"

"I've been trying to get recognized for half an hour, Mr. Chairman, but evidently you were unable to see me, so I came down to the well," Chisholm explained firmly. "I would just like to tell the caucus why I vehemently reject my committee assignments."

She delivered comments she had prepared. Pointing out that the House had only nine Black members, she argued the leadership had a moral duty to place those few in positions "[w]here they can work effectively to help this nation meet its critical problems of racism, deprivation, and urban decay," unlike the spot she had been given on subcommittees on forestry and rural development. "I think it would be hard to imagine an assignment that is less relevant to my background or to the needs of the predominantly Black and Puerto Rican people who elected me, many of whom are unemployed, hungry, and badly housed, than the one I was given," she charged. And then, she presented a resolution, directing the leadership to find a different assignment for her.

Surprisingly, the resolution passed. Her gambit had worked.

Chisholm would soon end up on the Veterans Affairs Committee. Afterward, however, her colleagues did not congratulate her. Instead, they expressed sympathy for what they regarded as her political death. Her defiance would, they predicted, mark her for permanent exclusion and irrelevancy at the hands of a vengeful leadership. She responded that they might be right. Perhaps she wouldn't serve in Congress as long as some of her colleagues. But "[s]ometimes somebody has to start trying to change things, start to say something, do something, be politically expendable."

Back in her district, early in her term, Chisholm gave roaring speeches about how she was standing up to the power of "the Man" in Washington. Her audiences loved it. She was angry and disgusted with many of her colleagues and their conflicts of interest and inactivity, calling senior leaders "reactionaries, bigots and mediocrities" and the Congress itself "drugged and inert." Addressing a group of Black women at a New York hotel after only a few weeks in office, she spoke with a rolling cadence of accented syllables, combining familiarity with her audience and explosive energy in her words. "Oh, everyone is being so *kind* to me. They have *such good* advice. They tell me, Shirley, you're just a freshman and you have to keep quiet as a freshman." She paused and stood back from the mic, allowing a ripple of laughter to pass through the audience at the idea of her keeping quiet. "I listen sweetly to them and then I say, 'Gentlemen, thank you for your advice. I understand what you're saying. But when I get up there on the floor of Congress, I'm sure you'll understand that I am speaking with the pent-up emotions of the community.'"

With a smile, she concluded, "The one thing the people in Washington and New York are afraid of in Shirley Chisholm is *her mouth*."

The audience exploded.

Still, Chisholm would quickly learn that what she said wasn't entirely true. They weren't afraid in Washington. Within months of arriving in Congress, she gave her maiden speech on the House floor, a scorching denunciation of the war in Vietnam and military spending that she believed was consuming the funds needed for programs addressing poverty. She concluded by saying she would not vote for any defense appropriations until that disparity was reversed. Chisholm later admitted that she expected a reaction from the House—in the movies, her powerful words would have been met with applause and colleagues gathering around to say she had persuaded them. But instead, she walked back to her seat in silence, and overheard one member say to another, "You know, she's crazy."

After less than two years in office, Chisholm came to the conclusion that she could not pass much legislation, and probably would not last long in Congress. Her real value, in her view, would be to help individual constituents as they navigated problems with the government, and use her voice nationally to push for change—and that, she did constantly, speaking at campuses and forums across the country. Politically, however, fighting Shirley Chisholm had met her match. She needed a new strategy. And so, to take the fight to the next level and spread her message wider, she astonishingly chose—a mere four years into her eventual fourteen years in Congress—to run for a higher office.

She decided to run for president.

Few expected Chisholm to win the presidency in 1972. The story of her attempt, however, has become legendary—of her courageous, disorganized, underfunded campaign, and how it opened the eyes of women, African Americans, and young people to the potential to speak boldly and change politics. Chisholm made it all the way to the Democratic National Convention in Miami, heard her name placed in nomination, and saw thousands of delegates erupt in cheers as she came up to a huge lectern and looked down over their sea of faces. "What I noticed most were the older black men and women," she later recalled. "Some were crying, and their faces were so full of joy that they looked in pain. I thought I could read their lives' experiences in their faces at that instant, and I know what it was they felt. For a moment they really believed it: 'We have overcome.'" That symbolic moment made the campaign worth it in her view. As Chisholm had explained, "I ran for the presidency, despite hopeless odds, to demonstrate sheer will and refusal to accept the status quo."

That was the fighting Shirley Chisholm, with inspiring symbolic power. But the fighting part of Chisholm wasn't all of her, or even the most important part of her service. For she was, like all people, multidimensional. Later in her career, she would accomplish a lot without fighting, pushing through legislation improving millions of Americans' lives and collaborating with politicians who had far different worldviews than her own. As she would say later, "belief in the right of another to hold and publicly advocate the contrary point of view without having his motives impugned and his character maligned seems to be a fundamental tenet of our political system." Indeed, Chisholm believed that, if anything, such "tolerance and mutual respect is fundamental to democracy's survival."

It was, perhaps, that same spirit, at least in part, that motivated her visit to George Wallace's hospital room in Maryland on that fateful day in June of 1972.

Wallace, for his part, was an unabashed admirer of Chisholm.

No one would have expected that.

He had made his name in 1963, with a nationally televised inauguration address as governor of Alabama, in which he shouted, "In the name of the greatest people that have ever trod this earth, I draw a line in the dust and toss the gauntlet before the feet of tyranny, and I say, segregation now, segregation tomorrow and segregation forever." Later that year, he stood in a doorway at the University of Alabama in Tuscaloosa to physically block two Black students from registering for classes, until President Kennedy forced him to back down by ordering in the National Guard.

School segregation remained a burning issue in the 1972 campaign. The US Supreme Court had ruled it unconstitutional in 1954, but by the time the Civil Rights Act passed, ten years later, 99 percent of Black children in the South still attended segregated schools. By 1971, the problem persisted, including in Northern cities. To address the problem, courts ordered busing to mix children among schools, which was met with intense opposition. In 1972, Florida put an advisory vote on the ballot over busing, further raising the temperature of the opposition. Wallace sought to convert that opposition into votes as he pursued the Democratic nomination for president.

Chisholm argued that the optimal solution to school segregation would be open housing—even as a member of Congress, she had been redlined out of buying a house in Brooklyn—but, in the overheated political environment of 1972, she believed she could not give an equivocating answer on busing while some voters living in racially segregated areas bemoaned potential harm to their schools. And so, in her stump speech, she would ask, "Where were you when for years Black children were being bused out of their neighborhoods and carried miles on old rattletrap buses to go down back roads to a dirty school with a tarpaper roof and no toilets? If you believed in neighborhood schools, where were you then? I'm not going to shed any crocodile tears for you now that you've discovered the busing problem."

As Wallace and Chisholm both campaigned in rural Florida, he heard what she was saying about busing and began to praise what he believed to be her courage and candor—a comment that, conveniently, allowed him to criticize the mainstream Democratic candidates by comparison. He said Chisholm was the only candidate other than himself whose statements on busing were the same in the North and the South.

She agreed.

Chisholm vigorously and vehemently opposed Wallace's views. But she also compared Wallace's candor, in her view, with what she contended was intentional vagueness on the part of the other Democratic candidates. Facing what many deemed a no-win busing issue politically, the leading Democrats had largely ducked, with hedging and vacillating answers. Chisholm charged hard against such inconsistency, and in her trademark style, contended that those muddled answers reflected what she believed to be hypocrisy on racial issues. Of course, one of her primary reasons for running had been to force the other candidates to take positions on her issues. And she wouldn't let up.

By the time Wallace was shot, he was leading the popular vote and had won primaries in Florida, Tennessee, and North Carolina. The day after the shooting, he won Michigan and Maryland. But with the assassination attempt, it all came to a grinding halt. His campaign ended, and his future became unclear. Three weeks later, Chisholm had nothing to gain by visiting him in the hospital. To the contrary, she believed she had already lost votes because of his praise in Florida.

She went to visit him in the hospital anyway.

When she visited him in his room, Wallace said, "Is that really you, Shirley? Have you come to see me?" The bullet in his spine caused severe pain as well as paralysis. They held hands.

Wallace began to cry. Chisholm started crying, too.

She said, "You and I don't agree, but you've been shot, and I might be shot, and we are both the children of American democracy, so I wanted to come see you."

Then they prayed together.

Doctors sent her out after about fifteen minutes. But Wallace did not want her to go. He briefly clung to her hands.

Outside, Chisholm ran into a waiting throng of media staking out the hospital. Although she had told no one she was coming, the visit generated more press than any other event in her campaign.

"It seemed to me that the excessive attention paid to what I intended to be a simple, private expression of human sympathy and concern was, in another way, a revelation of the same sickness in public life that leads to assassinations," she later wrote.

As Wallace had anticipated, the news hurt her politically. His image conflicted too strongly with hers. And given his segregationist record, many of her supporters could not understand why she would visit him.

Some deemed it unforgivable.

One of Chisholm's committed convention delegates, an African American from Texas, threatened to withdraw his support. Another supporter, an exceptionally talented college student in Oakland who had organized the entire campaign in northern California, was ready to quit when she confronted Chisholm. "How could you do that?" the young Black student asked her. "He's a segregationist and he's trying to maintain the status quo you're trying to change." Chisholm responded to the young woman with a wag of her finger. "Little girl," she said, "sometimes we have to remember we're all human beings, and I may be able to teach him something, to help him regain his humanity. . . . You always have to be optimistic that people can change. . . . I know people are really angry, but you have to rise to the occasion if you're a leader, and you have to break through and you have to open and enlighten other people who may hate you."

The young volunteer would later state that the lesson reenergized her. She kept working on the campaign and went to the Miami convention with Chisholm. And in 1998, over a quarter century later, Barbara Lee would be elected to represent Oakland in Congress, where she, over time, would become to many an icon herself. "What she said to me took root," Lee recalled, decades later.

In July 1972, Chisholm's underfunded presidential campaign came to a dispiriting end at the national convention in Miami. Though she received the votes of 152 delegates, the convention descended into a contentious fight that ultimately led to the nomination of another candidate, George McGovern. Later that fall, President Nixon would win reelection by a landslide.

Back in her Brooklyn district, Chisholm still had to win reelection to her seat on Congress. And the reaction to the Wallace meeting, potentially, put that at risk. She spoke to two large community gatherings full of angry voices, making the same points she had explained to Lee and others. Feeling her political future was on the line, she brought out her strongest voice and seemed to grow in height, determined to share with her supporters the good she hoped to cultivate in the same.

Many voters strongly disagreed. But their respect for Chisholm remained intact.

She was reelected by a large margin.

As Chisholm returned to Congress after the 1972 election, she appeared to approach the job in a new way, working to build coalitions and using the process to pass legislation. In 1973, she worked behind the scenes to pull together labor and women's organizations to support a bill to increase the minimum wage and apply it, for the first time, to domestic workers. And to complete the coalition, she called on an unlikely ally—George Wallace, who was grateful to her and eager to help. He contacted southern members of Congress to vote for the legislation and helped it pass. While President Nixon vetoed the bill, a similar measure would eventually become law the following year, in 1974.

The hospital visit had profoundly affected Wallace, according to his daughter, Peggy Wallace Kennedy. "Daddy was overwhelmed by her truth, and her willingness to face the potential negative consequences of her political career because of him—something he had never done for anyone else," Wallace Kennedy said. "Shirley Chisholm planted a seed of new beginnings in my father's heart."

A few years later, in 1979, some contend that Wallace showed how those seeds had grown. He entered a Baptist church in Montgomery, Alabama, alone but for an attendant rolling his wheelchair, and, sitting before the Black congregation, apologized and asked for forgiveness. He also made trips that year to apologize to civil rights leaders he had opposed. In 1965, as Alabama governor, Wallace had vowed to stop a civil rights march from Selma to Montgomery, sending state troopers who beat down the marchers on what became known as Bloody Sunday at the Edmund Pettus Bridge. In 1979, he begged forgiveness from the leader of that same march, whom the troopers had brutally injured: John Lewis.

Lewis accepted Wallace's apology.

In 1982, Wallace ran for governor of Alabama for the last time. Many voters thought his conversion was sincere. Others believed it to be blatant opportunism. The historical record offers few answers. What the record does show is that he won that final campaign, and according to some estimates, received significant support from the state's Black electorate.

Later, as a member of Congress, Lewis wrote about the experience in a *New York Times* opinion column. "The very essence of the civil rights movement was its appeal to the conscience of those who beat us with batons, attacked us with dogs and stood defiantly at the schoolhouse door," he wrote. "When I met George Wallace, I had to forgive him, because to do otherwise—to hate him—would only perpetuate the evil system we sought to destroy."

Chisholm contributed to many legislative accomplishments throughout the 1970s, working within the system. She advocated for the Equal Rights Amendment, legislation requiring equality in women's sports, federal support for day care and more, lending her political acumen and skills to secure passage of landmark legislation. She also became a mediator between interests to make legislative progress on support for struggling schools and community colleges, while working on many other issues behind the scenes.

Nearly a decade into her career, her service came full circle, when in 1977 she collaborated with conservatives on the Agriculture Committee—which she had once scorned—to rewrite a farm bill helping her constituents. Testifying for the legislation on behalf of the Congressional Black Caucus, her rhetorical strength shined through once again, as she declared, "There are still millions of Americans among us whose health and whose lives will depend upon how well we, as legislators, write and enact the food stamp program in the Ninety-fifth Congress. As long as we have impoverished citizens who cannot get enough to eat, or who cannot afford the kind of food which will provide them with healthy diets, then I do not believe that our national nutrition policy is sufficient."

Through the 1970s and into the 1980s, Chisholm became increasingly frustrated by the nation's political shift, which came at the same time as a long economic malaise that hit hardest at the low-income families she represented. Fights in Congress became defensive battles against cuts to food and educational programs. Usually, that defense failed. Meanwhile, 40 percent of adult males in Chisholm's district were unemployed. As Chisholm told a reporter in 1982, "When I go home on weekends, eight out of ten people say, 'I am not interested in what legislation you put in this week, I am not interested, Shirley, I want a job. I want something to do.' Then, depending on their level of frustration, some of them will curse me: 'You haven't done me any good, I put you in office.' Week after week, I hear this. Boy, it began to get to me. I got to the point where I didn't want to go to my office. It got to the point where I had to steel myself for abuse."

Chisholm also had become deeply enmeshed with machine politics in Brooklyn and deal making in Washington. To get things done for her community, she had, by necessity, become skilled at utilizing the system that she had once resisted and denounced. Liberal and African American allies criticized her as she advanced into leadership in the House and worked with political bosses at home, claiming she had made compromises of the kind she once condemned as cowardice. And when she voted with conservatives, or supported White candidates against Black opponents, they charged that she was betraying her cause for personal power.

Some of that criticism went back to the Wallace episode, as well as to her strong support for the appointment of Republican Nelson Rockefeller as vice president in 1974. After Nixon resigned and Vice President Gerald Ford became president, Ford appointed Rockefeller, pursuant to the Twenty-fifth Amendment, which required confirmation by both houses of Congress. Some Democrats believed Rockefeller should be disqualified because of his response to the Attica Prison riot in 1971, when he was governor of New York. But Chisholm, controversially, championed his confirmation on the floor of the House.

Chisholm also developed close working relationships with conservative southern members of the House, including her fellow colleague on the Rules Committee, Republican Trent Lott, of Mississippi, who would later state that he respected her courage, voting with her more than any other Democrat on the committee. Those relationships allowed her to be both independent and effective. Indeed, according to the former staff director of the Congressional Black Caucus, Dr. Barbara Williams-Skinner, Chisholm's relationship with Republican colleagues would pay off numerous times, including when securing funds for school lunch programs. "She had developed relations with some of the more conservative members from the farm states who she could go to, whom she wasn't meeting over an issue for the first time," Dr. Williams-Skinner said.

As she prepared to retire from Congress, in 1982, Chisholm remained proud of her friendships with Lott, Rockefeller, and Wallace. She said she had remained loyal to Rockefeller because he had shown her kindness when she was in the New York legislature. Lott was a helpful committee colleague, and Wallace had become an admirer and ally.

"I don't take one incident of a person's total life and hang the person with it forever," she told a reporter, as that year's election campaign for her Brooklyn seat progressed without her. "Just like George Wallace standing in the door of the University of Alabama preventing Black young people from attending . . . I went to the hospital when he was shot in 1972, and later he was the man who helped get the votes on minimum wage for Black women . . . I believe there is good in everybody. Maybe that's a weakness I have."

After she left Congress, Chisholm first taught college classes and then finally retired to Florida, where she fully disconnected from the political scene. It was there that she passed away in 2005, at the age of eighty.

In the decades that followed her retirement, Chisholm would be discovered and rediscovered by the American public and, in time, elevated as an icon for equality and justice. Most admirers focused on the early part of her journey, especially her groundbreaking presidential run, where her ability to speak truth to power had been on full display. She had been among the most eloquent speakers of her age because her honesty allowed her to be direct and forceful in a way many politicians fear to be. That, indeed, was the fighting Shirley Chisholm who inspired many.

And yet, her legacy is far more complex than that.

Chisholm was a fighter, to be sure. But she was also a passionate bridge builder, without regard for the political consequences. And at a time when the country was as divided as any other era in modern American history, she found ways, as President Abraham Lincoln so eloquently urged more than a century before, to appeal to "the better angels of our nature." Doing so often came with a heavy price for her politically and personally. But she did it anyway. For as she'd later say, "I'd like them to say that Shirley Chisholm had guts. That's how I'd like to be remembered."

9

Barbara Jordan

★ ★ ★ ★ ★ ★ ★ ★ ★

You cannot change the minds of even good men and women overnight—at least not on every issue. If you respect differences, you will also respect the ability of other thoughtful people to struggle internally with a problem and come to an answer somewhat different than your own.

—BARBARA JORDAN

On the evening of July 12, 1976, the crowd at Madison Square Garden in New York City was raucous. The delegates, who had gathered for the Democratic National Committee's Presidential Convention, had been mostly passive and subdued throughout the day. But the mood had changed dramatically as soon as one of the evening's keynote speakers walked purposefully towards the lectern, high above the boisterous crowd. As she stepped forward, thousands of delegates stood up and erupted in thunderous applause. Their sustained standing ovation was the longest of the convention at that point. Citizens, elected officials, and activists from every corner of the country joined together in cheering her on. There was, it seemed, not a single person in the arena who didn't know exactly who she was.

Of course, that made sense. For this was not Congresswoman Barbara Jordan's first rendezvous with history.

Two years earlier, she had given a speech during the hearings on the impeachment of President Richard Nixon that crystalized the legal issues of the Watergate scandal for many Americans, elevating a sober constitutional analysis above political theater. Her voice of profound dignity, authority, and indignation had, to many, embodied the deepest values of the republic. That speech had helped, at least in part, speed President Nixon's slide into resignation, just two weeks later. And it made Jordan an instantly revered and admired figure. Members of the media named her the best-known member of Congress while she was still in her first term.

Everyone wanted to hear what she had to say tonight.

Just before Jordan's appearance at the arena in New York City, convention organizers replayed part of her Watergate speech. The audience erupted. Walter Cronkite narrated the scene of cheering and flag-waving enthusiasm for a huge television audience, noting that the convention gathered to nominate the governor of Georgia, Jimmy Carter, for president, seemed to be coming to life for the first time.

Jordan stepped forward with a smile.

As she gestured to calm the excited throng, she began her keynote address by recalling the long history of the Democratic Party. Her opening sentences were not particularly profound. But her deep, almost musical voice denoted the importance of her words. She spoke slowly, drawing out her syllables with the drawl of her native Texas but sharpening their edges with the northeastern vowels and inflection she had developed during her time in law school at Boston University. As a child listening to Baptist preachers in Houston—her own father among them—she had picked up the rhythmic rise and fall of their sentences. That strict upbringing had also taught her to say each word with percussive clarity in her enunciation. A former colleague from the Texas state senate had once said of Jordan that she had "the voice of God." Jordan herself, however, understood her gifts as mere tools to do good work, and her opportunity to use them as the product of work done by others who came before her. She brought the convention to that very point as she finished discussing the one-hundred-forty-four-year past of the Democratic Party leading to that hot summer evening in 1976.

"There is something different about tonight. There is something special about tonight," she said, as if teasing the audience. "What is different? What is special?"

"I, Barbara Jordan, am a keynote speaker."

She finished that statement with a huge smile and a twist of delight in her voice that set off a wild ovation in the hall, celebrating the elevation of the first Black woman ever to speak in her capacity to a major party convention. The delegates roared with approval and satisfaction until she quieted them down once again.

"A lot of years have passed since 1832, and during that time it would have been most unusual for any national party to ask a Barbara Jordan to deliver a keynote address. But tonight, here I am. And I feel that notwithstanding the past that my presence is one additional bit of evidence that the American Dream need not forever be deferred."

The optimism of that statement continued throughout her speech, as she proclaimed of the American people, "We are attempting on a larger scale to fulfill the promise of America. We are attempting to fulfill our national purpose, to create and sustain a society in which all of us are equal." She spoke in visionary strokes, making broad statements that seemed to take in the entire country and all its people. But her goal was not to inflate her own importance, or even the importance of her own party.

Jordan was on a mission of healing. And she intended her speech to advance that cause.

The previous ten years had left America damaged, adrift, and severely divided. After the riots and political assassinations of the 1960s, the tragedy and loss of life of the Vietnam War, and the criminality and disgrace of Watergate, Americans' faith in their institutions had fallen to a new low. Jordan knew that. A convention keynote speaker in her role would typically be called upon to extoll the nominee and denigrate the other party. But Jordan would never even mention Carter's name. And her criticism of the Republicans was barely implied—in fact, she said more about mistakes made by her own party. Instead, with directness and utter confidence, she inspired and uplifted her listeners, calling for a new national community to reconnect Americans into a shared sense of purpose.

She called upon them to renew America.

"A nation is formed by the willingness of each of us to share in the responsibility for upholding the common good," she told her enormous audience, as it grew quiet with the weight of her words. "A government is invigorated when each one of us is willing to participate in shaping the future of this nation. In this election year, we must define the common good and begin again to shape a common future. Let each person do his or her part. If one citizen is unwilling to participate, all of us are going to suffer. For the American ideal, though it is shared by all of us, is realized in each one of us."

The crowd grew quieter, still.

The power of the speech made the audience less responsive as it neared its conclusion, as Jordan pulled the delegates into rapt concentration on her words. As she concluded, however, applause began, and then steadily rose, as those on the floor slowly realized they had just heard one of the most unique and important speeches of the century. The next day, buttons appeared at the convention calling for Jordan to be named the vice presidential nominee. Audiences watching on television responded with their sense of inspiration as well. Barry Goldwater, the conservative former Republican nominee for president, said it had been "the most electrifying speech I've ever heard." To this day, decades later, experts in rhetoric continue to study the speech, and identify Jordan as one of the greatest orators of the century. Indeed, in 1999, as the twentieth century ended, one team of scholars looked back on all the American political speeches of the last one hundred years and rated her keynote address as the fifth greatest, behind only the most important speeches of Martin Luther King Jr., Franklin Roosevelt, and John Kennedy. Her Watergate speech was ranked not far behind.

Jordan would be mentioned widely as a potential president after her convention triumph. One scholar identified her as the most famous African American woman in the country. But, just two years later, at the young age of forty-two, and a mere three terms into her nascent career in the Congress, Jordan did what many deemed unthinkable.

She retired.

Jordan was grappling with serious health setbacks, including multiple sclerosis, which she had largely kept from public view. And despite her great political power, she also had a burgeoning feeling of futility as one of four hundred thirty-five representatives in the House. She had worked a grueling schedule that denied her much time with loved ones, and her intense privacy kept most friends at bay, not knowing much about her or feeling close.

Jordan left at the top, leaving one to wonder what else she might have accomplished as one of the most talented speakers and skilled politicians of the country. When she died in 1996, at the age of fifty-nine, her primary claims on history were the firsts associated with her name, including being the first African American elected by Texas to serve in Congress and the first to give a convention keynote address.

But, perhaps most important of all, she was the first American with the nation's ear who successfully made sense of the dilemma of a president who failed to fulfill his constitutional oath, and to define the just consequences for that failure. At the time, she was only thirty-seven years old. And the historical record reveals, quite surprisingly, that her Watergate remarks had been barely planned and were nearly extemporaneous. But, in that moment, she interpreted the work of James Madison and the other framers of the republic in a way that citizens could understand and that cut to the heart of a crisis that threatened to break the political system.

Those words still resound as her living legacy, heard and used today.

As a young woman, Jordan rose rapidly in politics, and she expressed some annoyance at being regarded as a prodigy born with her talents. Instead, she had made herself a great speaker through study and performance. And she had perfected the craft of political negotiation while working cooperatively with lawmakers who routinely called her foul racist names. In a Texas senate where one member consistently referred to her with racial slurs, Jordan figured out how to work the system and its complex rules, becoming so powerful she won the ability to draw her own congressional election district, which then sent her to Washington with more than 80 percent of the vote. On the floor of the US House, her delegation insisted on standing with her as she was sworn in, with some members who not much earlier would have denied her the right to serve becoming obsequious attendants to her power.

Few people could have accomplished this.

Jordan's rise began at an early age. As a student at Houston's Wheatley High School, she entered speech contests, bringing home trophies to the school and standing in front of the other students to receive her honors. One oratorical competition that she won took her all the way to Chicago, to represent Texas in a national speech-making event. She won that national contest, too. Returning to Houston, a reporter for a local newspaper, the *Houston Informer*, wrote an article about her. She told him, "It's only a milestone I've passed; it's just the beginning."

In 1952, Jordan's ambition to become a lawyer brought her to Texas Southern University (TSU), which the state had founded five years earlier to avoid having to allow African Americans to attend the University of Texas. The talented debate coach there, Tom Freeman, had seen her on stage in high school and recruited Jordan onto a team that became legendary, with her as one of its two stars. After defeating the local competition, the TSU students traveled to the northeast to take on students at the nation's most famous universities. Jordan was surprised to find them no smarter—and many not as talented—as her own classmates. The team was so successful that Harvard University brought its debate team to Texas to face off. They ended in a draw.

Traveling the country exposed Jordan to discrimination she hadn't experienced in her early life. To leave the South, the team had to drive great distances, because no hotel would allow them to stay, and at bathroom breaks they would be directed to outhouses behind service stations rather than the bathrooms indoors. But in the North, the team could eat in any restaurant they could afford. In 1954, when the US Supreme Court ruled school segregation unconstitutional, Jordan witnessed the heavy backlash in Texas, including ten pro-segregation bills introduced in the legislature, which a young legislator named Henry Gonzalez would famously filibuster in the state senate. By the time she graduated from college, she later wrote, "I woke to the necessity that someone had to push integration along in a private way if it were ever going to come."

Jordan attended law school at Boston University—barely able to afford tuition and barely passing due to what she contended was poor preparation in her segregated Texas school, aside from the stellar debate coach there. The experience transformed her, beyond adding the Boston edge to her voice. "I was doing sixteen years of remedial work in thinking," she later recalled. "You had to think and read and understand and reason. I really cannot describe what that did to my insides and to my head. I thought: *I'm being educated finally.*"

After graduating, as a new lawyer she set up her own law practice at her parents' kitchen table back in Texas, handling wills, divorces, and other basic neighborhood legal matters. But she found none of it interesting, much less challenging.

Jordan's real energy went into politics.

In the fall of 1960, she walked into the downtown Houston campaign office for John Kennedy and Lyndon Johnson. There, she met the liberal Democratic activists who controlled the party in the county and who had already racially integrated their ranks. The group's leader quickly recognized Jordan's talent—she already had the voice, air of authority, and physical presence that would either inspire or intimidate others throughout her life—and she was assigned to work in various precincts, canvassing and organizing voters to turn out. But the party discovered her greatest contribution by chance, when a speaker scheduled to talk at a Black church became ill and had to cancel.

"I was selected to do the pitch," Jordan recalled. "I was startled with the impact I had on people. Those people were just as turned on and excited as if some of the head candidates had been there to talk about the issues. When I got back to the local headquarters that night—we would usually close up about twelve or one o'clock—they said, 'Look, we are going to take you off the [mailing] lists and the envelopes and put you on the speaking circuit.'"

At twenty-four years old, Jordan became a key campaign asset. She spoke not only to every African American church and civic organization, but also to workers of all races gathered in union halls and Democratic organizations across the city. And she motivated Kennedy's supporters to do more—to get out the vote. When the Democratic ticket narrowly won Texas, and with its electoral votes barely won the White House, Jordan could justifiably take some of the credit for the extraordinary turnout in the Houston precincts where she had worked. And in that process, she had become a local political rising star with a future of her own.

Jordan lost races for the state house shortly thereafter, in 1962 and 1964, running under an electoral system that was designed to reduce urban voting power. In 1965, however, a judge ordered redistricting, and in 1966, she easily won a state senate seat representing Houston's African American core, where she was already the most popular political leader. Community leaders felt profound pride to send the first African American and the only woman to the state senate. However, they didn't expect her to accomplish much there, recalled one local leader, the head of the YMCA at the time. Many saw the upper chamber as the state's most exclusive and wealthy private club. Jordan and the small bloc of liberal Democrats elected that year would face long odds.

But Jordan approached the challenge much the same way she would take on obstacles throughout her life. She figured out the system.

In this case, that meant studying meticulously the arcane rules of the body. One day, utilizing a confusing parliamentary maneuver, she nearly passed an anti-pollution bill. When the state senate's previous master of the rules—State Senator Dorsey Hardeman, the most influential member of the body, and among its most conservative members— asked what she was doing, Jordan told him, "It's simple, I'm using the tricker's trick." She recalled his response. "Hardeman could not contain his appreciation for what I was doing, nor his mirth." Jordan and Hardeman were soon fast friends, working together on issues on the state senate floor and enjoying drinks together after session.

Some credited Jordan's success to, in large part, her not aligning solidly with her liberal colleagues, instead remaining mostly a free agent who could work with anyone. And, sometimes, she gave her vote to conservatives, with strings attached. "I was not coming carrying the flag and singing 'We Shall Overcome.' I was coming to work," she later recalled. Her strategy contributed to one of the successes of which she was most proud.

A bill was advancing that would have restricted voter registration. To keep it from reaching the floor, Jordan needed the votes of eleven state senators, including hers. "I made a list of ten senators who were in my political debt," she later explained. "I went to each one and said I was calling in my chit."

When she met the sponsor to tell him, he admitted, "I, too, can count; the bill is dead, Barbara."

Jordan made her politics work by managing relationships in the Capitol. Her personality was private and reserved; indeed, many people who met her found her to be icily efficient. But she knew how to rise to the occasion. At one political dinner dance for senators held annually, the prospect of inviting an African American woman to the event created a panic behind the scenes. But, of course, "[w]ithin three minutes after she arrived, she was at the center," recalled state senator Don Kennard, who had joined her at the dinner. "Just by being so gracious and charming she literally compelled even the biggest racists to be gracious and charming, too. . . . She didn't make them feel evil or guilty." Jordan's reputation rose quickly, and she became the consummate insider, joining her colleagues in late-night meetings that featured poker, scotch, and political deals.

By the time she had been in the state senate three years, Jordan was a power player—a good friend of both the governor and lieutenant governor and serving in many important committee roles. In one of those roles, as vice chair of the redistricting committee, she would draw the lines for a new congressional district required by the 1970 census. Liberal colleagues complained, however, that she didn't push hard enough for their causes. Students criticized her, too, especially after she served on a state senate committee that produced what critics labeled a weak report about problems at a Black college that had led to protests and a riot. But Jordan's strategy of working within the system was bearing fruit. Her success and positive reports from conservative Democrats in Texas reached all the way to the president of the United States, Lyndon Johnson, who had been their leader before becoming the nation's chief executive. And he became key to her further rise.

Johnson was in trouble late in his second term, his popularity damaged by the Vietnam War and pushback over civil rights. In February 1967, he called a meeting of the nation's top civil rights leaders to the White House. Jordan was astonished to receive a telegram requesting her attendance. She made the journey to Washington. And she sat, awestruck, at a table with President Johnson and many of the most important figures in the civil rights struggle.

As the president outlined his legislative program on civil rights and called for opinions, he turned to her. "Barbara, what do you think?" the president asked.

She was so flustered she could barely remember what she said.

But President Johnson was impressed.

A week later, the White House planted a positive mention of her performance at the meeting in a national newspaper column. Johnson liked her and came to consider her a friend. And in part, he felt some responsibility for her success, since the Voting Rights Act he had championed and signed into law in 1965 had helped enable her political career. Johnson's press secretary, George Christian, would later recall that "President Johnson was just proud of her. Pure and simple. He used to brag about her whenever he got a chance."

When Johnson traveled to Texas to speak, he insisted Jordan introduce him. And when she ran for Congress in 1972, he headlined a fund-raiser. She won a resounding victory.

In Washington, members of the Congressional Black Caucus formulated a strategy to place her on the Armed Services Committee, where they did not have a member. But former President Johnson had other plans. He told her she belonged on the Judiciary Committee. And he called the right people to make it happen. In fact, one of those calls interrupted Arkansas Representative Wilber Mills on his fishing vacation. The powerful Ways and Means chair, who had tried to assign her colleague, Shirley Chisholm, to the Agriculture Committee, gave Jordan first seniority among freshmen on Judiciary.

Several Black Caucus members weren't happy about Jordan's choice of committee. Nor were they pleased with her vote for Carl Albert as Speaker of the House, rather than the caucus's protest vote for an African American candidate. But Jordan didn't suffer much from her colleagues' disapproval. She had arrived in the Congress with her own clout. And even those who initially disliked Jordan's style would, ultimately, concede she was effective. As one Democratic caucus member said at the time, those who "had been running things in Washington for decades, are now bowing and scraping to Barbara. . . . They can't help noticing her, not just because she's Black and a woman, but mainly because they knew she's so much smarter than most of them and there's no way they can pull the wool over her eyes on *anything*. Whether they like her or not, they've got to respect her, and in Washington your contacts and the respect you get are mighty important things."

Jordan's maiden speech protested President Nixon's impoundment of appropriated funds, with which he disbanded the Office of Economic Opportunity and programs for health, housing, and education. She charged his action was unconstitutional. Further, the Democratic leadership in the House had, in her view, dragged its feet to respond to Nixon's order. And so, Jordan helped mount a protest of freshmen on the House floor, coordinating a resolution and speeches. Her own speech cited the *Federalist Papers* to defend the balance of powers written into the Constitution.

"Those few words, encrusted with tradition, customs, and statutes over the years, provide the basis for two co-equal branches of the federal government," she declared, in her booming voice. "In 1973, this delicate balance has been destroyed. The president, flouting the Constitution, laws, and tradition is attempting to completely dominate all decisions about how and where the federal government is to spend money. . . . The president goes even further, however, by dismantling agencies and programs of which he disapproves. . . . I do not think that the Founding Fathers intended faithful execution of the law to encompass death of legislation by execution." The protest was successful, ultimately leading to a whole new budgetary process for the Congress.

For Jordan, it was but a preview of her biggest historic role.

In 1972, operatives for the president's reelection campaign broke into the Democratic National Committee headquarters in the Watergate building in Washington to steal documents and place listening devices. They got caught, and a week later, on June 23, President Nixon met with top aides to direct an illegal cover-up, including an attempt to use the Central Intelligence Agency to block an investigation of the burglary by the Federal Bureau of Investigation. A secret recording system installed for Nixon's own use captured the meeting. Investigations over the next year—by reporters, the FBI, special prosecutors, and the Congress—exposed ever-deeper patterns of political dirty tricks, lawbreaking, and cover-ups. Finally, in February 1974, the issue fell to the Judiciary committee, which the House had charged with reviewing the evidence and considering drafting articles of impeachment.

The nation was deeply divided.

No "smoking gun" evidence had yet convinced the majority of observers that the president was personally involved, and he had resisted subpoenas to release the White House tapes through a series of court appeals. His popularity collapsed in the polls, but still, most Americans did not believe he should be impeached. Partly, the scandal was so complex and layered that it was difficult to follow the different allegations and storylines. Many of President Nixon's defenders muddied the waters further by claiming he had not known about any wrongdoing other than garden-variety political hardball—not crimes. Besides that, no president had faced impeachment since Andrew Johnson in 1868. Indeed, there was little consensus as to what kind of action would even constitute an impeachable offense under the Constitution's vague category of "high crimes and misdemeanors."

The committee worked in secret to protect the reputations of those accused. Jordan reserved judgment, uncertain about whether the president's actions merited the ultimate punishment of impeachment, and further, feeling deeply that removing a president was an action too terrible to contemplate. But she took her task as seriously as any in her life, bringing to it her customary thoroughness and thoughtfulness. As the committee's lawyers gathered documents and interviewed witnesses—and as the president's lawyer presented his counterarguments—Jordan listened and read everything, including 650 statements and 7,200 documents contained in big black notebooks she locked in a safe in her office at night. She met with respected experts to understand how to define an impeachable offense. She read all that she could find about impeachment, including the previous impeachment proceedings against federal judges. She even went to the National Archives and lined up with the tourists to see the original parchment copy of the Constitution, a copy of which she already carried every day in her purse. And she read the minutes of the Constitutional Convention, the ratifying conventions in each of the original states, and the *Federalist Papers*. As the days and weeks passed, she sat back in her chair and listened, taking copious notes and forming her own ideas on slips of paper she saved together for later use.

Speaking to a reporter, she explained what was at stake that focused her attention so severely. Jordan didn't want to remove a president—but she felt passionately about preserving the Constitution and allowing it to live to fulfill the promises in it. "Listen," she told him, "I salute the flag, I get goose pimples over the National Anthem and 'God Bless America.' I don't apologize for it. I feel very keenly about the necessity for this country to survive as a republican form of government having as its supreme law a constitution which remains inviolate. I feel this quite strongly, and that is what's operating with me. The long-range hope I have for this country is that it will grow stronger and that everybody can feel that they're in it, that it really does belong to us. There are many of my constituents who are Black and are poor who still do not feel that this country belongs to them, that the deal they have gotten is sour. They feel they are just going to live every day the best they can until they live no longer. I want to see the day when we—everybody—can feel like we belong here, that this country has to survive because we have to survive, that our future is bound up in the future of the nation."

After months of study and testimony, the immense weight of the evidence moved Jordan and her committee colleagues toward the duty they would face.

In February 1974, the committee requested the audio tapes. Two months later, in April, the White House provided heavily edited transcripts, which later proved to be inaccurate. The committee subpoenaed the tapes. Nixon defied the subpoena.

And so, in May, the committee began all-day closed meetings to sift the evidence, led by its legal counsel. Jordan sat back and listened, but she was becoming convinced. "When we began to sift through this whole morass, this mountain of information, that is when it all began to jell," she said. "I can't point to any specific revelation which caused the mood of the committee to shift, but around mid-April, the partisan acrimony was reduced. People started to listen and make decisions."

By July 1974, the committee prepared to debate articles of impeachment in public. Chairman Peter Rodino, a Democrat from New Jersey, proposed giving each of the thirty-eight members a fifteen-minute opening statement before moving on to the work at hand.

Shocking her colleagues, Jordan objected.

The freshman legislator argued, earnestly, that the evidence should simply speak for itself. Of course, she got little support—indeed, her colleagues, she recalled, thought she was foolish for suggesting they pass up the biggest national television audience any of them were ever likely to have. The Senate Watergate hearings the summer before had arrested the attention of the nation in a way few political events had done before or have since. Seventy-three percent of Americans watched some of the hearings, and a quarter of people watched them for ten hours or more. With the conclusion of the long, painful saga in their hands, the House Judiciary Committee could be sure everyone would be watching them. Their job would be either to end the threat of impeachment that hung over the president or to endorse impeachment charges that could lead to his removal.

The committee would proceed with public debate.

A moment of decision would soon be at hand.

On July 24, the committee began its public consideration of the articles. The committee went in order of seniority. Rodino spoke first, addressing the packed room in the Rayburn House Office Building, where audience members had lined up for hours to secure a seat. Wall-to-wall television coverage brought the summer to a halt across the country. Rodino reviewed the historical context of the hearing, the facts, and the task before the committee. The ranking member followed, praising Rodino's statements about the committee's task—many Republicans noted Rodino's fairness and the bipartisan function of the committee— but then asked for a postponement until the Nixon tapes would be available. The Supreme Court had just validated the subpoenas. Instead, Rodino let the morning's business proceed. He would bring President Nixon's delaying tactics to an end.

As a freshman, Jordan's turn to speak would not come on the first day. And, at least initially, she truly intended to say nothing at all. In fact, she still had not talked publicly about her vote.

"I was still just reading my sources and trying to be sure that I understood the charge and the offenses," she later wrote in her autobiography. "I was not going to impeach Richard Nixon because I didn't like him."

As the long day of speeches wore on, and as people approached her in excitement asking about what she would say, Jordan eventually decided she had to clarify her position and say her piece. Her skills of oratory were already well known in Washington. A woman approached her to say she had done the math to figure out when Jordan's turn would come, saying, "I'm having half a dozen people come over to my house so we can sit there and listen to you." Television and the newspapers had covered every speech, picking apart the words and counting how many members would vote to impeach.

Jordan could not remain silent.

At the dinner break on the second day, July 25, at about 5:30 p.m., she realized that her turn would come that evening, after the committee reconvened at 8:30. She went to her office to decide what she would say. In one sense, she appeared to have left this important task to the very last moment. Other members had literally been preparing for weeks. But in a larger sense, she had prepared most of her life, developing her skills of judgment and extraordinary ability to speak, hold an audience, and help those listening to her to understand.

That evening, she went into her office with her notes and ideas written on slips of paper. And she told her staff—for the first time—that she had decided to vote for impeachment. She then asked her secretary to stay late to type up the notes she would give to her. As the time approached, she sat at her desk, assembling the scribbled notes, connecting them into larger thoughts, and then handing the papers to the secretary in the outer office to type. For reference, she also had a chart she had commissioned from her legislative assistant, which quoted impeachment standards from America's founders and relevant precedents, matching them one by one to the president's alleged offenses.

As 8:30 p.m. approached, an aide handed her the sheets of papers fresh from the typewriter.

The committee was ready to reconvene.

Jordan walked into the committee room, carrying her four pages of typed and annotated notes and the chart.

Her colleagues were already seated. The room was ablaze with television lights.

Jordan sat along the lower tier of the two rows of the committee's long desks, her bright red dress standing out like a beacon against the brown wood behind her. Under Rodino's direction, the room, with every seat filled, had maintained a solemn silence as the members spoke, without applause or other reaction to what they said. All the members of the committee were lawyers, and many used their time with speeches like legal briefs, reviewing detailed evidence that recounted confusing references to names and meetings on certain days, attempting to zero in on what the president knew and when he knew it, but those presentations likely confused many of the millions of Americans watching at home. Others waved broadly at the facts and simply gave their opinion of what they had learned.

Jordan's speech would be very different.

Her turn came third that evening, at about 9:00 p.m., coincidentally when the prime-time television audience across the country was at its largest.

Rodino called on her.

Jordan leaned over her notes, the white pages reflecting into the cameras from her glasses. In her crisp, strong voice, she began slowly speaking. Over the next thirteen minutes, she would explain the role of the committee, the demands of the Constitution and intent of the founders, and how the president's acts lined up with the specific words

handed down through time. And somehow, she would distill the investigation to its essence and place before America the gravity and simplicity of the choice to uphold its founding document.

She began by placing herself in the context of that day's task:

"Earlier today we heard the beginning of the Preamble to the
Constitution of the United States, 'We the people.' It is a very
eloquent beginning. But when that document was completed
on the seventeenth of September in 1787, I was not included in
that 'We the people.' I felt somehow for many years that George
Washington and Alexander Hamilton just left me out by mistake.
But through the process of amendment, interpretation, and court
decision I have finally been included in 'We, the people.' Today, I
am an inquisitor. I believe hyperbole would not be fictional and
would not overstate the solemnness that I feel right now. My
faith in the Constitution is whole, it is complete, it is total. I am
not going to sit here and be an idle spectator to the diminution,
the subversion, the destruction of the Constitution."

The room remained still.

In the next section of her speech, Jordan quoted Alexander Hamilton, the ratification conventions, and Woodrow Wilson to define the
purpose and standards for impeachment, summarizing those sources
by concluding, "Common sense would be revolted if we engaged upon
this process for petty reasons. Congress had a lot to do. Appropriations,
tax reform, health insurance, campaign finance reform, housing, envi-
ronmental protection, energy sufficiency, mass transportation. Pettiness
cannot be allowed to stand in the face of such overwhelming problems.
So today we are not being petty. We are trying to be big, because the
task we have before us is a big one."

Next, Jordan turned to the evidence. She referenced only two dates,
the date of the break-in, June 17, 1972, and the date when Nixon took
charge of the cover-up, June 23, 1972 (although, at the time she spoke,
the "smoking gun" tape concerning his personal direction had not yet
been released). She plainly stated that the evidence showed Nixon did
know of his campaign's illegal activities by that date. Then, in the final
devastating section of the speech, Jordan juxtaposed the criteria for

impeachment stated by the founders with President Nixon's actions. Four times she repeated the same pattern: the words of the founders, followed by the description of his misconduct, and then the founder's words, repeated once again.

Finally, she concluded:

"James Madison, again at the Constitutional Convention: 'A president is impeachable if he attempts to subvert the Constitution.'

"The Constitution charges the president with the task of taking care that the laws be faithfully executed, and yet the president has counseled his aides to commit perjury, willfully disregard the secrecy of grand jury proceedings, concealed surreptitious entry, attempted to compromise a federal judge while publicly displaying his cooperation with the process of criminal justice.

"'A President is impeachable if he attempts to subvert the Constitution.'

"If the impeachment provision in the Constitution of the United States will not reach the offenses charged here, then perhaps that eighteenth-century Constitution should be abandoned to a twentieth-century paper shredder. Has the president committed offenses and planned and directed and acquiesced in a course of conduct which the Constitution will not tolerate? That is the question. We know that. We know the question. We should now forthwith proceed to answer the question. It is reason, and not passion, which must guide our deliberations, guide our debate, and guide our decision."

When she concluded, the audience remained silent.

Rodino called on the next member to speak. And Jordan had no idea the impression she had made or if her speech had even been successful.

After the work of the evening was completed, she walked with an aide to an exit from the Rayburn building. As she prepared to leave, she saw an odd scene—her vehicle was surrounded by people. Not knowing their intent, she decided she would charge through the crowd without looking or responding.

And then, as she stepped out of the door of the building, a huge cheer went up. People near and far raised fists and waved. One person yelled, "Right on," while another declared, "I knew that when you talked, you were going to base whatever you were going to say on the law if you had to go back to Moses." The next day, letters and telegrams began pouring in. Someone set up twenty-five billboards along highways in Houston that read, THANK YOU, BARBARA JORDAN, FOR EXPLAINING THE CONSTITUTION TO US.

Jordan had become an overnight folk hero.

CBS News declared she had the best mind on the committee. The *Washington Post* reprinted her remarks in full. But the letters that arrived tell the story best.

"All of us who love the Mosaic of this precious land that is our own bless you for your Forceful, Scholarly, Eloquent and Epic statement of the case. Now you belong to the ages. 'Free at last.'"

Another: "I am not from Texas, nor am I Black. Probably I am best described as a cynical and disillusioned observer of the American political process. For the first time in quite a while, I am encouraged."

From an aged woman in Miami who said she watched the speech in tears: "I will die with renewed belief that there is still a vast store of honesty, truth and honor among the men and women we have elected to serve us—you have restored my faith in our government."

A hundred-year-old Black man from Texas, born during Reconstruction, praised her eloquence, attesting "I know you had some bad days to make it where you are today."

Many more wrote to say they had been convinced of Nixon's guilt. "This White, Yankee Republican would be honored some future date to campaign for our first Black, first woman president if you were the candidate. . . . Do not weary of your task. We need your honest, forceful voice." *New York Times* columnist Anthony Lewis summed up the mood. "The hope for national healing as we purge ourselves of Watergate was the stronger as the committee acted because we could see the process at work," he wrote. "To see the committee was to see ourselves as guardians of the Constitution, and that was strangely reassuring."

The committee voted for impeachment, with seven of the seventeen Republicans joining in voting for at least one article, along with all twenty-one Democrats, completing the committee's work on July 30, 1974. Public opinion turned in favor of impeachment at the same time, with polls showing support for removing President Nixon from office breaking above 50 percent as the committee voted. A week later, he released a full transcript of the meeting on June 23, 1972, which showed he had personally ordered the cover-up. The last of his support fell away.

On August 8, the president announced his resignation.

A new period of reform began for a vindicated Congress. Jordan played her part, as a busy legislator, most notably by helping pass improvements to the Voting Rights Act in 1975 and adding enforcement mechanisms for other civil rights laws. But she also became something of a puzzle to some in the later part of her short congressional career. Jordan had risen in politics through compromise and the studied accumulation of power, something that had never been given to her as a gift or by her demand, but because she operated within the political system better than most, on the terms that existed when she entered it.

But her Watergate speech had made her another kind of figure.

It had, in many respects, vaulted her to the Mount Olympus of American politics. Her fame came upon her appeal to conscience, logic, and reason, expressed clearly and directly, helping restore Americans' sense of patriotism and the people's faith in our system of government. But, with such fanfare, also came fierce criticism. For some of those who had not known her before, that new image failed to mesh with the reality of Jordan's pragmatic approach to lawmaking, and how she got to the place where she could make her famous speech. And Jordan would receive harsh criticism from other supporters who disagreed with some of her later decisions, including her work as chair of the US Commission on Immigration Reform.

Jordan would address her admirers and her critics alike in a speech made long after she left the public stage. After retiring from Congress in 1978, she worked for more than a decade as a professor at the University of Texas in Austin. And although still able to enthrall a huge audience—as she did at the 1992 Democratic National Convention in New York City that nominated Bill Clinton for president—she led a private life, struggling with declining health and confined to a wheelchair. From that vantage point, looking back, she spoke in Chicago to a group of philanthropists.

"It is dangerous to enter the struggle to establish a civil society as a purist if, as a purist, you are unwilling to take in others and be flexible," she explained. "You can have principles that are at the core of your position: we don't kill, we don't maim, we respect the dignity of the individual, and it is essential that we hate bigotry and intolerance. And on these principles, I certainly advocate a purist position. But there are times when you must get off the purist position if you are going to come to a consensus or resolution of the issues. You cannot change the minds of even good men and women overnight—at least not on every issue. If you respect differences, you will also respect the ability of other thoughtful people to struggle internally with a problem and come to an answer somewhat different than your own."

Her defense of the Constitution was one of those principles that Jordan never did compromise. As she told the nation in her Watergate speech, "My faith in the Constitution is whole, it is complete, it is total." And on the day she died in 1996, when her loved ones opened her purse to take out her personal effects, they found her copy of the Constitution still there.

Faithful to the end.

Epilogue

On the morning of May 17, 2022, I attended a rare Joint Session of Congress, convened in the House chamber and presided over by the vice president and the Speaker of the House. My colleagues and I had gathered together to hear from the prime minister of the Hellenic Republic (otherwise known as Greece), Kyriakos Mitsotakis. The session included all the time-honored formality typically accorded a head of state. But the most interesting part of the session that day was not the pomp and circumstance.

The prime minister's address was, in a word, captivating. And I found the insights he shared about the potential fate of democratic republics across the globe—including our own—to be particularly compelling. Perhaps that was because I was fully immersed, at the time, in the historical record of the nine figures that I had identified for this book. Or maybe, it was because joint sessions now seemed to remind me and many of my colleagues of the most fateful joint session we had participated in—the electoral vote count the year before, on January 6, 2021. Whatever the reason, democracy, republicanism, and our country's destiny were very much top of mind.

Prime Minister Mitsotakis began his speech by describing the birth of democratic philosophies in Greece over two thousand years ago, and then, the rebirth of those same principles in 1776 on the other side of the Atlantic Ocean, when America's founders constructed our republic. "The birth of democracy in ancient Athens," he explained, "brought about an explosion of the creative spirit in Greece that produced the architecture, the art, the drama, and the philosophy that have shaped western civilization ever since." But, Mitsotakis added, "The establishment of democracy in the United States has brought about the greatest expansion of human freedom and human progress the world has ever known."

He couldn't have been more right.

I was deeply enthralled as he described the longevity and historical reach of the democratic principles and values governing our respective republics—passing like an Olympic torch, from its ancient parentage in Athens to America's founders, and through the many congressional leaders I had been researching for this book. I suspect that those Americans who watched Mitsotakis's address on television were just as impressed as I was. Regrettably, however, the Congress did little that day to display our commitment to the democratic ideals he applauded.

Fewer than a hundred representatives and senators showed up for the address.

The symbolism was ironic, and instructive. A Congress that had, over decades, largely ceded to partisanship and dysfunction by abandoning our basic work of debate and deliberation, with many speeches given to empty seats and C-SPAN cameras, had skipped a session for a foreign leader who sought to warn us about threats to democracy and the urgent need for its defense. Still, I was grateful to my colleagues who had attended. And as I glanced across the chamber, I saw many of them—on both sides of the aisle—listening carefully, reading their copies of Mitsotakis's words as he pulled the audience from daily political concerns to consider the foundation of the Constitution and the country that we were sworn to protect.

"I am more worried about the internal fragmentations of our democracies than I fear the threat of arrogant despots," the prime minister calmly warned, pointing, in particular, to the threats posed by social media and the like. "There are three major forces that collectively bind together successful democracies. Social capital, and by that, I mean the extensive social networks, with high levels of trust, so admired by Alexis de Tocqueville when he visited the United States in the 1830s. Strong institutions. And common stories—common stories that forge a unified national identity. All three are being threatened today, at the same time authoritarian regimes are questioning our ability to deliver prosperity for all our citizens. They are offering their people a Faustian deal: to trade political freedom and individual rights for high levels of growth and individual economic well-being. Many unfortunately are willing to accept it. These are some of the challenges we face today. And that is why making our democracies more resilient is such an important priority for our generation."

I agree.

The stories we tell can certainly make our republic more resilient. And as I sat in the House chamber, listening to the prime minister's words, I thought immediately of the nine people profiled in these pages. Their stories are part of America's national identity, and in many respects, reflect our country at its best. Each of them, patriotic citizens from very different walks of life and every corner of our country, who, somehow and someway, found themselves serving in the People's House. And there they mustered the political and moral courage to do what they believed was right.

Times have certainly changed since the days of Joseph Rainey and William Wilson. So have the challenges that America faces. Each generation is called upon to address its own unique challenges, some of which appear to metastasize just as quickly as we recognize them. But the stories of the public servants detailed in this book can inspire all of us *today*—in the here and now—to strive to tackle these obstacles head-on and to contribute to our great country during a time of such heated political division. And as we reflect upon the heavy odds these humble public servants faced, and the lonely battles that they waged— some successful, and many others not—we can keep our own hopes alive for national progress and the continual renewal of the indomitable American spirit that has animated our country since its founding.

None of the individuals profiled in this book was perfect. They all had flaws, and each made mistakes. A few were lionized in their time. Others were soon forgotten. Some were the targets of assassination attempts, which they barely survived. All of them were subjected to fierce and harsh criticism, including from their own allies and supporters. And each, at one point or another, experienced political defeats.

In November 2014, years before I was elected to the Congress, I lost a political race for the first time, a statewide campaign to become the secretary of state in Colorado. It was a close race, and one that I had believed I would win. Deeply stung by the loss, and with my six-year term on the University of Colorado Board of Regents quickly coming to an end, I was skeptical as to whether I would ever seek political office again. A few weeks after the election, a friend shared with me a quote from our nation's twenty-sixth president, Theodore Roosevelt, that I hadn't come across before. I wrote down his words on a scrap of paper, which I've kept in my wallet ever since, a reminder of the importance of civic activism and avoiding the fear of failure. For as President Roosevelt aptly observed over a century ago:

> "It is not the critic who counts; not the man who points out how the strong man stumbles, or where the doer of deeds could have done them better. The credit belongs to the man who is actually in the arena, whose face is marred by dust and sweat and blood; who strives valiantly; who errs, who comes short again and again, because there is no effort without error and shortcoming; but who does actually strive to do the deeds; who knows great enthusiasms, the great devotions; who spends himself in a worthy cause; who at the best knows in the end the triumph of high achievement, and who at the worst, if he fails, at least fails while daring greatly, so that his place shall never be with those cold and timid souls who neither know victory nor defeat."

Every person in this book was truly in the arena. They knew, all too well, the splendor of victory and the bitter pain of defeat. And the political battles that they waged—win or lose—all had one common element at their core: political courage.

As nebulous a phrase as that may be, one can see it clearly and unmistakably in these pages. For some, it meant making tough and unpopular compromises and demonstrating the political savvy to make unconventional allies in the pursuit of some level of progress, however small, for their constituency and their country. For others, it meant demonstrating the courage to convince their constituents to go against the grain of their own preferences in the pursuit of larger and loftier goals. And to others still, it required a fearlessness to take on powerful interests, and at times, their own political party.

While any political battle can be hard, taking on members of one's own party has perhaps become among the most difficult. We live in deeply polarized times. And when political leaders fail to demonstrate the moral courage to challenge conventional party orthodoxy, particularly when such positions are wrongly conflated with the truth, the consequences for any republic can be dire.

George Washington wisely recognized this fact. In 1795, he wrote to his secretary of war about a political conflict in Boston. "Much indeed to be regretted, party disputes are now carried to such a length, and truth is so enveloped in mist and false representation, that it is extremely difficult to know through what channel to seek it," President Washington wrote. "This difficulty to one, who is of no party, and whose sole wish is to pursue with undeviating steps a path which would lead this country to respectability, wealth, and happiness, is exceedingly to be lamented. But such, for wise purposes, it is presumed, is the turbulence of human passions in party disputes, when victory more than truth is the palm contended for."

The hyper-polarization that President Washington complained of has only worsened since he wrote of it centuries ago. Yet, there are still moments when our national conscience is shaken awake. When Americans are reminded of what it means to choose country over party. And what it costs.

When serving as a House manager during the presidential impeachment trial in February 2021, I had multiple opportunities to address the United States Senate. I was nervous every time I stepped into the chamber and took the lectern, but none more so than when delivering a closing argument on the final day of the trial. I had spent quite a bit of time—and many late nights—preparing what to say for my closing statement. To me, the facts were clear. And the law was even clearer. But clearest of all was the political courage that would be required of the Republican senators who dared to oppose the former president and concur with our theory of the case. Each of them was surely aware, as I was, that through all three prior presidential impeachments in American history, only one senator had ever cast a vote to convict a president of his own party.

The political consequences of doing so would be severe.

I had spent much of the trial sitting on the Senate floor. And occasionally, as I glanced across the chamber at the small, wooden senatorial desks, some of which dated to the nineteenth century, my mind would wander. I thought about the senators throughout history who had sat at those desks and served in the hallowed chamber, and the weighty matters they had debated. And I thought often about Senator Edmund G. Ross, in particular, whom President Kennedy had profiled, imagining him sitting in that same room among us as he cast the deciding vote to acquit President Andrew Johnson more than one hundred fifty years ago. One way to potentially convince the senators arrayed before us, I decided, was to try to dispose of the cynicism that has so corroded our political system, and instead, bring to life the kind of courage Kennedy had written about in his *Profiles*.

It was, to be sure, an idealistic approach, and perhaps a naïve one at that. Many pundits contended that political allegiance would win the day. And they would turn out to be mostly right. But my fellow managers and I refused to accept it. And we would put forth the best arguments that we could muster to combat that cynicism.

"I am the youngest member of our manager team by quite a few years," I said, "so perhaps I am a bit naïve, but . . . I don't believe their effort is going to work, and here is why: because I know what this body is capable of. I may not have witnessed it, but I have read about it in the history books. I have seen the C-SPAN footage, archives, sometimes have watched them for hours—yes, I have actually done that—and the history of our country in those books and in those tapes, the history of this country has been defined right here on this floor."

I then reminded the senators of the history that had occurred in the room where they were sitting: the passage of the Thirteenth Amendment, ending slavery, and the Declaration of War in World War II, on December 8, 1941. And I noted the courage of the individuals who had served there—people like Senator John Sherman Cooper, of Kentucky, a conservative southerner who cast his vote in favor of the Civil Rights Act in 1964, despite the political cost—a name I hoped would resonate specifically with Minority Leader Mitch McConnell of Kentucky, who had interned for the late Senator Cooper decades before. "We have certainly had our struggles," I continued, "but we have always risen to the occasion when it mattered most, not by ignoring injustice or cowering to bullies and threats, but by doing the right thing, by trying to do the right thing, and that is why so many nations around the world aspire to be like America . . . they look to us because we have been a guiding light, a North Star in these moments because the people who sat in your chairs, when confronted with choices that define us, rose to the occasion."

Referring to brave votes made by senators of the past—the kind Kennedy profiled as courageous—I then told the Senate, "There are moments that transcend party politics and that require us to put country above our party because the consequences of not doing so are just too great. Senators, this is one of those moments." And I concluded by saying, "I firmly believe that our certification of the electoral college votes in the early hours of January seventh, our refusal to let our Republic be threatened and taken down by a violent mob, will go down in history as one of those moments too. And I believe that this body can rise to the occasion once again today. . . . And the stakes—the stakes—could not be higher, because the cold, hard truth is that what happened on January sixth can happen again. [For] I fear, like many of you do, that the violence we saw on that terrible day may be just the beginning."

Ultimately, as we know, fifty-seven senators voted for conviction—well short of the sixty-seven required under our Constitution. Still, among them were seven Republican senators, each of whom did something that had happened only once before in the entirety of American history. They voted to convict a president of their own political party. And they had done so despite strong political headwinds and fierce opposition among their constituencies at home. While disappointed, of course, in the overall outcome, I was grateful for the decision made by those seven senators to choose country over party, which would surely come at a cost.

Others would pay a heavy price for making the same choice. My congressional neighbor to the north, Liz Cheney, represented the State of Wyoming in Congress and was the third-highest ranking Republican in the House when she broke with most in her caucus by voting in favor of impeachment. Months later, she lost her position in party leadership. And ultimately, her principled vote for impeachment and decision to serve as vice-chair of a congressional committee charged with investigating the attack on the Capitol would result in the end of her congressional career, as she lost her next primary election.

Many readers may agree with my view regarding her actions, and the actions of all the aforementioned public servants.

Others will surely not.

But the core question we must all ask ourselves is the same one posed by President Kennedy in *Profiles in Courage* decades ago: must individuals "conscientiously risk their careers only for principles which hindsight declares to be correct, in order for posterity to honor them for their valor?"

Every generation must answer President Kennedy's question, and must do so honestly, and on their own terms.

What we can say, with certainty, is that dramatic acts of political courage are rare. Otherwise, we would not note and celebrate them. And when those acts do occur, celebrate them we must. For they reflect a commitment and dedication to the Constitution that inspires every generation to demonstrate the same, as they rise to confront the challenges facing our country. The remarkable individuals described in this book remind us that political leadership means much more than doing what is popular or what the party faithful demand. For at its best, it consists of doing what is right—of following the dictates of the Constitution, and one's own conscience, even when those decisions may be unpopular and lead to censure or exclusion.

Our nation's second president, John Adams, once laid bare his "fear that in every elected office, members will obtain an influence by noise, not sense. By meanness, not greatness. By ignorance, not learning. By contracted hearts, not large souls." As he concluded plainly, "there must be decency and respect."

His fears ring true today.

In the frenzied political environment that we find ourselves in, devoid of nuance and empathy while simultaneously bursting with empty noise, a jaded cynicism and unhealthy skepticism of our ability to rise above it becomes all too common. We must fight that temptation. The public servants profiled in this book—ordinary people, who did extraordinary things—show us the way. With their strong voices, and even stronger hearts, they found the courage to speak truth to power, even when their political party, or own self-interest, made it far easier to go along with the prevailing view.

Every American has the capacity to do the same.

As citizens, we each have a solemn responsibility to contribute to this magnificent experiment in self-governance, gifted to us by the founders, to be guarded and protected by the generations to follow. The challenges we face are significant. And the odds may be long. But every time the United States has been tested, our country, powered by the courage and conviction of patriots, has ultimately risen to the occasion. I'm confident we will do so again, and that America's best days truly lie ahead. Of that much, I am sure.

Acknowledgments

It has been the honor of my life to represent the best congressional district in the country—Colorado's 2nd Congressional District—which stretches all the way from the Wyoming border to the cities of Fort Collins, Estes Park, Lafayette, and Boulder, and includes some of the most iconic mountain communities in America. And I'm profoundly grateful to the people of my community—for giving me the opportunity to represent them, and for all I have learned from them as I've endeavored to serve during such a tumultuous time in our country's history. The support of my wonderful community, and incredible family and friends, has been immeasurable.

Of course, I am most grateful to my amazing wife, Andrea, whose assistance in editing this book was instrumental. While Simon & Schuster's editing team was superb, Andrea's support, keen editing skills, and ability to curb superfluous verbiage remains unmatched.

Thank you to former Simon & Schuster Publisher Dana Canedy for believing in this project, and to Simon & Schuster Executive Editor Bob Bender, for his sage insights and unwavering commitment to seeing this book to its conclusion. To have one's book shaped by the same editor who previously edited the books of one of America's greatest writers, the late David McCullough, is a special privilege indeed. I also want to acknowledge the invaluable contribution of researcher and writer Charles Wohlforth, with whom I collaborated on this book and for whose assistance I am deeply grateful. My sincere thanks to Dana, Bob, Charles, Associate Editor Johanna Li, research assistant Julia Wohlforth, copyeditor Patricia Romanowski Bashe, designer Carly Loman, art director Jackie Seow, and the publicity and marketing teams at Simon & Schuster.

The Library of Congress is a special place. The largest library in the world, it has existed in one form or another since 1800, save for its destruction by British forces in 1814 (after which former President Thomas Jefferson sold his own library to Congress so that it could begin anew). As the library itself explains it, "Jefferson's belief in the power of knowledge and democracy has shaped the Library's philosophy of sharing its rich, often unique collections, and services, as widely as possible." My gratitude to the reference librarians and archivists there for all the meticulous work they perform to achieve that important goal. The extensive records of congressional proceedings and floor debates maintained by the library, some of which took place over a century ago, proved to be essential research material for this book. The Library of Congress truly is a national treasure, and it is my sincere hope that, having read this book, you may decide to make the trip to Washington and grace its halls.

I also want to acknowledge the many libraries, universities, and archives that provided critical research materials, including the Joseph Mark Lauinger Memorial Library at Georgetown University, the Jacob Rader Marcus Center of American Jewish Archives (which maintains the papers of Adolph Sabath), the Margaret Chase Smith Library, and the Dolph Briscoe Center for American History of the University of Texas at Austin (which maintains the papers of Henry Gonzalez), among others.

And lastly, I'd like to acknowledge one final person—you, the reader, for picking up this book. Deciding to read the book of any politician is surely a gamble, particularly in this day and age, when such books, like so much of our modern political rhetoric, are often designed to endear the author to those who share their worldview. I've humbly tried to do something different. Having come across such captivating historical narratives, which encapsulate so well the boundless American spirit, I decided, if given the opportunity, to follow the Library of Congress's credo—to share them as widely as possible. I hope you enjoy the stories as much as I've enjoyed telling them.

Notes

Prologue

7 *ever written in American history*: Many scholars believe this essay was written by James Madison, although the Library of Congress notes Alexander Hamilton may also have been the author of this portion: James Madison, "Federalist No. 63," in Alexander Hamilton, John Jay, and James Madison, *The Federalist Papers* (Project Gutenberg Etext, 1992).

7 *"any particular profession or religious faith"*: James Madison, "Federalist No. 52," in Alexander Hamilton, John Jay, and James Madison, *The Federalist Papers* (Project Gutenberg Etext, 1992).

9 *"we are all mortal"*: John F. Kennedy, "Commencement Address at American University," Washington, DC, July 10, 1963.

10 *"most heroic act in American history"*: John F. Kennedy, *Profiles in Courage, 50th Anniversary Edition* (New York: HarperPerennial, 2006), 115.

11 *"future guardians of the liberties of the country"*: George Washington, "Eighth Annual Message of George Washington, December 7, 1796," in *A Compilation of the Messages and Papers of the Presidents*, by Joint Committee on Printing of the House and Senate (Bureau of National Literature, 1897).

12 *"the same year that my parents came to the United States"*: *Congressional Record*, 116th Congress, 1st Session (June 4, 2019), 4293.

1: Joseph Rainey

No full-length biography of Rainey exists, but this chapter relies on, among other sources, the Committee on House Administration of the US House of Representatives, *Black Americans in Congress, 1870–2007* (Washington, DC: US Government Printing Office, 2008), which was also an important source for other chapters. For the political history of Reconstruction generally, the chapter relied heavily on the work of Eric Foner, and in particular, *Reconstruction: America's Unfinished Revolution, 1863–1877*, updated ed. (New York: HarperPerennial, 2014).

17 *"more welcome than death"*: Bertram Wyatt-Brown, "The Civil Rights Act of 1875," *The Western Political Quarterly* 18, no. 4 (December 1965), 763–75.

18 *the Civil War's 720,000 lost lives*: J. David Hacker, "A Census-Based Count of the Civil War Dead," *Civil War History* 57, no. 4 (December 2011), 307–48.

18 *secure its passage*: *Congressional Globe*, 42nd Congress, 2nd Session (1872), 3382–83.

18 *wisdom of his famous intellect*: Committee on House Administration of the US House of Representatives, *Black Americans in Congress, 1870–2007*, 31; *Congressional Record*, 43rd Congress, 1st Session, 2 (1874), 3413.

18 *"rights here as well as others"*: *Congressional Record*, 43rd Congress, 1st Session, 2 (1874), 3413 (emphasis added).

19 *"chosen advocate for freedom"*: The quote and those following from the speech are found at *Congressional Record*, 43rd Congress, 1st Session, 2 (1874), 3412–14.

20 *oratory skills and integrity*: "The Negro as a Ruler," *Georgetown Enquirer*, January 5, 1881.

21 *one of the six African American Congressmen at the time*: *Congressional Record*, 41st Congress, 3rd Session (1871), 881–82.

21 *financial success and status in the community*: Cyril Outerbridge Packwood, *Detour-Bermuda, Destination-US House of Representatives: The Life of Joseph Hayne Rainey* (Hamilton, Bermuda: Baxter's Limited, 1977).

22 *"possessed a strength of character"*: Packwood, *Detour-Bermuda, Destination-US House of Representatives*.

22 *allowing them no political rights*: Richard Zuczek, "Black Codes," *South Carolina Encyclopedia*, University of South Carolina, Institute for Southern Studies, May 17, 2016, https://www.scencyclopedia.org/sce/entries/black-codes/.

22 *nullifying the codes*: Committee on House Administration of the US House of Representatives, *Black Americans in Congress, 1870–2007*, 29.

22 *chair of the Finance Committee*: *Black Americans in Congress*, 62; George C. Rogers, *The History of Georgetown County, South Carolina*, 1st ed. (Columbia: University of South Carolina Press, 1970), 443.

22 *compulsory public education for all*: Rogers, *History of Georgetown County*, 443.

23 *political rights of all South Carolinians*: Ibid.

23 *committee itself was then threatened*: Matthew Lynch, *Before Obama: A Reappraisal of Black Reconstruction Era Politicians* (Santa Barbara, CA: ABC-CLIO, 2012), 132.

24 *"every sentence was pronounced"*: "The Negro Representative—How He Looks, &c," *Cleveland Daily Plain Dealer*, December 14, 1870.

24 *prosecute their attackers*: Committee on House Administration of the US House of Representatives, *Black Americans in Congress, 1870–2007*, 34–35, 64.

24 *"loyal men of the southern States"*: *Congressional Record*, 42nd Congress, 1st Session, 1 (1871), 102.

25 *act would be unconstitutional*: Eric Foner, 629–35.

25 *"the body politic of the South"*: *Congressional Globe*, 42nd Congress, 1st Session, 1 (1871), 393–95.

26 *"I earnestly hope the bill will pass"*: Foner, *Reconstruction: America's Unfinished Revolution, 1863–1877*.

26 *tamp down the violence*: Foner, *Reconstruction*, 629–35.

27 *mandated the desegregation of schools*: Wyatt-Brown, "The Civil Rights Act of 1875," 763.

27 *"exterminated in this country"*: *Congressional Record*, 43rd Congress, 1st Session (1874), 406.

27 *private conduct of Americans*: Wyatt-Brown, "The Civil Rights Act of 1875," 766.

28 *reincorporated into the democratic system*: Robert W. Burg, "Amnesty, Civil Rights, and the Meaning of Liberal Republicanism, 1862–1872," *American Nineteenth Century History* 4, no. 3 (October 2003), 43–45. See also Wyatt-Brown and Foner for accounts of these events.

29 *"this discrimination must cease"*: *Congressional Record*, 43rd Congress, 1st Session (1874), 344.

29 *precipitating a decline as well in his health*: Dennis Hidalgo, "Charles Sumner and the Annexation of the Dominican Republic," *Itinerario* 21, no. 2 (July 1997), 51–65; Wyatt-Brown, "The Civil Rights Act of 1875," 767–68.

31 *"at your hands, lo! these many days"*: *Congressional Globe*, 42nd Congress, 2nd Session (1872), 3382–83. These pages also contain details on the preceding events in the House, the number of amnesties granted, and the quotations and facts in the following paragraphs.

32 *devised a clever strategy to outmaneuver him*: E. Bruce Thompson, *Matthew Hale Carpenter, Webster of the West*, 1st ed. (Madison: State Historical Society of Wisconsin, 1954), 160–65. Thompson and Wyatt-Brown detail the events described in this paragraph.

32 *"where are the equal rights of the colored race?"*: Wyatt-Brown, "The Civil Rights Act of 1875," 769.

32 *gain enough support to go forward*: *Congressional Globe*, 42nd Congress, 2nd Session (1872), 3932.

32 *power to enforce its protections*: Foner, *Reconstruction*, 725–28.

33 *wake of his death, without amendments*: Wyatt-Brown, "The Civil Rights Act of 1875."

34 *urgent necessity for the Civil Rights bill*: *Congressional Record*, 43rd Congress, 1st Session (1875), 556. The entire exchange with Vance is found at this citation.

35 *"I will keep that oath"*: *Congressional Record*, House, 43rd Congress, 1st Session (1874), 458.

36 *accorded us without this enactment*: *Congressional Record*, 43rd Congress, 1st Session (1875), 343–44.

37 *essentially ending Reconstruction*: Details on the passage and results of the Civil Rights Act of 1875 are detailed in Committee on House Administration of the US House of Representatives, *Black Americans in Congress, 1870–2007*, 35–42.

38 *he was elected to the US Senate*: Foner, *Reconstruction*, 780.

38 *blamed the Reconstruction South Carolina government for the deaths*: The Committee on House Administration of the US House of Representatives, *Black Americans in Congress, 1870–2007* (Washington, DC: US Government Printing Office, 2008), 65–66.

38 *even larger body of his supporters descended on the scene*: Luis-Alejandro Dinnella-Borrego, *The Risen Phoenix: Black Politics in the Post–Civil War South*, illustrated ed. (Charlottesville and London: University of Virginia Press, 2016), 1–2.

2: Josiah Walls

This chapter draws largely on the only detailed biography of Walls, Peter D. Kingman, *Josiah Walls: Florida's Black Congressman of Reconstruction* (Gainesville: University Presses of Florida, 1976).

44 *Walls did not vote for the bill*: For a discussion of these events, each of these members' votes, and Walls's decision, see Committee on House Administration of the US House of Representatives, *Black Americans in Congress, 1870–2007* (Washington, DC: US Government Printing Office, 2008), 35–42.

46 *"the great sea of oblivion"*: For Walls's speech and the events leading to it, see *Congressional Record*, 43rd Congress, 2nd Session (1875), 2109–10; Appendix, 166–70.

47 *in any former Confederate state*: Joe Martin Richardson, *The Negro in the Reconstruction of Florida, 1865–1877*, 1st ed. (Tallahassee: Florida State University, 1965), 193.

47 *in another Virginia town*: Klingman, *Josiah Walls*, 6.

48 *often physically threatened*: Detailed discussion of education in Florida during this period is found in Richardson, *The Negro in the Reconstruction of Florida, 1865–1877*, 155–93.

49 *"only about six years ago"*: *Congressional Globe*, House, 42nd Congress, 2nd Session (1872), 808–10.

49 *stable source of funding*: Richardson, *The Negro in the Reconstruction of Florida, 1865–1877*, 154–93.

49 *lack of education remained noticeable*: Richardson, *The Negro in the Reconstruction of Florida, 1865–1877*, 283.

49 *near Tallahassee, 153 were killed*: Luis-Alejandro Dinnella-Borrego, *The Risen Phoenix: Black Politics in the Post–Civil War South*, illustrated ed. (Charlottesville and London: University of Virginia Press, 2016), 79–80.

50 *paperweights for the legislators' desks*: Klingman, *Josiah Walls*, 22.

50 *existing public school system today*: Klingman, *Josiah Walls*, 27.

53 *another election contest*: As noted above, Walls's biography, including the facts detailed in the previous pages, can be found in Klingman, *Josiah Walls*.

54 *"whose need is as great as ours"*: "Proceedings of the Southern States Convention of Colored Men, Held in Columbia, SC, Commencing October 18, Ending October 25, 1871" (Columbia, SC: Carolina Printing Co., 1871), Colored Conventions Project Digital Records, 48–49.

54 *unused federal buildings in Florida as schools*: *Congressional Globe*, 42nd Congress, 3rd Session (1872), 220; Richardson, *The Negro in the Reconstruction of Florida, 1865–1877;* Klingman, *Josiah Walls*.

55 *MacIntyre did not interrupt again*: *Congressional Globe*, House, 42nd Congress, 2nd Session (1872), 808–10. All the following quotes from this speech are found in these pages.

56 *the bill passed on its final vote*: Klingman, *Josiah Walls*, 77–78.

56 *Walls would draw the line*: The Committee on House Administration of the US House of Representatives, *Black Americans in Congress, 1870–2007* (Washington, DC: US Government Printing Office, 2008), 90–91.

57 *with rights for former slaves*: Klingman, *Josiah Walls*, 78–79.

57 *"at the hands of every lover of justice"*: Dinnella-Borrego, *The Risen Phoenix*, 84.

57 *he firmly declared*: Richardson, *The Negro in the Reconstruction of Florida, 1865–1877*, 292.

58 *as one reporter attested*: Klingman, *Josiah Walls*, 124–25.

58 *to become lawyers without passing the bar*: Klingman, *Josiah Walls*, 22.

58 *"most pronounced slave oligarchy that has ever existed among men"*: Stephen Middleton, *Black Congressmen During Reconstruction: A Documentary Sourcebook* (Westport, CT, and London: Praeger, 2002), 379.

60 *"past disagreements will be blotted out"*: Middleton, *Black Congressmen During Reconstruction*, 372–73. Each of the quotations from this speech on the previous pages is from this source.

61 *one other vote besides his own*: Klingman, *Josiah Walls*, 119.

61 *rendering some unable to operate*: Richardson, *The Negro in the Reconstruction of Florida, 1865–1877*, 194–96.

62 *such cemeteries were later destroyed*: The events described on this page and the previous page, from February 1884 through Walls's death, are covered by Klingman, *Josiah Walls*, 141–44.

3: William B. Wilson

The key source for Wilson's life, and this chapter, is Roger Ward Babson, *W. B. Wilson and the Department of Labor* (New York: Brentano's, 1919), with many additional details from John Lombardi, *Labor's Voice in the Cabinet: A History of the Department of Labor from Its Origin to 1921* (New York: Columbia University Press, 1942).

66 *to bring about that change*: Roger Ward Babson, *W. B. Wilson and the Department of Labor*, 1–15. The opening pages of this chapter rely on this source.

66 *"toward higher planes with more splendid ideals"*: Babson, *W. B. Wilson and the Department of Labor*, 4.

67 *"judicial mind than that of Secretary Wilson"*: John Lombardi, *Labor's Voice in the Cabinet: A History of the Department of Labor from Its Origin to 1921* (New York: Columbia University Press, 1942), 105–13.

67 *"that I have been fair"*: Babson, *W. B. Wilson and the Department of Labor*, 231–232.

69 *"cut on the back of my head"*: "A Scotch Eviction Led to the American Cabinet," *New York Times*, March 3, 1914, sec. v, 6.

70 *"under certain conditions"*: Babson, *W. B. Wilson and the Department of Labor*, 54.

71 *"order of the court to stop breathing"*: Babson, *W. B. Wilson and the Department of Labor*, 51.

71 *"'so take it any way you like'"*: "A Scotch Eviction Led to the American Cabinet," 6.

72 *a budget of millions of dollars*: Babson, *W. B. Wilson and the Department of Labor*, 55–56; Lombardi, *Labor's Voice in the Cabinet*, 85–89.

72 *"men and citizens"*: Jonathan Grossman, "The Coal Strike of 1902: Turning Point in US Policy," *Monthly Labor Review*, June 1974, https://www.dol.gov/general/aboutdol /history/coalstrike#54.

72 *"the property interests of the country"*: Grossman, "The Coal Strike of 1902: Turning Point in US Policy."

73 *Mitchell to visit the White House*: Babson, *W. B. Wilson and the Department of Labor*, 118.

73 *equals with their employers*: Grossman, "The Coal Strike of 1902: Turning Point in US Policy."

74 *None had passed*: Babson, *W. B. Wilson and the Department of Labor*, 147–50.

74 *"backing up [certain] Congressmen"*: Lombardi, *Labor's Voice in the Cabinet*, 61.

74 *And, surprisingly to many, he won*: Ibid. Wilson became the first Scottish immigrant to be elected as a Democrat to the People's House from Pennsylvania.

75 *"an account of my stewardship"*: Babson, *W. B. Wilson and the Department of Labor*, 125.

75 *"his conciliatory methods"*: Babson, *W. B. Wilson and the Department of Labor*, 124.

75 *before the Social Security Act passed*: Lombardi, *Labor's Voice in the Cabinet*, 81–82.

76 *office secretary and aide*: Babson, *W. B. Wilson and the Department of Labor*, 36.

77 *echoed through the House*: *Congressional Record*, 60th Congress, 1st Session (April 29, 1908), 5430–433. The account of the speech and debate over these pages rely on this source.

77 *a cross-examination*: Karen Poulson, "Historic Documentation Record Western Stone Company (Keepataw Site)" (Illinois Department of Transportation: Archaeological Research, Inc., n.d.), http://arch-res.com/pdf_files/Quarry.pdf.

79 *erupted into sustained applause*: *Congressional Record*, 60th Congress, 1st Session (April 29, 1908), 5430–433.

80 *an iron worker from Illinois*: Lombardi, *Labor's Voice in the Cabinet*, 62–63. This source covers the political situation leading up to Wilson's chairmanship.

80 *"economic conditions and requirements"*: Lombardi, *Labor's Voice in the Cabinet*, 82–83.

81 *"take root and grow"*: Babson, *W. B. Wilson and the Department of Labor*, 127.

81 *"cooler days of the autumn"*: *Congressional Record*, 62nd Congress, 2nd Session (June 10, 1912), 8863.

81 *didn't feel he had to block*: *Congressional Record*, 62nd Congress, 2nd Session (June 10, 1912), 8871–72.

82 *with a point of order*: *Congressional Record*, 62nd Congress, 2nd Session (June 10, 1912), 8877.

82 *"accomplish some good"*: *Congressional Record*, 62nd Congress, 2nd Session (June 10, 1912), 8854.

83 *"I would be opposed to the bill"*: Congressional Record, 62nd Congress, 2nd Session (June 10, 1912), 8866–68. This citation details the debate described between Wilson and Madden.

84 *job would actually come into existence*: Lombardi, *Labor's Voice in the Cabinet*, 75. The facts and details concerning Wilson's appointment rely on this source.

85 *"The Secretary of Labor is recognized for five minutes"*: Congressional Record, 62nd Congress, 2nd Session (March 3, 1913), 4804.

85 *morning of March 4, Inauguration Day*: Congressional Record, 62nd Congress, 2nd Session (March 3, 1913), 4831.

87 *those Palmer had rounded up*: Lombardi, *Labor's Voice in the Cabinet*, 336–49.

87 *his limited fame would suggest*: "W. B. Wilson Dies; Leader of Labor; End Comes on Train in South to the Nation's First Secretary of Labor," *New York Times*, May 26, 1934.

87 *"to their communities, and to their nation"*: Babson, *W. B. Wilson and the Department of Labor*, 240–241.

4: Adolph Sabath

This chapter relied heavily on a political biography of Sabath published in two articles, Burton A. Boxerman, "Adolph Joachim Sabath in Congress: The Early Years, 1907–1932," *Journal of the Illinois State Historical Society* 66, no. 3 (Autumn 1973) and "Adolph Joachim Sabath in Congress: The Roosevelt and Truman Years," *Journal of the Illinois State Historical Society* 66, no. 4 (Winter 1973). Also, a critical source for vivid details was John R. Beal's "Adolph J. Sabath," in *Public Men in and Out of Office*, ed. John Thomas Salter (Chapel Hill: University of North Carolina Press, 1946).

92 *"piqued, dissatisfied, and disgruntled"*: John R. Beal, "Adolph J. Sabath," in *Public Men in and Out of Office*, ed. John Thomas Salter (Chapel Hill: University of North Carolina Press, 1946), 203.

92 *questionable circumstances*: "Homage to Wilson: Clark Leads House Democrats to Seagirt Mecca," *Washington Post*, July 21, 1912, 1.

93 *twenty-fourth consecutive term in the House*: "Adolph Sabath Dies; in House for 23 Terms," *Chicago Daily Tribune*, November 6, 1952, 1.

93 *longtime political opponents*: United States 83rd Congress House, 1st Session, 1953 and United States Congress, *Memorial Services Held in the House of Representatives of the United States: Together with Remarks Presented in Eulogy of Adolph Joachim Sabath, Late a Representative from Illinois* (Washington, DC: US Government Printing Office, 1953).

93 *"always found a champion"*: Boxerman, "Adolph Joachim Sabath in Congress: The Roosevelt and Truman Years," 443.

94 *fifteen years old*: Beal, "Adolph J. Sabath."

94 *magistrate for criminal cases*: Remarks of Barratt O'Hara, in United States 83d Congress House, 1st Session, 1953, and United States Congress, *Memorial Services Held in the House of Representatives*, 32.

95 *stroke of good luck*: Boxerman, "Adolph Joachim Sabath in Congress: The Early Years, 1907–1932," 328.

95 *his career to public service*: Remarks of Rep. Ray Madden, in United States 83rd Congress House, 1st Session, 1953, and United States Congress, *Memorial Services Held in the House of Representatives*, 58.

96 *"I never in a Turkish bath perspired more"*: Beal, "Adolph J. Sabath," 200.

97 *"and I am one of them"*: Emphasis added. *Congressional Record, 60th Congress*, 1st Session (January 20, 1908), 881–82. Each of the quotations from Sabath's speech is found here.

97 *"oppressed people of the earth"*: Ibid, 881.

97 *where in the nation they lived*: Boxerman, "Adolph Joachim Sabath in Congress: The Early Years, 1907–932," 330.

98 *from Great Britain, Ireland, Scandinavia, and Germany*: US Census Bureau, "Historical Statistics of the United States, 1789–1945," using census.gov (1949), https://www2.census.gov/library/publications/1949/compendia/hist_stats_1789 -1945/hist_stats_1789-1945-chB.pdf.

98 *"increased year to year"*: Woodrow Wilson, *A History of the American People* (New York: Harper & Brothers, 1902), 212–13.

98 *courting William Jennings Bryan to come to his side*: James Chace, *1912: Wilson, Roosevelt, Taft and Debs—The Election That Changed the Country* (New York: Simon & Schuster, 2009), 126–32. Details regarding Wilson described over the following paragraphs are derived from this source.

99 *taken out of context*: Don Wolfensberger, "Woodrow Wilson, Congress and Anti-Immigrant Sentiment in America: An Introductory Essay" (Congress and the Immigration Dilemma: Is a Solution in Sight?, Woodrow Wilson International Center for Scholars, 2007).

99 *resolutions of denunciation*: Hans Vought, "Division and Reunion: Woodrow Wilson, Immigration, and the Myth of American Unity," *Journal of American Ethnic History* 13, no. 3 (Spring 1994), 24–50.

99 *His campaign was in real trouble*: Chace, *1912*, 136–37.

99 *little chance to win*: Chace, *1912*, 142.

100 *win on the forty-sixth ballot*: Chace, *1912*, 146–58

101 *"should be encouraged"*: "Homage to Wilson: Clark Leads House Democrats to Seagirt Mecca," *Washington Post*, January 21, 1912.

102 *"poison our minds against him"*: *Congressional Record*, 62nd Congress, 2nd Session, Appendix (December 9, 1911), 790–806

102 *"every promise he made me he carried out"*: Beal, "Adolph J. Sabath," 204.

103 *he came back satisfied*: Boxerman, "Adolph Joachim Sabath in Congress: The Early Years, 1907–932," 332.

103 *"some sixty or seventy percent of Turks"*: *Congressional Record*, 63rd Congress, 2nd Session (January 30, 1914), 2597.

103 *"who are across the Mediterranean"*: *Congressional Record*, 63rd Congress, 2nd Session (February 4, 1914), 2904–5.

104 *"despicable practices of these foreign countries"*: *Congressional Record*, 63rd Congress, 2nd Session (January 30, 1914), 2600.

104 *"have done for our country"*: *Congressional Record*, 63rd Congress, 2nd Session (February 4, 1914), 2904.

105 *"these immigrants to possess"*: *Congressional Record*, 63rd Congress, 2nd Session (January 30, 1914), 2599.

105 *"Fight of Sabath Futile"*: "Bars Up to Aliens: House Test Vote Indicates the Passage of Burnett Bill," *Washington Post*, January 31, 1914, 1.

106 *predicting he would sign it*: *Congressional Record*, 63rd Congress, 2nd Session (January 30, 1914), 2627.

106 *"a permanent home and a new opportunity"*: *Congressional Record*, 63rd Congress, 2nd Session (February 4, 1914), 2904–905.

106 *weighed in with their opposition*: Wolfensberger, "Woodrow Wilson, Congress and Anti-Immigrant Sentiment in America: An Introductory Essay," 10–11.

106 *the announcement was made*: "President Hears Immigration Views; 500 Men and Women at White House For and Against Burnett Bill," *New York Times*, January 23, 1915, 10; *Congressional Record*, 63rd Congress, 3rd Session (February 4, 1915), 3015.

107 *"restriction, not selection"*: "Immigration Veto Sent to Congress; President Rejects Bill," *New York Times*, January 29, 1915, 4.

107 *to support the president*: Ibid.

108 *"make this country their home"*: *Congressional Record*, 63rd Congress, 3rd Session (February 4, 1915), 3063–64.

108 *for it to be checked twice*: "House Upholds Veto of the Alien Bill; Friends of Measure Fail by Four," *New York Times*, February 5, 1915, 1; *Congressional Record*, 63rd Congress, 3rd Session (February 4, 1915), 3077–078.

108 *of people already in the US as of 1890*: Claudia Goldin, "The Political Economy of Immigration Restriction in the United States, 1890 to 1921," in *The Regulated Economy: A Historical Approach to Political Economy*, ed. Gary D. Libecap and Claudia Goldin (Chicago: University of Chicago Press, 1993).

109 *for over forty years, until 1965*: Wolfensberger, "Woodrow Wilson, Congress and Anti-Immigrant Sentiment in America: An Introductory Essay," 13.

109 *diplomatic decisions in support of the country*: Boxerman, "Adolph Joachim Sabath in Congress: The Roosevelt and Truman Years," 437–40.

109 *recognizing Czechoslovakia as a nation*: Boxerman, "Adolph Joachim Sabath in Congress: The Early Years, 1907–1932," 335–36.

110 *in Záboří, in honor of his mother*: "Czech Honor for Sabath: Native Village Makes Dean of House Honorary Citizen," *New York Times*, September 7, 1947, 22.

110 *"anything very effective to implement it"*: Beal, "Adolph J. Sabath," 208–09.

110 *"as tender as his mind was vibrant"*: Remarks of Barratt O'Hara, in United States 83rd Congress House, 1st Session, 1953, and United States Congress, *Memorial Services Held in the House of Representatives of the United States: Together with Remarks Presented in Eulogy of Adolph Joachim Sabath, Late a Representative from Illinois* (Washington, DC: US Government Printing Office, 1953), 50.

111 *"we shall not look upon his like again"*: Remarks of John McCormack, *Memorial Services Held in the House of Representatives of the United States, Together with Remarks Presented in Eulogy of Adolph Joachim Sabath, Late a Representative from Illinois*, 83rd Congress, 1st Session, 1953 (Washington, DC: Government Printing Office, 1953), 57.

5: Oscar Stanton De Priest

For De Priest's early biography and service in Congress, this chapter draws largely on Harold F. Gosnell, *Negro Politicians; The Rise of Negro Politics in Chicago* (Chicago: University of Chicago Press, 1935). A key source on the "restaurant incident" in particular was Elliott M. Rudwick, "Oscar De Priest and the Jim Crow Restaurant in the US House of Representatives," *Journal of Negro Education* 35, no. 1 (1966), 77–82, https://doi.org/10.2307/2293932.

115 *he was not welcome*: Elliott M. Rudwick, "Oscar De Priest and the Jim Crow Restaurant in the US House of Representatives," 77–82.

116 *bloodstains on the concrete*: Gosnell, *Negro Politicians; The Rise of Negro Politics in Chicago*, 165. The details and description of De Priest's family and childhood rely on this source.

117 *"signal for a fight"*: Ibid., 166.

118 *"The chance, the suspense, interests me"*: Ibid., 167–68.

118 *crowds were said to have followed him in the street*: Ibid., 180–82.

119 *the great majority of whom were Black*: Jonathan S. Coit, "'Our Changed Attitude': Armed Defense and the New Negro in the 1919 Chicago Race Riot," *Journal of the Gilded Age and Progressive Era* 11, no. 2 (April 2012), 225–56.

119 *White woman who had shot an African American man*: Coit, "'Our Changed Attitude': Armed Defense and the New Negro in the 1919 Chicago Race Riot," 249.

119 *bring food to his neighborhood so families could eat*: Henry Louis Gates and Evelyn Brooks Higginbotham, *African American Lives* (New York: Oxford University Press, 2004), 229.

120 *"rescued all of them" from the mob*: William L. Clay, *Just Permanent Interests: Black Americans in Congress, 1870–1991* (New York: Amistad Press, 1992), 69.

120 *His actions had made him famous*: Coit, "'Our Changed Attitude': Armed Defense and the New Negro in the 1919 Chicago Race Riot."

120 *Chicago's mayor, "Big Bill" Thompson*: Gosnell, *Negro Politicians; The Rise of Negro Politics in Chicago*, 176.

120 *would likely do as he dictated*: Gosnell, *Negro Politicians; The Rise of Negro Politics in Chicago*, 80, 182.

120 *for the majority Black district*: Parke Brown, "Madden's Death May Seat Negro," *Chicago Tribune*, April 28, 1928, 2.

120 *"'by God, there'll be one there'"*: Gosnell, *Negro Politicians; The Rise of Negro Politics in Chicago*, 80, 182.

121 *challenged his nomination*: Ibid., 182–83.

121 *if he quit his campaign*: Maurine Christopher, *Black Americans in Congress* (New York: Thomas Y. Crowell, 1976), 170.

121 *while he was under indictment*: Gosnell, *Negro Politicians; The Rise of Negro Politics in Chicago*, 182–83.

121 *the judge dismissed the case*: Associated Press, "De Priest Charges Dropped in Chicago," *Washington Post*, April 14, 1929, 16.

122 *"all Members of the body at once"*: *Congressional Record*, 71st Congress, 1st Session (April 15, 1929), 26.

122 *"I will not be a 'Black' congressman"*: Kenneth Eugene Mann, "Oscar Stanton De Priest: Persuasive Agent for the Black Masses," *Negro History Bulletin* 35, no. 6 (1972), 134–37.

122 *occupied by southern Democrats*: Ibid., 134.

122 *breach of etiquette*: Rudwick, "Oscar De Priest and the Jim Crow Restaurant in the US House of Representatives," 77–82.

122 *"I am going to have it"*: Patrick G. Eddington, "Oscar De Priest: Black Congressional Pioneer," *Defending Rights & Dissent Blog* (blog), February 26, 2021, www .rightsanddissent.org/news/oscar-de-priest-black-congressional-pioneer/.

122 *remove his name from the door*: Mann, "Oscar Stanton De Priest: Persuasive Agent for the Black Masses."

123 *"a lonely figure" isolated in the back row*: Gosnell, *Negro Politicians; The Rise of Negro Politics in Chicago*, 183.

123 *Civilian Conservation Corps to prohibit discrimination*: The Committee on House Administration of the US House of Representatives, *Black Americans in Congress, 1870–2007* (Washington, DC: US Government Printing Office, 2008), 282A.

123 *for equality for African Americans*: David Day, "Herbert Hoover and Racial Politics: The De Priest Incident," *Journal of Negro History*, 65, no. 1 (1980), 6–17.

124 *censuring First Lady Hoover*: Annette B. Dunlap, "Tea and Equality: The Hoover Administration and the De Priest Incident," *National Archives Records Administration* 47, no. 2 (2015), 16–22.

124 *letters, and resolutions of their own*: Ibid.

124 *"fighting eternally for his rights"*: Associated Press, "De Priest Calls Legislators of Dixie Cowards," *Chicago Daily Tribune*, July 2, 1929, 1.

124 *"the privileges he has taken"*: Dunlap, "Tea and Equality: The Hoover Administration and the De Priest Incident."

125 *"organizing and standing together"*: Mann, "Oscar Stanton De Priest: Persuasive Agent for the Black Masses."

125 *"He looks like a fighter"*: Gosnell, *Negro Politicians; The Rise of Negro Politics in Chicago*, 192.

125 *speech in Birmingham, Alabama*: Ibid., 185–86.

125 *He went anyway*: Christopher, *Black Americans in Congress*, 171.

125 *long after he left office*: Patrick G. Eddington, "Oscar De Priest: A Congressional Death Threat J. Edgar Hoover Ignored," *Cato at Liberty* (blog), February 26,

2021, https://www.cato.org/blog/oscar-de-priest-congressional-death-threat-j -edgar-hoover-ignored.

125 *fear that could turn out voters*: Gosnell, *Negro Politicians; The Rise of Negro Politics in Chicago*, 185.

125 *"new courage, new inspiration"*: Ibid.

126 *"anything to do with the restaurant"*: Associated Press, "De Priest to Force Vote on Color Line," *New York Times*, January 24, 1934, 3. De Priest's quote in the previous paragraph is found in the same article.

126 *allow all African Americans to eat there*: "De Priest in House Raises Race Issue," *New York Times*, January 25, 1934, 26.

126 *if he would simply hold back from making a fiery speech*: Ibid.

126 *committee to be appointed by the Speaker*: *Congressional Record*, 78th Congress, 2nd Session (January 24, 1934), 1275.

127 *with greater chances of success*: Rudwick, "Oscar De Priest and the Jim Crow Restaurant in the US House of Representatives," 78. Each of the quotes in the paragraph is found in this source.

128 *De Priest's petition kept growing*: Ibid., 78–80. Rudwick's article details the events in the previous paragraph.

131 *"instead of just twelve million of them"*: *Congressional Record*, 78th Congress, 2nd session (March 21, 1934), 5047–049. All quotations from De Priest's speech of March 21, 1934, over the previous pages, are found at this citation.

131 *"before I came here"*: *Congressional Record*, 73rd Congress, 2nd Session (March 23, 1934), 5253–255.

132 *"the idle of every race and creed"*: Associated Press, "Arthur Mitchell, an Ex-Lawmaker," *New York Times*, May 10, 1968, 47.

133 *public accommodations within the District of Columbia*: Rudwick, "Oscar De Priest and the Jim Crow Restaurant in the US House of Representatives," 77.

133 *dying in 1951 at age eighty*: Christopher, *Black Americans in Congress*, 175.

133 *sacred documents left behind*: Shelley Stokes-Hammond, "Pathbreakers: Oscar Stanton De Priest and Jessie L. Williams De Priest," *White House Historical Association* (web), n.d, http://www.whitehousehistory.org.

6: Margaret Chase Smith

Smith's own autobiography was a key source for this chapter: Margaret Chase Smith, *Declaration of Conscience*, ed. William C. Lewis Jr. (New York: Doubleday, 1972), as well as Patricia Ward Wallace's *Politics of Conscience: A Biography of Margaret Chase Smith* (Westport, CT: Praeger, 1995).

137 *all the more untenable to Smith*: Smith, *Declaration of Conscience*, 7. Smith's book provides the details for the opening paragraphs of this chapter.

139 *"fear, ignorance, bigotry, and smear"*: Smith, *Declaration of Conscience*, 13–17. The entire speech is found on these pages.

139 *her words led newspapers nationally*: William S. White, "Seven GOP Senators Decry 'Smear' Tactics of McCarthy," *New York Times*, June 2, 1950, 1.

140 *The plane landed safely*: Wallace, *Politics*, 73; Gregory P. Gallant, *Hope and Fear in*

Margaret Chase Smith's America: A Continuous Tangle (Lanham, MD: Lexington Books, 2014), 69.

140 *in Maine's rural communities*: Janann Sherman, "Senator-at-Large for America's Women: Margaret Chase Smith and the Paradox of Gender Affinity," in *The Impact of Women in Public Office*, ed. Susan J. Carroll (Bloomington and Indianapolis: Indiana University Press, 2001), 93–95.

140 *obituary in the* Portland Press Herald: Wallace, *Politics of Conscience*, 56; Sherman, "Senator-at-Large for America's Women: Margaret Chase Smith and the Paradox of Gender Affinity," 94.

141 *she trounced him, too*: Wallace, *Politics of Conscience*, 48–51.

141 *her own life as "simple but useful:"* Eileen Keerdoja, "The Feisty Lady from Maine," *Newsweek*, September 15, 1980, 20.

142 *sent on an inspection trip*: Wallace, *Politics of Conscience*, 59–62.

142 *if they were found to be infected*: Janann Sherman, *No Place for a Woman: A Life of Senator Margaret Chase Smith* (New Brunswick, NJ: Rutgers University Press, 2001), 59–61.

142 *study and solve the problems*: Phyllis A. Hall, "Crisis at Hampton Roads—The Problems of Wartime Congestion, 1942–1944," *The Virginia Magazine of History and Biography* 101, no. 3 (July 1993), 405–32.

142 *intensely dedicated, like her*: Gallant, *Hope and Fear in Margaret Chase Smith's America*, 55.

142 *she could potentially ask*: Wallace, *Politics of Conscience,* 63.

142 *although they never married*: Associated Press, "William C. Lewis Jr. Is Dead; Air Force Brigadier General," *New York Times*, May 29, 1982, 2.

143 *picked up by the vice squad*: Sherman, *No Place for a Woman*, 59–61.

143 *"certainly deserved a better chance"*: Robert H. Mason, "Girls Behind Norfolk Jail Bars Visited by Congresswoman," *Norfolk Virginia Pilot*, March 27, 1943, 1.

143 *not punishment for missing work*: Gallant, *Hope and Fear in Margaret Chase Smith's America*, 52–53.

143 *six hundred thousand women to join in wartime production*: Wallace, *Politics of Conscience*, 67.

143 *which seemed supportive*: *Congressional Record*, 78th Congress, 2nd Session (March 9, 1944), 2454.

143 *"take care of their children"*: Sherman, *No Place for a Woman*, 64–65.

144 *The full appropriation was approved*: *Congressional Record*, 78th Congress, 2nd Session (March 9, 1944), 2454–457. These pages contain the debate, including the quotations from Smith in the preceding paragraphs.

144 *many of which were adopted*: Wallace, *Politics of Conscience*, 56, 64–66; Susan J. Carroll, *The Impact of Women in Public Office* (Bloomington: Indiana University Press, 2001), 103. These sources detail the tour described in the previous two paragraphs.

145 *to rise further in the military*: Wallace, *Politics of Conscience*, 69.

146 *"she worries over it just like a baby"*: Frank Graham, *Margaret Chase Smith: Woman of Courage* (New York: John Day Company, 1964), 44.

146 *sent a telegram of support*: Wallace, *Politics of Conscience*, 70.

146 *"most logical source of replacement"*: Josephine Ripley, "A Questionable Limit on Woman Power," *Christian Science Monitor* (March 29, 1948).

146 *"dressed and clean at all times"*: House of Representatives, Committee on Armed Service, Subcommittee No. 3, "Organization and Mobilization," July 23, 1947, Margaret Chase Smith Library.

147 *with the amendment deleting regular status for women*: Smith, *Declaration of Conscience*, 87–89; LBH to Smith, "Undated Note," n.d., folder Permanent Status for Women, Margaret Chase Smith Library.

147 *the only person to vote against it*: Smith, *Declaration of Conscience*, 87–89.

149 *"the years that both of us have served in this body"*: Smith, *Declaration of Conscience*, 92–93. Each of the quotes and details of this incident over the previous pages are from this source.

150 *"as the Senate did, or they do not"*: *Congressional Record*, 80th Congress, 2nd Session (April 21, 1948), 4714–715.

151 *"wisely and soberly consider"*: *Congressional Record*, 80th Congress, 2nd Session (April 21, 1948), 4717.

152 *"under the misnomer of Reserve"*: *Congressional Record*, 80th Congress, 2nd Session (April 21, 1948), 4718.

152 *"a crusade with her"*: Smith, *Declaration of Conscience*, 95.

152 *"how to operate in Congress"*: Gallant, *Hope and Fear in Margaret Chase Smith's America*, 51. The account regarding Secretary Ickes and quotes concerning the same are found in this source.

153 *hundreds of thousands of mothers and babies each year*: Wallace, *Politics of Conscience*, 69.

153 *for the next fifty years*: Sources for the foregoing paragraph are: Alexander Wooley, "The Fall of James Forrestal," *Washington Post*, May 23, 1999; Gallant, *Hope and Fear in Margaret Chase Smith's America*, 56–58, 72.

154 *"reply on your part is imperative"*: Smith to Forrestal, "Draft Letter," April 22, 1948, folder Permanent Status for Women, Margaret Chase Smith Library; Smith, *Declaration of Conscience*, 96–98.

154 *supported that position all along*: Forrestal to Smith, "Letter," April 30, 1948, folder Permanent Status for Women, Margaret Chase Smith Library.

154 *Truman's signature on July 12, 1948*: House of Representatives, "Women's Armed Services Integration Act of 1948, Report No. 2052," Conference Report, 80th Congress, 2nd Session, May 26, 1948; Gallant, *Hope and Fear in Margaret Chase Smith's America*, 65.

154 *"I lost all the battles except the last one"*: Wallace, *Politics of Conscience*, 72.

154 *71 percent of the vote*: Office of History and Preservation, Office of the Clerk, US House of Representatives, *Women in Congress, 1917–2006* (Washington, DC: Government Printing Office, 2006), 198–199.

154 *government service had come to an end*: Rachel Slade, "The Moment That Presaged Margaret Chase Smith's Downfall," *Down East Magazine*, May 2020, https://downeast.com/history/the-downfall-of-margaret-chase-smith/.

155 *"you kind of like to try"*: Office of History and Preservation, Office of the Clerk,
US House of Representatives, *Women in Congress, 1917–2006* (Washington, DC:
Government Printing Office, 2006), 200.

7: Henry B. Gonzalez

A pair of lengthy magazine profiles provided much helpful support for this chapter: Robert Stowe England, "Profile: The Spicy Politics of Henry Gonzalez,"
Mortgage Banking 51, no. 5 (February 1991), 38 and "The Political Desires of
Chairman Gonzalez," *Mortgage Banking* 51, no. 6 (March 1991), 34. For details
on his early life, see Eugene Rodriguez, *Henry B. Gonzalez: A Political Profile*
(New York: Arno Press, 1976).

159 *a very different conclusion*: Christopher Hitchens, "No Fool on the Hill," *Harper's* 285, no. 1709 (October 1992), 84. The entirety of Hitchens's observations on
this page are drawn from this article.

160 *reading books and government documents*: Ibid.

161 *"a view of the whole ground"*: Thomas Jefferson, "First Inaugural Address"
(Washington, DC, March 4, 1801).

162 *"crumbled institutional situation"*: *Congressional Record*, 100th Congress, 2nd
Session (July 28, 1988), 19540, 19542.

162 *"he goes after it"*: Tom Kenworthy, "Gonzalez's Pugnacious Populism," *Washington Post*, December 6, 1989.

163 *Henry had been born in Texas*: Rodriguez, *Henry B. Gonzalez*, 31–39; England,
"The Political Desires of Chairman Gonzalez," 34. This paragraph and the preceding paragraph rely on these sources.

163 *worked in a public housing agency*: Rodriguez, *Henry B. Gonzalez*, 39–45; England, "Profile: The Spicy Politics of Henry Gonzalez," 38.

163 *"catching the public eye for some time"*: Rodriguez, *Henry B. Gonzalez*, 61.

164 *he was shot at in the street*: Rodriguez, *Henry B. Gonzalez*, 63–72.

164 *longer than anyone before in Texas history*: Rodriguez, *Henry B. Gonzalez*,
78–82.

164 *"had slammed the doors and buried the keys"*: Dugger quoted in Molly Ivins,
"The Late Henry B. Was a Boxer, Not a Saint," *Fort Worth Star-Telegram*, November 30, 2000, 11. Ronnie Dugger, "The Segregation Filibuster of 1957," *Texas
Observer*, May 7, 1957, 1–2.

165 *"I listened to him all night"*: Kenworthy, "Gonzalez's Pugnacious Populism."

165 *"'a new land of hope'"*: Rodriguez, *Henry B. Gonzalez*, 80–81.

165 *"passion for justice that animated the whole"*: Molly Ivins, "The Late Henry B.
Was a Boxer, Not a Saint," *Fort Worth Star-Telegram*, November 30, 2000, 11.

165 *known across the country*: James W. Riddlesperger Jr and Anthony Champagne,
Lone Star Leaders: Power and Personality in the Texas Congressional Delegation
(Fort Worth: Texas Christian University Press, 2011), 155.

166 *vacated by a Kennedy appointment*: Rodriguez, *Henry B. Gonzalez*, 110–12. The
preceding paragraphs about Gonzalez's relationship with the Kennedys rely on
this source.

166 *Lyndon Johnson, a Texan, visited to campaign for Gonzalez*: Rodriguez, *Henry B. Gonzalez*, 113–16.

166 *focusing on his courage*: Edward M. Kennedy, "Remarks Delivered by Senator Kennedy on Presenting the Profile in Courage Award to Henry B. Gonzalez" (Boston, Massachusetts, September 11, 1994), John F. Kennedy Presidential Library and Museum, https://www.jfklibrary.org/events-and-awards/profile-in-courage-award/award-recipients/henry-gonzalez-1994.

166 *never seriously challenged again*: Rodriguez, *Henry B. Gonzalez*, 113–16; Riddlesperger and Champagne, *Lone Star Leaders*, 155.

166 *Gonzalez's strongest interest*: England, "The Political Desires of Chairman Gonzalez."

167 *"most divisive period in our society since the Civil War"*: Henry B. Gonzalez, "The Relinquishment of Co-Equality by Congress," *Harvard Journal on Legislation* 29, no. 2 (Summer 1992), 331–56.

168 *"the king will be restored to his throne"*: Ibid.

168 *decisions he considered unconstitutional*: "Gonzalez, Henry B. | US House of Representatives: History, Art & Archives," United States House of Representatives: History, Art & Archives, accessed July 8, 2022, https://history.house.gov/People/Listing/G/GONZÁLEZ,-Henry-B—(G000272)/.

168 *supporters from San Antonio denounced him*: Jennifer Dixon, "That's Just Henry," Associated Press, January 28, 1991, found in 149.K.14.4F, Henry B. Gonzalez Correspondence and news clippings, 1991–1994, Bruce Vento Papers, Minnesota History Center, Minnesota Historical Society.

168 *causes they believed he could never win*: "Gonzalez, Henry B. | US House of Representatives: History, Art & Archives."

168 *"not be able to eat chalupas"*: Pete Hamill, "Henry B. Gonzalez," in *Profiles in Courage for Our Time*, ed. Caroline Kennedy (New York: Hyperion, 2002), 104.

168 *a $2,500 bank account*: Paul Houston, "Rep. Gonzalez: He Packs a Punch," *Los Angeles Times*, July 15, 1990.

168 *"vote for Gonzalez!"*: Ivins, "The Late Henry B. Was a Boxer, Not a Saint," 11.

168 *"mismatched coffee mugs"*: Elaine Sciolino, "Washington at Work; Eccentric Still but Obscure No More, Texan Leads Inquiry on Iraq Loans," *New York Times*, July 3, 1992, sec. A, 15.

169 *clashes with top committee staff*: Riddlesperger and Champagne, *Lone Star Leaders*, 157.

169 *ultimately validate his charges*: The Nader Letter, "Comeback Chairman," 1996, found in folder 2004-127-402, Henry B. Gonzalez Papers, Briscoe Center for American History, University of Texas at Austin.

169 *"keeping the issue alive"*: Riddlesperger and Champagne, *Lone Star Leaders*, 157; Marilyn Mendoza, "Forty Years Ago, US District Judge Wood Assassinated in San Antonio by Woody Harrelson's Father," *San Antonio Express-News*, May 29, 2019.

169 *angering Latino activists by his lack of support*: England, "Profile: The Spicy Politics of Henry Gonzalez," 43–46.

169 *"Mexican American, so much the better"*: Jan Jarboe Russell, "The Eternal Chal-
     lenger," *Texas Monthly*, September 20, 1992.

170 *working his way up in seniority*: England, "The Political Desires of Chairman
     Gonzalez."

170 *not an easy time to work on public housing*: England, "Profile: The Spicy Politics
     of Henry Gonzalez."

170 *contributed by the institutions he oversaw*: Jess Bidgood, "Fernand St Germain,
     Legislator Tied to S.&L. Crisis, Dies at 86," *New York Times*, August 21, 2014.

170 *when it was his turn to be chair*: England, "Profile: The Spicy Politics of Henry
     Gonzalez."

171 *ultimately reaching $124 billion*: Federal Reserve Bank of St. Louis, "Savings and Loan
     Crisis 1980–1989," Federal Reserve History, 2013, https://www.federalreservehistory
     .org/essays/savings-and-loan-crisis.

171 *threat to fight like Davey Crockett*: Paul Houston, "Rep. Gonzalez: He Packs a
     Punch," *LA Times*, July 15, 1990.

171 *"think nothing of it"*: England, "Profile: The Spicy Politics of Henry Gonzalez."

171 *"a fair, bipartisan way"*: Ibid.

171 *"Henry would be uncontested winner"*: Riddlesperger and Champagne, *Lone Star
     Leaders*.

172 *in seventeen years*: "US Housing Programs Overhauled," in *CQ Almanac 1990*,
     46th ed. (Washington, DC: Congressional Quarterly, 1991), 631–56; England,
     "Profile: The Spicy Politics of Henry Gonzalez."

173 *destroyed more families' finances*: England, "Profile: The Spicy Politics of Henry
     Gonzalez"; "Lincoln Savings Scandal Examined in Hearings," in *CQ Almanac
     1989*, 45th ed. (Washington, DC: Congressional Quarterly, 1990), 133–39.

173 *as he closed in on the facts*: England, "Profile: The Spicy Politics of Henry Gon-
     zalez"; Kenworthy, "Gonzalez's Pugnacious Populism."

173 *"when he became chairman"*: Kenworthy, "Gonzalez's Pugnacious Populism."

174 *Congressional interference in their work*: Lincoln Savings & Loan, Day 1 Part 1
     (C-SPAN Video, October 26, 1989), https://www.c-span.org/video/?9696-1/lincoln
     -savings-loan-day-1-part-1.

174 *"battled to protect the taxpayer"*: "Lincoln Savings Scandal Examined in Hear-
     ings," in *CQ Almanac 1989*, 45th ed. (Washington, DC: Congressional Quarterly,
     1990), 133–39.

174 *"cost the nation and the financial industry heavily"*: Lincoln Savings & Loan, Day
     1 Part 1 (C-SPAN Video, October 26, 1989), timecode 4:30, https://www.c-span
     .org/video/?9696-1/lincoln-savings-loan-day-1-part-1.

174 *"I was a sheriff without a gun"*: Lincoln Savings and Loan, Day 3, Part 1 (C-SPAN
     Video, 1989), timecode 42:00–48:00, https://www.c-span.org/video/?9837-1/lincoln
     -savings-loan-day-3-part-1.

175 *"It was a quid pro quo"*: "Lincoln Savings Scandal Examined in Hearings," in *CQ
     Almanac 1989*, 133–39.

175 *allowed no staff witnesses to attend*: "Panel Probes Senators' Aid to Keating," in
     CQ Almanac 1990, 46th ed. (Washington, DC: Congressional Quarterly, 1991).

175 *four and a half years in prison:* Robert D. McFadden, "Charles Keating, 90, Key Figure in '80s Savings and Loan Crisis, Dies," *New York Times,* April 2, 2014. One of the senators involved, John McCain, would go on to become a two-time presidential candidate and earn deserved praise from members of both parties for his repeated instances of political courage.

175 *"still over there a-moldering away":* England, "Profile: The Spicy Politics of Henry Gonzalez."

175 *the role of the Reagan White House:* Ibid.

176 *when chairs would be elected:* Paul Starobin, "Double Trouble," *National Review,* January 12, 1991, 58–63, found in 149.K.14.4F, Henry B. Gonzalez Correspondence and news clippings, 1991–1994, Bruce Vento Papers, Minnesota History Center, Minnesota Historical Society.

176 *"ranking Republican of the committee in a television ad":* England, "Profile: The Spicy Politics of Henry Gonzalez."

176 *charged Wylie had been responsible for the S&L crisis:* Gary Martin, "Gonzalez Unlikely to Face Challenge," *San Antonio Express-News,* December 6, 1992, found in folder 2004-127-402, Henry B. Gonzalez Papers, Briscoe Center for American History, University of Texas at Austin.

176 *"I admire him very much":* Starobin, "Double Trouble."

176 *"where the Democrats were hit hardest":* England, "Profile: The Spicy Politics of Henry Gonzalez."

177 *"legislative mugging that failed":* Starobin, "Double Trouble."

177 *seventy-one bills as chair:* Various letters and articles contained in folder 2004-127-402, Henry B. Gonzalez Papers, Briscoe Center for American History, University of Texas at Austin.

177 *he "can be difficult":* Richard L. Berke with Stephen Labaton, "A Difficult Season for Banks Trying to Lobby Capitol Hill," *New York Times,* February 19, 1991; *Congressional Record,* 106th Congress, 2nd Session (December 5, 2000), 26241.

177 *another financial crisis in that industry: Congressional Record,* 106th Congress, 2nd Session (December 5, 2000), 26242.

178 *Gonzalez's picture hanging beside it:* Houston, "Rep. Gonzalez: He Packs a Punch."

178 *"pressed down by injustice and prejudice":* Kennedy, "Remarks Delivered by Senator Edward M. Kennedy on Presenting the Profile in Courage Award to Henry B. Gonzalez."

179 *"eradicate disease, and house the people":* Henry B. Gonzalez, "Remarks on Receiving the Profile in Courage Award" (speech, Boston, MA, September 11, 1994), John F. Kennedy Presidential Library and Museum, https://www.jfklibrary.org/events-and-awards/profile-in-courage-award/award-recipients/henry-gonzalez-1994. The quote in the previous paragraph also comes from this source.

179 *"personally very tough for him":* Andrew Taylor, "Two Seek to Replace Gonzalez as Panel's Ranking Member," *Congressional Quarterly* (November 16, 1996),

3282, found in folder 2004-127-402, Henry B. Gonzalez Papers, Briscoe Center for American History, University of Texas at Austin.

179 *"social justice for all Americans"*: Hon. Jesse L. Jackson Jr., to US House of Representatives (November 14, 1996), found in folder 2004-127-402, Henry B. Gonzalez Papers, Briscoe Center for American History, University of Texas at Austin.

179 *a joint letter of support*: Hon. Ed Pastor and Hon. Donald M. Payne to Democratic Colleagues (November 18, 1996), found in folder 2004-127-402, Henry B. Gonzalez Papers, Briscoe Center for American History, University of Texas at Austin.

180 *"This guy defines the Democratic Party's values"*: Andrew Taylor, "Regarding Henry," *Congressional Quarterly* (November 23, 1996), 3305, found in folder 2004-127-402, Henry B. Gonzalez Papers, Briscoe Center for American History, University of Texas at Austin.

181 *"I will not disappoint you"*: Undated typescript, "The Honorable Henry B. Gonzalez Before the Democratic Caucus," found in folder 2004-127-402, Henry B. Gonzalez Papers, Briscoe Center for American History, University of Texas at Austin. Quotes from Gonzalez's speech in the previous paragraphs come from this source.

181 *He withdrew*: Andrew Taylor, "Regarding Henry."

181 *"My gosh, the spirit moved me"*: Juliet Eilperin, "Emotional Plea Keeps Gonzalez in Banking Spot," *Roll Call* 42, no. 40 (November 21, 1996), 1, found in folder 2004-127-402, Henry B. Gonzalez Papers, Briscoe Center for American History, University of Texas at Austin. LaFalce's quote in the previous paragraph also comes from this source.

182 *as one of their trade journals reported*: Steve Cocheo, "Gonzalez to Leave Congress," *ABA Banking Journal* 89, issue 10 (October 1997).

182 *"for the people than Henry B. Gonzalez of Texas"*: *Congressional Record*, 106th Congress, 2nd Session (December 5, 2000), 26246.

8: Shirley Chisholm

This chapter relies heavily on Chisholm's own words in two autobiographies and a book of published interviews: Shirley Chisholm, *Unbought and Unbossed* (Boston: Houghton Mifflin, 1970), *The Good Fight* (New York: Harper & Row, 1973), and *Shirley Chisholm: The Last Interview and Other Conversations* (Brooklyn: Melville House, 2021).

185 *"We're all animals"*: Chisholm, *The Good Fight*, 93–95.

185 *fired multiple bullets into Wallace*: William Greider, "Wallace Is Shot, Legs Paralyzed; Suspect Seized at Laurel Rally," *Washington Post*, May 16, 1972, 1.

186 *kept a private schedule*: Chisholm, *The Good Fight*, 93–95. Chisholm's quote in the previous paragraph is also from this source.

186 *with the opposite message*: Ibid., 67–69.

187 *"the most dangerous racist in America"*: Jonathan Capehart, "How Segregationist George Wallace Became a Model for Racial Reconciliation," *Voices of the Movement*, Episode 6, transcript in the *Cape Up* series, *Washington Post*, May 16, 2019,

https://www.washingtonpost.com/opinions/2019/05/16/changed-minds-recon
ciliation-voices-movement-episode/.

187 *lodged next to his spine*: Greider, "Wallace Is Shot."

187 *let her neighbors decide*: Chisholm, *Shirley Chisholm: The Last Interview and Other Conversations*, 91–94; Anastasia Curwood, "Black Feminism on Capitol Hill: Shirley Chisholm and Movement Politics, 1968–1984," *Meridians* 13, no. 1, Duke University Press (2015), 204–32.

188 *"a catalyst for change in America"*: Chisholm, *The Last Interview*, 119.

188 *"Even Mother was almost afraid of me"*: Chisholm, *Unbought and Unbossed*, 4.

188 *behavioral expectations high*: Chisholm, *Unbought*, 4–18.

188 *she stood ramrod erect her whole life*: Chisholm, *The Last Interview*, 87.

189 *"defy, or even question"*: Chisholm, *Unbought*, 6.

189 *racial slurs and overt discrimination*: Chisholm, *Unbought and Unbossed*, 4–18.

189 *"Power concedes nothing without a struggle"*: Ibid., 10–15, 135–38.

190 *to fulfill the goal of political participation*: Ibid.; Chisholm, *The Last Interview*, 68. The previous paragraph is based on these sources as well.

191 *"incomprehensible to most politicians"*: Chisholm, *Unbought and Unbossed*, 32–37.

191 *"start changing right then"*: Ibid., 47–52.

192 *unemployment insurance to domestic workers*: Ibid., 60–63.

192 *"more to a party than its leadership"*: Ibid.

192 *"go back to being a professional educator"*: Susan Brownmiller, "This Is Fighting Shirley Chisholm"; *New York Times*, April 13, 1969.

193 *"You have to let them feel you"*: Ibid.; Chisholm, *Unbought and Unbossed*, 68–70.

193 *constantly greeted by passersby*: Brownmiller, "This Is Fighting Shirley Chisholm."

193 *"Yes sir, beat you to it today"*: Chisholm, *The Last Interview*, 80–84; Chisholm, *Unbought and Unbossed*, 79.

195 *"badly housed, than the one I was given"*: Ibid., 84. The previous quote is found on this same page.

195 *"do something, be politically expendable"*: Ibid., 80–85.

195 *"drugged and inert"*: Ibid., 100–07.

195 *"afraid of in Shirley Chisholm is her mouth"*: Brownmiller, "This Is Fighting Shirley Chisholm."

196 *"You know, she's crazy"*: Chisholm, *Unbought and Unbossed*, 96–98.

196 *"forums across the country"*: Ibid., 89–90.

196 *"believed it: 'We have overcome'"*: Chisholm, *The Good Fight*, 2.

196 *"refusal to accept the status quo"*: Ibid., xii.

197 *"fundamental to democracy's survival"*: Ibid., 99.

197 *"segregation forever"*: Samara Freemark and Joe Richman of Radio Diaries, "'Segregation Forever': A Fiery Pledge Forgiven, But Not Forgotten," *All Things Considered* (NPR, January 10, 2013), https://www.npr.org/2013/01/14/169080969/segregation -forever-a-fiery-pledge-forgiven-but-not-forgotten.

197 *ordering in the National Guard*: Debbie Elliott, "Wallace in the School-house Door," *Morning Edition* (NPR, June 11, 2003), https://www.npr .org/2003/06/11/1294680/wallace-in-the-schoolhouse-door.

197 *the problem persisted, including in Northern cities*: M. Costello, "School Busing and Politics," *CQ Editorial Research Reports 1972* (vol. I), http://library.cqpress .com/cqresearcher/cqresrre1972030100; Pedro A. Noguera, "US Schools Are Not Racially Integrated Despite Decades of Effort," *The Conversation*, May 13, 2022, https://theconversation.com/us-schools-are-not-racially-integrated-despite-decades -of-effort-177849.

197 *pursued the Democratic nomination for president*: Costello, "School Busing and Politics."

198 *"now that you've discovered the busing problem"*: Chisholm, *The Good Fight*, 62.

198 *intentional vagueness on the part of the other Democratic candidates*: Ibid., 62–63; Associated Press, "Rep. Chisholm Visits Wallace," *Times-Picayune* (New Orleans), June 9, 1972.

198 *what she believed to be hypocrisy on racial issues*: Chisholm explained this view in her 1973 book, *The Good Fight* (pages 10–11).

198 *he won Michigan and Maryland*: R. W. Apple Jr., "Wallace Campaign Is Expected to Peak in Tuesday's Races," *New York Times*, May 14, 1972.

198 *because of his praise in Florida*: Chisholm, *The Last Interview*, 91–92.

199 *Then they prayed together*: Chisholm, *The Good Fight*, 97.

199 *why she would visit him*: Ibid., 97–99. The quotation in the previous paragraph is also from this source.

200 *"What she said to me took root"*: Capehart, "How Segregationist George Wallace Became a Model for Racial Reconciliation." The previous paragraph is also based on this source.

200 *respect for Chisholm remained intact*: Chisholm, *The Last Interview*, 91–92.

200 *a similar measure would eventually become law the following year, in 1974*: Barbara Winslow, *Shirley Chisholm: Catalyst for Change, 1926–2005* (Boulder, CO: Westview Press, 2014), 137–38; US Department of Labor, "History of Changes to the Minimum Wage Law: Adapted from Minimum Wage and Maximum Hours Standards Under the Fair Labor Standards Act, 1988 Report to the Congress Under 4(d)(1) of the FLSA," https://www.dol.gov/agencies/whd/minimum–wage /history.

200 *"a seed of new beginnings in my father's heart"*: Capehart, "How Segregationist George Wallace Became a Model for Racial Reconciliation."

201 *apologized and asked for forgiveness*: Ibid.

201 *support from the state's Black electorate*: Glenn T. Eskew, "George C. Wallace (1963–67, 1971–79, 1983–87)," *Encyclopedia of Alabama*, September 8, 2008, http://encyclopediaofalabama.org/article/h-1676.

201 *"the evil system we sought to destroy"*: John Lewis, "Forgiving George Wallace," *New York Times*, September 16, 1998, sec. A, 29.

201 *passage of landmark legislation*: Winslow, *Shirley Chisholm*, 137–139; Chisholm, *The Last Interview*, 108–109.

201 *many other issues behind the scenes*: Jacqueline Trescott, "Shirley Chisholm in Her Season of Transition," *Washington Post*, June 6, 1982.

201 *on behalf of the Congressional Black Caucus*: Martin Tolchin, "Urban-Rural Co-

alition Successful on Farm and Food Stamp Measure," *New York Times,* July 29, 1977.

202 *"do not believe that our national nutrition policy is sufficient"*: Committee on Agriculture, House of Representatives, 95th Congress, 1st Session, HR 4844, "Food Stamp Program, Hearings Before the Subcommittee on Domestic Marketing, Consumer Relations, and Nutrition and the Full Committee" (Washington, DC: Government Printing Office, 1977), 575.

202 *Usually, that defense failed*: Winslow, *Shirley Chisholm,* 139–141.

202 *"I had to steel myself for abuse"*: Trescott, "Shirley Chisholm in Her Season of Transition."

202 *betraying her cause for personal power*: Winslow, *Shirley Chisholm,* 144–46.

203 *his confirmation on the floor of the House*: Trescott, "Shirley Chisholm in Her Season of Transition."

203 *"issue for the first time"*: Ibid. The quotation from Chisholm two paragraphs later is from the same source.

204 *"the better angels of our nature"*: Abraham Lincoln, "First Inaugural Address," Washington, DC, March 4, 1861.

204 *"how I'd like to be remembered"*: Brownmiller, "This Is Fighting Shirley Chisholm."

9: Barbara Jordan

Mary Beth Rogers's biography on Jordan was a key source for this chapter: *Barbara Jordan: American Hero* (1998; repr., New York: Bantam Books, 2000).

208 *still in her first term*: Mary Ellen Curtin, "Reaching for Power: Barbara C. Jordan and Liberals in the Texas Legislature, 1966–1972," *Southwestern Historical Quarterly* 108, no. 2 (Texas State Historical Association, 2004), 210–31.

208 *the long history of the Democratic Party*: Barbara Jordan, Democratic National Convention Keynote Speech, 1976, Part 1, YouTube (TSU Jordan Archives, posted 2012), https://youtu.be/Bg7gLIx__-k.

208 *percussive clarity in her enunciation*: Rogers, *Barbara Jordan,* 22, 27, 76–86.

208 *"the voice of God"*: James W. Riddlesperger and Anthony Champagne, *Lone Star Leaders: Power and Personality in the Texas Congressional Delegation,* 1st ed. (Fort Worth: Texas Christian University Press, 2011), 183.

208 *"I, Barbara Jordan, am a keynote speaker"*: Barbara Jordan, "Democratic National Convention Keynote Address, New York, July 12, 1976," in Barbara Jordan, *Barbara Jordan: Speaking the Truth with Eloquent Thunder,* ed. Max R. Sherman (Austin: University of Texas Press, 2007), 34–40. Each of the following quotations from the speech is from this source.

209 *"realized in each one of us*: Jordan, "Democratic National Convention Keynote Address," 34–40.

210 *ranked not far behind*: Brian T. Kaylor, "A New Law: The Covenant Speech of Barbara Jordan," *Southern Communication Journal* 77, no. 1 (January 2012), 10–23.

210 *most famous African American woman in the country*: Rogers, *Barbara Jordan,* 236.

210 *one of four hundred thirty-five representatives in the House*: Riddlesperger and Champagne, *Lone Star Leaders*, 188.

210 *much about her or feeling close:* While Jordan never disclosed her sexual orientation publicly, in 2021, long after her death, the National Archives revealed that she had been the first lesbian to serve in Congress and identified her life partner—facts that many contend would have had serious political consequences for her career had they been made public in the 1970s. Jessie Kratz, "LGBTQ+ History Month: Barbara Jordan," *Pieces of History, National Archives* (blog), June 10, 2021, https:// prologue.blogs.archives.gov/2021/06/10/lgbtq-history-month-bar bara-jordan/.

211 *more than 80 percent of the vote*: Curtin, "Reaching for Power."

211 *"it's just the beginning"*: Barbara Jordan and Shelby Hearon, *Barbara Jordan, a Self-Portrait* (Garden City, NY: Doubleday, 1979), 67–68.

212 *"in a private way if it were ever going to come"*: Rogers, *Barbara Jordan*, 58.

212 *"I'm being educated finally"*: Ibid., 64.

213 *"'put you on the speaking circuit'"*: Ibid., 78.

213 *would face long odds*: Curtin, "Reaching for Power."

214 *enjoying drinks together after session*: Curtin, "Reaching for Power."

214 *"the bill is dead, Barbara"*: Ibid. Each of the quotes from these three paragraphs is from this source.

214 *"make them feel evil or guilty"*: Rogers, *Barbara Jordan*, 112.

215 *poker, scotch, and political deals*: Rogers, *Barbara Jordan*, 139–43.

215 *led to protests and a riot*: Curtin, "Reaching for Power."

215 *"brag about her whenever he got a chance"*: Rogers, *Barbara Jordan*, 130–34.

216 *"mighty important things"*: Ibid., 178–80.

217 *"death of legislation by execution"*: Ibid., 191.

217 *most Americans did not believe he should be impeached*: Andrew Kohut, "From the Archives: How the Watergate Crisis Eroded Public Support for Richard Nixon," *Pew Research Center* (blog), originally published August 8, 2014, republished September 25, 2019, https://www.pewresearch.org/fact-tank/2019/09/25/how-the -watergate-crisis-eroded-public-support-for-richard-nixon/.

218 *"bound up in the future of the nation"*: B. J. Phillips, "Recognizing the Gentleladies of the Judiciary Committee," *Ms.* 3, no. 5 (1974), 70–74.

219 *"People started to listen and make decisions"*: Ibid.

219 *watched them for ten hours or more*: Kohut, "From the Archives: How the Watergate Crisis Eroded Public Support for Richard Nixon."

220 *bring President Nixon's delaying tactics to an end*: US Congress, Debate on Articles of Impeachment; Hearings of the Committee on the Judiciary, 93rd Congress, 2nd Session, Pursuant to H. Res. 803 (Washington, DC: US Government Printing Office, 1974), 1–6.

220 *"so we can sit there and listen to you"*: Jordan, *Self-Portrait*, 184–185. This reference includes Jordan's quotation in the previous paragraph.

222 *"the destruction of the Constitution"*: US Congress, Debate on Articles of Impeachment, 111.

222 *"the task we have before us is a big one"*: US Congress, Debate on Articles of Impeachment, 112.

223 *"guide our debate, and guide our decision"*: US Congress, Debate on Articles of Impeachment, 113.

224 EXPLAINING THE CONSTITUTION TO US: Jordan, *Self-Portrait*, 193, 199.

224 *"restored my faith in our government"*: Rogers, *Barbara Jordan*, 271.

224 *"We need your honest, forceful voice"*: Jordan, *Self-Portrait*, 196–97.

224 *"that was strangely reassuring"*: Anthony Lewis, "The People Do Govern," *New York Times*, July 29, 1974.

225 *above 50 percent as the committee voted*: Kohut, "From the Archives: How the Watergate Crisis Eroded Public Support for Richard Nixon."

225 *enforcement mechanisms for other civil rights laws*: Riddlesperger and Champagne, *Lone Star Leaders*.

226 *"an answer somewhat different than your own"*: Rogers, *Barbara Jordan*, 238.

Epilogue

227 *"human progress the world has ever known"*: US House of Representatives, "Greek Prime Minister Address to Congress," C-SPAN Video, May 17, 2022, https://www.c-span.org/video/?520271-2/greek-prime-minister-warns-threat-democracy-address-congress.

228 *"an important priority for our generation"*: US House of Representatives, "Greek Prime Minister Address to Congress."

230 *"who neither know victory nor defeat"*: Kathleen Dalton, *Theodore Roosevelt: A Strenuous Life* (New York: Alfred P. Knopf, 2002), 359.

231 *"victory more than truth is the palm contended for"*: George Washington, *The Writings of George Washington; Being His Correspondence, Addresses, Messages, and Other Papers, Official and Private, Vol XI*, Jared Sparks (Boston: Russel, Shattuck and Williams and Hillard, Gray, and Co., 1836), 40.

232 *"defined right here on this floor"*: *Congressional Record*, 117th Congress, 1st Session (February 13, 2021), S727–S728.

232 *"confronted with choices that define us, rose to the occasion"*: Ibid.

233 *"that terrible day may be just the beginning"*: Ibid.

233 *"honor them for their valor?"*: John F. Kennedy, *Profiles in Courage, 50th Anniversary Edition*, 260.

234 *"there must be decency and respect"*: Letter from John Adams to Joseph Warren, April 22, 1776, found in *Sources and Documents Illustrating the American Revolution 1764–1788 and the Formation of the Federal Constitution*, 2nd ed., Samuel Eliot Morison (Oxford: Clarendon Press, 1961), 146.

Illustration Credits

p. 16   Brady–Handy photograph collection, Library of Congress.
p. 42   Brady–Handy photograph collection, Library of Congress.
p. 64   The John Mitchell Photographic Collection/Catholic University Special Collections.
p. 90   Harris & Ewing photograph collection, Library of Congress.
p. 114   National Photo Company Collection, Library of Congress.
p. 136   Library of Congress Prints and Photographs Division.
p. 158   University of Texas at San Antonio Special Collections.
p. 184   Library of Congress Prints and Photographs Division.
p. 206   US House of Representatives.

Index

Adams, John, 234
Adams, John Quincy, 8
Alabama, 116, 197, 201
Alabama, University of, 197, 203
Alachua County, Fla., 43, 49, 57
Albert, Carl, 194, 216
Alexander, Joshua, 85
Alexandria Lodge No. 1026 (African American fraternal organization), 22
American Federation of Labor (AFL), 72, 74, 79, 80, 83, 84, 103, 105, 106
Andrews, W. G. "Ham," 146, 147, 149, 151
Arnot, Pa., 68, 70, 71, 72
Athens, Greece, 227, 228
Austro-Hungarian Empire, 109

Babson, Roger, 67, 81, 87
Baltimore Afro-American, 127
Barbados, 188–89
Bar Harbor, Maine, 152
Beal, John R., 110
Beck, James Burnie, 36
Bedford-Stuyvesant neighborhood (Brooklyn), 190, 192–93
Belafonte, Harry, 191
Belknap, William W., 13
Bermuda, 21, 22
Bethel AME Church (Harlem), 125
Bill of Rights, 3, 8
Black, William K., 173–74
Black Codes, 22
Blaine, James G., 24

Blanton, Thomas, 129, 130
Bloody Sunday, 201
Blossburg, Pa., 74, 75, 87
Bohemia, 93, 103, 104
Bohemian Country Life, 102
Boston University, 208, 212
Breevort Houses, 192–93
Brookings Institution, 162
Brooklyn, N.Y., 186, 187, 188, 189, 198, 200, 202, 203
    Bedford-Stuyvesant neighborhood in, 190, 192–93
Brooklyn College, 189
Brooks, Preston, 18–19
Brown v. Board of Education, 164
Bryan, William Jennings, 95–96, 98, 100
Buchanan, Frank, 105
Burnett, John L., 103, 104, 108
Burns, Robert, 68
Bush, George H. W., 161
Bush (H.W.) administration, 176
busing, 185, 197, 198
Butler, Benjamin, 30, 35, 37

Cain, Richard, 44
Capitol, US, 8, 38, 159
    January 6th attacks on, 14, 233
    segregated dining room in, 115–16, 123, 125–33
Capone, Al, 118, 120
Carpenter, Matthew, 32
Carter, Jimmy, 208, 209
CBS News, 224

Central Intelligence Agency, 217

Chambers's Information for the People (encyclopedia), 68

Cheney, Liz, 233

Chicago, Ill., 94, 132, 179, 211, 225
De Priest's early political career in, 117–19, 120
Great Migration to, 117
immigrant communities in, 94, 97, 99, 104
1919 race riot in, 119–20

Chicago City Council, 133

Chicago Colosseum, 95

Children's Bureau, 80

Chinese Exclusion Act (1882), 98

Chisholm, Conrad, 186, 192

Chisholm, Shirley, 185–204
barriers broken by, 186, 188, 196, 204
on busing issue, 198
childhood and background of, 188–90
committee assignment pushback by, 193–95, 216
congressional campaign of, 192–93
in controversial hospital visit with Wallace, 186–88, 197, 198–99, 200, 202, 203
death and legacy of, 203–4
early political career of, 19–92
as increasingly willing to compromise and build coalitions, 200, 202–3
legislative accomplishments of, 200, 201–2, 203
political marginalization of, 195, 196
presidential campaign of, 185, 186, 188, 196, 198, 199–200, 204
strong, uncompromising voice of, 186, 187, 188, 193, 195–96, 197, 198, 200, 201–2, 204

Christian, George, 215

Civilian Conservation Corps, 123

civil rights, 6, 17-39, 44, 46, 57, 118, 163–65, 169, 178, 179, 215, 225

Civil Rights Act of 1875, 19, 21, 26–29, 35, 57, 58
opposition to, 17, 27, 30, 31, 34, 35, 36
passage of, 37, 43, 44, 45–46
provisions stripped from final version of, 32, 37, 45, 61
Rainey as picking up mantle for, 18, 19–20, 33–34, 35–36
strategy of linking Confederate amnesty bills to, 18, 21, 28, 29, 3–32, 33–34, 36, 37, 57
Walls as abstaining from vote on, 44–45, 60

Civil Rights Act of 1964, 8, 197, 232

civil rights movement, 2, 128, 201

Civil War, US, 6, 8, 17, 18, 19, 20, 21, 23, 25, 27, 33, 34, 44, 46, 49, 59, 62, 74
Black soldiers in, 35, 47–48

Clark, Champ, 96, 99, 100, 101

Cleveland, Grover, 103

Cleveland Daily Plain Dealer, 24, 36, 37

Clinton, Bill, 225

coal mines, coal miners, 6, 65–66, 67–68, 7–71, 75, 80
accidents in, 67, 69, 76, 77, 78–79
labor strikes in, 65, 67, 71–73
Wilson's attempt to establish bureau for, 76–79
Wilson's work in, 66, 67, 69–70

Cold War, 145, 146

Colorado, 1, 2, 4, 5, 67, 229

Colored People's Convention, 22

Columbia University, 190

Commerce and Labor Department, US, 74

Commission on Immigration Reform, US, 225

Confederate Army, 21, 23, 34, 47

Confederates, 23, 27, 35, 57, 60
amnesty bills for, 18, 20, 21, 23, 24–25, 27–28, 29–32, 57

Congressional Historian (website), 6

Congressional Record, 68, 102, 160

Conservative Party, 51

Constitution, US, 3, 8, 17, 25, 36, 39, 54, 115, 123, 124, 130, 133, 162, 168, 169, 218, 228, 233, 234
Article I of, 167
impeachment provision in, 223
Jordan's speeches on, 14, 207, 216–17, 221–22, 223, 224, 226
see also specific amendments

Constitutional Convention, 218, 223

Cook County Central Committee, 99

Cooper, John Sherman, 232

Cranston, Alan, 175

Cronkite, Walter, 208

C-SPAN, 12, 160, 228, 232

Cuba, 54, 58

Cuban missile crisis, 9

Czech-American Club, 94

Czechoslovakia, 109

Czech Republic, 93, 109

Darrow, Clarence, 118

"Declaration of Conscience, A" (M. C. Smith speech), 137, 138–39

Declaration of Independence, 3, 23, 59, 123, 124, 133

DeConcini, Dennis, 175

Democratic National Committee, 217

Democratic National Convention:
of 1896, 95
of 1912, 92, 99–100
of 1972, 196, 199–200
of 1976, 207, 208–10
of 1992, 225

Democratic Political Club, 94

Democratic Steering and Policy Committee, 179, 180

Democratic Study Group, 176

Depression, Great, 123, 163

De Priest, Alexander, 116

De Priest, Jessie, 123, 124, 133

De Priest, Mary, 116

De Priest, Oscar Stanton, 115–33
background and childhood of, 116–17
in congressional campaign, 12–21
criminal indictments of, 118–19, 121
critics of, 116, 123, 132
early political career of, 117–19, 120
in House segregated dining room battle, 124, 125–33
House swearing in of, 121–22
1919 Chicago race riot and, 119–20
public speaking engagements of, 124–25
real-estate business of, 117, 133
tea party incident and, 123–24, 126

desegregation, 185, 197, 198, 212, 213
see also segregation

Dominican Republic, 29

Douglass, Frederick, 53, 189

Dugger, Ronnie, 164–65

Dukakis, Michael, 161

Durango, Mexico, 163

Edmund Pettus Bridge (Selma, Ala.), 2, 201

education, 190, 201, 202
of former slaves, 48, 49, 56
immigrants and, 104, 108
as means for achieving equality, 45, 48, 49, 51, 55, 56, 62
as prohibited for slaves, 47, 48–49, 55
in Reconstruction, 47, 49
see also public education

Eighteenth Amendment, 123

Eisenhower, Dwight, 146, 151, 166

elections, US, 95, 98, 107
of 1870, 51–52, 54
of 1872, 27, 32, 36, 52, 54
of 1874, 34, 35, 43
of 1876, 37
of 1906, 74–75
of 1912, 91–93, 98–101, 102, 107
of 1928, 12–21
of 1960, 165–66, 212–13

elections, US (*cont.*)
    of 1964, 154
    of 1968, 192–93
    of 1972, 185, 186, 196, 198, 199–200,
        216
    of 1988, 161
Electoral College, 37
Elliott, Robert, 24–25, 29, 30, 31
Ellis Island, N.Y., 86
Equal Rights Amendment, 201

Farmer, James, 192
FBI (Federal Bureau of Investigation),
    125, 169, 217
Federal Deposit Insurance Corporation
    (FDIC), 161, 171
Federal Home Loan Bank, 173, 174
Federalist Papers, The, 7, 216, 218
Federal Reserve Board, 169
Fifteenth Amendment, 59, 62, 126
Finley, J. J., 60
First Amendment, 32
Florida, 43, 44, 45, 47-9 48, 50-52, 54, 57,
    61, 124, 125, 186, 197, 198, 203
Florida A&M University (Florida
    Normal College), 47, 61–62
Florida Republican Party, 50
Florida State Senate, 46–47, 49, 50,
    61
Ford, Gerald, 202
Forrestal, James, 151, 153–54
Forrestal, Jo, 153
Fourteenth Amendment, 20, 33, 49, 50,
    62, 123, 126, 132
Frank, Barney, 177, 179
Freeman, Tom, 212

Gavagan, Joseph, 13–31
General Accounting Office, 169
Georgetown, S.C., 21, 22, 38
Glasgow, Scotland, 65
Glenn, John, 175
Goldwater, Barry, 210

Gompers, Samuel, 72, 74, 80, 83, 84, 105,
    106
Gonzalez, Bertha, 163
Gonzalez, Charlie, 182
Gonzalez, Henry B., 159–82
    in backlash to S&L investigation, 160,
        175–77
    childhood and background of, 162–63,
        169, 178
    as civil rights champion, 163–65, 169,
        178, 179, 212
    death and funeral of, 182
    in defending power of Congress,
        167–68
    Democrats' efforts to remove from
        House Banking Committee, 175–7,
        179–81
    early political career of, 163–66, 169,
        181, 212
    in first congressional campaign, 166,
        178
    JFK assassination and, 166, 168–69
    in JFK presidential campaign, 165–66
    oratorical skills of, 160, 161, 163,
        164–65, 166, 178–79, 18–81
    Profile in Courage Award of, 177–79
    as refusing financial support or outside
        income, 160, 168
    S&L investigation headed by, 160, 162,
        172–75
    speeches to empty chambers by, 159,
        16–62, 164, 168, 170, 171
    Tonkin Gulf Resolution and, 167, 181
    in warnings of looming financial crisis,
        159, 160, 161–162, 170, 171
    as Washington outsider, 160, 166, 168,
        169, 170, 180
    as well-read and knowledgeable, 161,
        162–63, 164, 165, 180
Gonzalez, Leonides, 162, 163
Governor's Summer Cottage (New
    Jersey), 91–92, 99, 10–1
Grant, Ulysses, 26, 27, 29, 32, 46, 53, 60

Grant administration, 34
Gray, Edwin, 174–75
Great Depression, 123, 163
Great Migration, 117
Greece, 103, 227
Greeley, Horace, 27, 32, 36

Hamburg Massacre (1876), 37–38
Hamilton, Alexander, 222
Hamilton, Bermuda, 22
Hardeman, Dorsey, 214
Harlem, N.Y., 125, 190
Harvard University, 212
Hayes, Rutherford B., 37
Hearst, William Randolph, 98–99
Hellenic Republic, 227
History of the American People, A
    (Woodrow Wilson), 98, 108
Hitchens, Christopher, 159
Hoffman, Clare, 143
Holy Cross Hospital (Silver Spring,
    Md.), 186
Hoover, Herbert, 123
Hoover, J. Edgar, 125
Hoover, Lou Henry, 123, 124
House Agriculture Committee, 193–94,
    201, 216
House Appropriations Committee, 143
House Armed Services Committee, 216
    women's military integration bill
        debated in, 146–54
    see also House Naval Affairs
        Committee
House Banking, Finance and Urban
    Affairs Committee, 162, 17–77,
    181–82
    Democrats in attempts to oust
        Gonzalez from position in, 175–77,
        179–81
    Housing Subcommittee of, 170
    S&L investigation in, 162, 172–75
House Committee on Immigration, 96
House Foreign Affairs Committee, 167

House Judiciary Committee, 13–14, 30,
    35, 216
    Nixon impeachment hearings and,
        13–14, 207, 217–24
    Trump impeachment hearings and, 13,
        231
House Labor Committee, 74, 80, 81
House Naval Affairs Committee,
    141–42, 145–46, 153
    see also House Armed Services
        Committee
House Office buildings, 126, 173, 181,
    219–220, 223
House of Representatives, US, 1, 10, 38,
    51, 92, 100, 137, 169, 210
    bureau of mines debate in, 76–79, 80
    Confederate amnesty bills in, 18, 20,
        21, 23, 24–25, 27, 29–31, 32, 57
    Consent Calendar of, 147, 148, 149
    "hopper" bill-drop tradition in, 8
    immigration bills debated in, 12,
        96–97, 103–6, 107–8, 110
    Ku Klux Klan Act debate in, 24,
        25–26
    Labor Department debate in, 81–83
    Lanham Act debate in, 143–44
    loss of fiery debate in, 12
    as "People's House," 3, 4, 6, 7, 8, 182
    Philadelphia immigration station
        debate in, 96–97
    pro-labor legislation passed in, 80, 83,
        85–86
    Seaman's bill in, 84–86
    segregated dining room controversy
        at, 115–16, 124, 125–33
    Sumner day of remembrance in, 17–18,
        19–20, 33
    Sumner's civil rights bill in, 18, 19,
        3–31, 32, 33–37, 43, 44, 45–46, 57
    swearing-in process in, 121, 122
    Tonkin Gulf Resolution in, 167
    Trump impeachment hearings in, 10,
        13, 14

House of Representatives, US (*cont.*)
Women's Armed Services Integration
Act in, 145–52, 153–54
see also Congress, US; *specific House
committees*
House Rules Committee, 93, 109, 110,
127, 131, 203
House Veteran Affairs Committee,
195
House Ways and Means Committee, 193,
216
Houston, Tex., 208, 211, 213, 224
Houston Informer, 211
Howard University, 128
Hoyer, Steny, 182

Ickes, Harold, 152
Illinois, 99, 100, 116, 118, 121
immigrants, immigration, 1, 3, 6, 13, 45,
57, 68, 87, 92, 93, 225
in Chicago, 94, 97, 104
debates on legislative bills for, 12,
96–97, 103–9, 110
early 1900s wave of, 97–98
German immigrants, 98, 103, 104
Irish immigrants, 98, 103, 104
Italian immigrants, 98, 99, 103, 104
Jewish immigrants, 98, 104, 108
literacy tests proposed for, 103–4, 107,
108
opposition to, 96, 98–99, 103, 104–5,
107, 108
Polish immigrants, 98, 99, 103, 104
restrictions proposed for, 98, 103–9,
110
Sabath as champion for, 93, 94, 96–97,
102, 103–6, 109, 110
Sabath's background as, 91, 92, 93, 94,
95, 97, 105
Scandinavian immigrants, 98, 103,
104
William Wilson's background as,
65–66, 74, 75, 105

Woodrow Wilson's writings in
opposition to, 98–99, 100, 101, 102,
103, 108
Israel, 109
Ivins, Molly, 165

Jackson, Jesse, Jr., 179, 180
Jefferson, Thomas, 161
Jim Crow laws, 62, 124, 126, 127
see also segregation
John F. Kennedy Library Foundation,
177–78
Johnson, Andrew, 10, 14, 217, 232
Johnson, Lyndon B., 143, 166, 169, 212,
215–16
Jones, Mother, 72
Jordan, Barbara, 13–14, 207–26
ability to cultivate relationships and
compromise of, 214–15, 225,
226
barriers broken by, 21–11, 213
childhood and background of, 208,
211–12
congressional campaign of, 216
critics of, 215, 216, 225
death and legacy of, 21–11
at Democratic National Conventions,
207, 208–10, 225
fame and popularity of, 207–8, 210,
213, 220, 223–24, 225
health issues of, 210, 225
in JFK presidential campaign,
212–13
LBJ's relationship with, 215–16
maiden House speech of, 216–17
oratory skills of, 208, 210, 211, 212,
213, 220, 224
in Texas State Senate, 211, 213–15
Watergate speech of, 14, 207, 208, 210,
211, 22–24, 225, 226
at White House civil rights meeting,
215
Julius Caesar (Shakespeare), 26

Kazan, Abraham, 164
Keating, Charles, 162, 174–75
Kennard, Don, 214
Kennedy, Edward, 178
Kennedy, Jacqueline, 166
Kennedy, John F., 178–79, 197, 210, 231
    assassination of, 166, 168–69
    "Peace Speech" of, 9
    presidential campaign of, 165–66,
        212–13
    Profiles in Courage by, 9–10, 11, 14,
        178, 232, 233
Kennedy, Joseph, II, 179–80
Kennedy, Robert, 165, 166, 186
Kerwin, Hugh, 68, 76
King, Martin Luther, Jr., 2, 186, 187, 210
Ku Klux Klan, 20, 26, 45, 52, 55, 125
Ku Klux Klan Act (1871), 24, 25–26

Labor Department, US, 8–85
    William Wilson as first secretary of,
        66–67, 86–87
labor movement, 80, 101, 105
    strikes in, 65, 67, 71–73, 86
    William Wilson as union leader in, 67,
        69, 7–74
LaFalce, John, 179, 181
Langston, John Mercer, 53
Lanham Act (1946), 143–44
Leach, Jim, 171, 182
Lee, Barbara, 199–200
Lend-Lease program, 141
Lewis, Anthony, 224
Lewis, John, 1–2, 3, 4, 6, 13, 201
Lewis, Morris, 115, 125–26
Lewis, William, Jr., 138, 142–43, 147, 149,
        152, 153
Liberal Party, 192
Library of Congress, 1
Lincoln, Abraham, vii, 8, 22, 204
Lincoln Savings and Loan Association,
        162, 172–75, 176
literacy tests, 103–4, 107, 108

Long, Jefferson, 2–21
Longworth, Alice Roosevelt, 121
Longworth, Nicholas, 121–22
Longworth House Office Building, 181
Lott, Trent, 203
Lynch, John, 44

MacArthur, Douglas, 146
MacIntyre, Archibald, 54–55
Madden, Martin, 77, 82–83, 118, 120, 123
Madison, James, 7, 8, 211, 223
Magna Carta, 58
Maine, 139, 140, 141, 152-54
Mann, James Robert, 82, 84–85
Marianna, Fla., 52, 186
Marshall Plan, 145
McCain, John, 175, 254
McCarthy, Joseph, 6, 137, 139
McConnell, Mitch, 232
McCormack, John, 149, 194
McGovern, George, 200
Mexico, 162, 164
Mills, Wilber, 193–94, 216
Mitchell, Arthur, 132
Mitchell, John, 73, 84
Mitsotakis, Kyriakos, 227–29
Moore, J. Hampton, 82
"My Advice to Privileged Orders"
        (Gonzalez speech), 161–62

National Archives, 218
National Association for the
        Advancement of Colored People
        (NAACP), 123, 124, 128, 164, 191
National Guard, 197
Naval Academy, US, 23
Navy, US, 138, 141, 150, 153, 154, 167
    secret House executive session
        attended by officers of, 147, 151, 153
    WAVES in, 144–45, 153
Neal, Claude, 186
Nearing, William, 75
New Deal, 93, 109, 132

New National, 57
New York, N.Y., 98
New York Times, 192, 201, 224
Niblack, Silas, 51–52
Nimitz, Chester, 144, 146, 151
Nixon, Richard, 186, 200, 202,
    216–17
  Watergate scandal and, 13–14, 207,
    217–18, 219, 220, 221–23, 224,
    225
Norfolk, Va., 142–43
North Carolina, 129, 198
Nunn, Ira, 147, 148, 151, 153

Office of Economic Opportunity, 216

Palmer, A. Mitchell, 87
Panama Canal, 75
"Peace Speech" (Kennedy), 9
Pennsylvania, 66, 67–68, 72, 74, 78
Pentagon, 144, 145, 152, 153
People's Movement, 119
Philadelphia, Pa., 21, 98
  centennial celebration in, 59–60
  debate over immigration station in,
    96–97
Pickle, J. J., 171
Pilsen Youth Club, 94
Poland, 109
Portland, Maine, 152
Portland Press Herald, 140
Portugal, 140
Princeton University, 91
Profile in Courage Award, 177–79
Profiles in Courage (Kennedy), 9–10, 11,
    14, 178, 232, 233
public education, 23, 44, 48, 68, 192,
    201
  congressional debate on legislation for,
    54–56
  in Florida, 47, 50, 61
  segregation in, 27, 45, 50, 56, 6–61,
    164, 197–98, 212

Walls as strong advocate for, 44, 45, 46,
    47, 48–49, 51, 53–57, 61, 62
  see also education
Puerto Rico, 75

Rainey, Edward, 21
Rainey, Grace, 21
Rainey, Henry, 126, 132
Rainey, Joseph, 13, 14, 17–39, 116, 229
  background and early jobs of, 18,
    21–22
  death of, 38
  early political career of, 22–23
  as first Black congressman in history,
    18, 20, 23–24, 38, 44
  Ku Klux Klan Act and, 24, 25–26
  legacy of, 38–39
  oratorical skills of, 19, 20, 24, 34,
    36–37
  as picking up mantle for Sumner's civil
    rights bill, 18, 19–25, 33–34, 35–39
  in run for Congress, 23
  Sumner eulogized by, 18, 19–20, 33
Rainey, Susan, 21–22
Rapier, James, 44, 116
Rayburn House Office Building, 173,
    219–220, 223
Reagan, Ronald, 12, 161
Reagan administration, 170, 174, 175
Reconstruction, 2–21, 22–23, 27, 28, 33,
    34, 35, 38, 44, 52, 53, 60, 61, 116,
    224
  education in, 47, 49
  end of, 37, 38, 45, 58, 62
  racial violence in, 2–21, 23, 45, 46,
    49–50, 58
Republican National Convention:
  of 1928, 120
  of 1964, 154
Riegle, Donald, 175
Rockefeller, Nelson, 202–3
Rodino, Peter, 219–20, 221, 223
Roosevelt, Eleanor, 189–90, 191

Roosevelt, Franklin D., 93, 109, 141, 152, 210

Roosevelt, Theodore, 73, 93, 102, 121, 229–30

Ross, Edmund G., 10, 14, 231–32

Roth, Toby, 173

Sabath, Adolph, 91–111
  Bryan's friendship with, 95–96
  as champion for immigrants, 93, 94, 96–97, 102, 103–6, 107–8, 109, 110
  childhood of, 93–94
  congressional accomplishments of, 109, 110
  death and legacy of, 93, 11–11
  immigrant background of, 91, 92, 93, 94, 95, 97, 105
  kind and considerate demeanor of, 91, 110
  as leader in Chicago immigrant community, 94, 97
  Woodrow Wilson's quest for endorsement by, 91–93, 100, 101, 102, 110

Sabath, Babette, 93–94, 110

Sabath, Joachim, 94

Sabath, Joseph, 110

Saipan, 144

San Antonio, Tex., 160, 162, 163, 165, 166, 168, 169, 178
  Gonzalez funeral in, 182

San Antonio City Council, 163–64

S&L crisis, *see* savings and loan crisis

San Fernando Cathedral (San Antonio), 182

San Francisco, Calif., 142

Santa Anna, Antonio López de, 164

savings and loan crisis, 161, 169, 17–75, 176, 179
  backlash to Gonzalez's investigation of, 160, 175–77
  politicians implicated in, 160, 162, 170, 172, 173, 174, 175

Gonzalez's investigation of, 160, 162, 172–75

Scotland, 65, 75, 103

Sea Girt, N.J., 91, 99, 10–1, 102

Secret Service, 186

segregation, 27, 28, 60, 107, 122, 124, 132, 197, 199, 212
  Gonzalez's opposition to, 164–65, 179, 212
  House dining room battle over, 115–16, 124, 125–33
  of schools, 27, 45, 50, 56, 6–61, 164, 197–98, 203, 212
  see also desegregation

Senate, US, 3, 7, 10, 17, 18, 38, 74, 83, 84, 85, 101, 106, 154, 162, 173
  Brooks's violent attack on Sumner in, 18–19
  Confederate amnesty bills in, 27–28, 29, 32
  dining room at, 122, 128
  M. C. Smith's "Declaration of Conscience" speech in, 137, 138–39
  Sumner's civil rights bill in, 17, 27, 28, 29, 30, 32, 33
  Trump impeachment trials in, 14, 231–33
  Watergate hearings in, 219
  Women's Armed Services Integration Act passed in, 146, 147, 149, 150, 152, 154
  see also Congress, US

Senate Banking Committee, 174–75

Senate Judiciary Committee, 27, 28

Senate Select Committee on Ethics, 175

Seventeenth Amendment, 3

Shafer, Paul, 148, 151

Shakespeare, William, 26

Short, Dewey, 149, 15–51, 153

Sickles, Daniel, 22

Slaughterhouse decision, 33, 35

slavery, slaves, 8, 18, 21, 25, 27, 44, 47,
    48, 58, 59, 116
    education of former, 48, 49, 56
    laws prohibiting education of, 47,
        48–49, 55
    Sumner's opposition to, 18, 19, 26–27,
        33
    Thirteenth Amendment in abolishing
        of, 8
Smalls, Robert, 38
Smith, Adam, 68
Smith, Clyde, 14–41
Smith, Margaret Chase, 137–55
    as advocate for women in the military,
        138, 141, 144–46, 147–52, 153–54
    in alleviating Maine's oil shortage, 152
    background of, 140
    in congressional campaigns, 14–41,
        154
    "Declaration of Conscience" speech
        of, 137, 138–39
    on inspection tour of war in Pacific,
        144
    Lanham Act supported by, 143–44
    in near plane crash, 139–40
    presidential campaign of, 154
    pro-defense position of, 141, 145, 154
    in tour of wartime coastal
        communities, 142–44
Social Security Act (1935), 75
South Carolina, 21-3, 25-6, 28, 37-8
South Carolina State Senate, 22
Southern States Convention of Colored
    Men, 53–54
Soviet Union, 9, 145
Spain, 58, 163
State Conference of the Colored Men of
    Florida, 61
State Department, US, 109
St. George port, 21–22
St Germain, Fernand, 170, 171
St. Hill, Charles, 189
St. Hill, Ruby, 188, 189

Sullivan, Roger, 100, 101, 102
Sulzer, William, 81, 84
Sumner, Charles, 18, 21, 22, 27–28, 29,
    30, 32, 44, 57
    as abolitionist and civil rights
        champion, 17, 18, 19–20, 21, 26–27,
        33
    Brooks's violent attack on, 18–19
    civil rights bill proposal of, see Civil
        Rights Act of 1875
    House day of remembrance for, 17–18,
        19–20, 33
Supreme Court, US, 37, 132, 197, 212,
    220
    Brown v. Board of Education decision
        of, 164
    Slaughterhouse decision of, 33, 35

Taber, John, 143
Taft, William Howard, 79, 83–84, 85, 86,
    102, 103
Texas, 12, 124, 161, 163, 164, 165, 166,
    211, 212, 213, 215
Texas, University of, 211–12
Texas Observer, 164
Texas Southern University (TSU),
    211–12
Texas State Senate, 160, 164–65, 181, 208,
    211, 213–15
Thirteenth Amendment, 8, 12, 232
Thompson, "Big Bill," 120
Tilden, Samuel, 37
Time, 165
Titanic, sinking of (1912), 80
Tobias, Channing, 127
Tocqueville, Alexis de, 228
Tonkin Gulf Resolution, 167
Treasury Department, US, 38, 160
Truman, Harry, 93, 109, 153, 154
Trump, Donald J., 14
    impeachment hearings and trials of, 13,
        213–33
Twenty-fifth Amendment, 167, 202

Union military, 21, 22, 23, 35, 47–48
unions, 67, 69, 70, 72–74, 79, 80, 82, 83, 84, 98
see also labor movement
United Mine Workers of America (UMW), 72–73, 84
Unity Democratic Club, 191

Vance, Robert, 33–34
Van Zandt, James, 146
Vento, Bruce, 175–76, 177, 179, 181
Vietnam War, 154, 196, 209, 215
Vinson, Carl, 141–42, 144, 145–46
Virginia, 142
Viva Kennedy campaign committee, 165–66
voter intimidation, 24, 28, 37, 49–50, 51–52
Voting Rights Act (1965), 215, 225

Wallace, George, 185–86, 197, 198, 20–1, 203
  Chisholm's controversial hospital visit with, 186–88, 197, 198–99, 200, 202, 203
Wallace Kennedy, Peggy, 200
Walls, Helen "Ella," 48, 61
Walls, John, 47
Walls, Josiah T., 43–62, 116
  as abstaining from Civil Rights Act vote, 44–45, 60
  as advocate for public education, 44, 45, 46, 47, 48–49, 51, 53–57, 61, 62
  background of, 43–44, 45, 47, 55
  congressional campaigns of, 51–53, 54, 60, 61
  death and legacy of, 62
  as director of Florida A&M University, 47, 61–62
  early political career of, 49–50, 51
  education of, 45, 47, 48, 56
  farming ventures of, 45, 50, 51, 56, 57–58, 61

  in fight for Sumner's civil rights bill, 57, 58, 60
  in Florida State Senate, 46–47, 49, 50, 61
  military service of, 45, 47–48, 49
  partisan accusations of election irregularities against, 46, 52–53, 54, 60
  in public education bill debates, 54–56
  Southern States Convention of Colored Men and, 53–54
  in speech supporting Philadelphia centennial celebration, 59–60
  State Conference of the Colored Men of Florida and, 61
  teaching career of, 45, 47, 48, 49
Walls, Nettie, 61, 62
Wall Street Journal, 169
War Manpower Commission, 143
Warren, Lindsay, 115, 116, 126, 129, 131, 132
Warsoff, Louis, 190
Washington, George, 11, 222, 23–31
Washington Post, 101, 105, 162, 173, 224
Washington Tribune, 125
Watergate scandal, 13–14, 209, 217–25
  Jordan's speech on, 14, 207, 208, 210, 211, 22–24, 225, 226
Wealth of Nations (A. Smith), 68
Webster, William, 169
Western Stone Company, 118
Wheatley High School (Houston), 211
Whittemore, Benjamin, 23
Williams-Skinner, Barbara, 203
Wilson, Adam, 65, 68, 69, 78–79
Wilson, Agnes, 69–70
Wilson, Helen, 65, 68
Wilson, Henry, 17
Wilson, William B., 65–87, 229
  in attempts to establish bureau of mines, 76–79, 80
  blacklisting and false arrests of, 67, 70, 71

Wilson, William B. (*cont.*)
  calm demeanor and rational approach
    of, 66, 67, 74, 75, 77, 81, 85
  coal mining jobs of, 66, 67, 69–70, 77,
    79
  conciliatory approach of, 67, 74, 75, 81
  congressional campaign of, 74–75
  in creation of Labor Department,
    66–67, 8–85, 86
  death and legacy of, 87
  farming by, 67, 71
  hardscrabble childhood of, 65–66,
    67–69, 76, 77
  as House Labor Committee chair, 80,
    81
  immigrant background of, 65–66, 74,
    75, 105
  Seaman's bill of, 80, 84–86
  as secretary of labor, 66–67, 86–87
  self-education of, 68–69, 76
  as union leader, 67, 69, 7–74
  workers' rights as concern of, 66, 75,
    76–79, 80, 82, 83, 84–86
Wilson, Woodrow, 66, 67, 83, 84, 98–103,
    100, 101, 102, 103, 105-110, 222
Women Accepted for Volunteer
    Emergency Service (WAVES),
    144–45, 153
Women's Armed Services Integration
    Act (1948), 145–52, 153–54
Women's Army Corps (WACs), 144, 146
World War I, 12, 67, 86, 106, 108, 109,
    119
World War II, 109, 138, 141–42, 144–45,
    145, 151, 153, 232
Wylie, Chalmers, 176

Yorktown, Battle of, 47

Záboří, Bohemia, 109–10